GREAT BRITONS

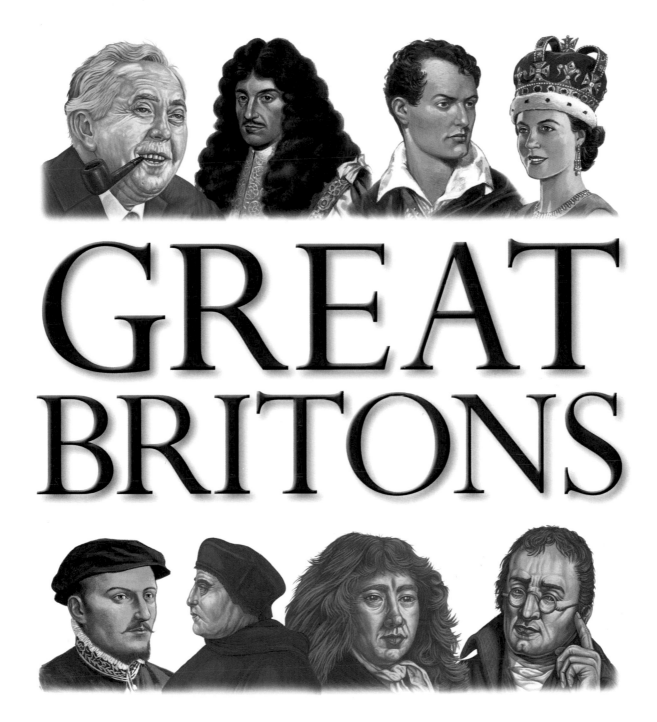

GREAT BRITONS

fiona macdonald

Miles Kelly

PUBLISHING

First published in 2004 by
Miles Kelly Publishing Ltd
Bardfield Centre, Great Bardfield, Essex CM7 4SL

Copyright © Miles Kelly Publishing Ltd 2004

10 9 8 7 6 5 4 3 2 1

Publishing Director: Anne Marshall
Project Manager: Kate Miles
Design: Sally Boothroyd
Picture Research: Liberty Newton
Copy editor: Ann Kay
Repro: DPI Colour

British Library Cataloguing-in-Publication Data
A catalogue record for this book is available from the British Library

ISBN 1-84236-453-7
Contact us by e-mail: info@mileskelly.net
Visit our website: www.mileskelly.net

Printed in China

how to use this book

The features described below will help you get the best from *Great Britons*. The symbols next to each entry allow you to navigate through the book by theme. The frequent fact panels supply additional information about the personalities, lists of their works and brief chronologies.

ARTISTS AND DESIGNERS

MEDICAL SCIENTISTS

ENTERTAINERS

KINGS, QUEENS AND NOBILITY

EXPLORERS AND TRAVELLERS

COMPOSERS AND MUSICIANS

POLITICAL LEADERS, PHILOSOPHERS, REFORMERS AND CAMPAIGNERS

RELIGIOUS FIGURES

SCIENTISTS AND INVENTORS

MILITARY LEADERS

SPORTS STARS

WRITERS, POETS AND ESSAYISTS

Main entry
Concise but informative text on the life and works of over 500 people from every corner of the British Isles.

Delius, Frederick
(1862–1934)
Musician

Born in Yorkshire of German descent, Delius composed music based on traditional English tunes, in a graceful, romantic style. He continued to compose, with the help of a devoted friend, even after he lost the ability to see and speak.

▲ ROYAL BALLET
Dancers from the company founded by Ninette de Valois.

de Valois, Dame Ninette (Edris Stannus)
(1898–2001)
Dancer

Born in Ireland, de Valois danced in France before settling in London to found her own ballet school. She began to create very successful new ballets of her own, and to direct dancers in new productions of existing ballets. In 1931, she founded her own ballet company, which later became the Sadlers Wells Ballet and then, in 1956, the Royal Ballet.

A woman of great imagination, skill and determination, de Valois worked closely with choreographer Sir Frederick Ashton to promote British ballet and to make her company one of the best in the world. She also founded the Royal Ballet School, to train dancers from a very young age.

Dewar, Sir James
(1842–1923)
Scientist

Inventor of the vacuum flask, which keeps contents warm or cold, Dewar worked in cryogenics – the science of freezing. He was the first to discover how to produce large quantities of liquid oxygen and liquid hydrogen (both are now used in space rockets), and to cool substances down to almost absolute zero (-459.67 °F/-273.15 °C).

Dickens, Charles
(1812–1870)
Writer

Born into a poor family (his father was imprisoned for debt), 12-year-old Dickens was sent to work in a factory and became determined to make a better life for himself. He began by writing newspaper reports. His first novel, *The Pickwick Papers*, was published in instalments in a popular magazine when Dickens was only 24. It was a great success, and he became famous.

Dickens produced many more novels and short stories. All combine dramatic plots, vivid character sketches, humour, and social criticism. Dickens was shocked by the miserable conditions in which many ordinary people had to live and work. He also used his skill as a writer to campaign for many causes, such as banning slavery.

NOVELS BY CHARLES DICKENS

1836 *The Pickwick Papers*	1854 *Hard Times*
1839 *Oliver Twist*	1857 *Little Dorrit*
1839 *Nicholas Nickleby*	1859 *A Tale of Two Cities*
1841 *The Old Curiosity Shop*	1861 *Great Expectations*
1841 *Barnaby Rudge*	1865 *Our Mutual Friend*
1843 *Martin Chuzzlewit*	1870 *Edwin Drood**
1848 *Dombey and Son*	
1850 *David Copperfield*	*unfinished when
1853 *Bleak House*	Dickens died

Dirac, Paul
(1902–1984)
Scientist

Son of a Swiss father and a British mother, Dirac worked in a new and exciting form of mathematics known as quantum mechanics. This is used by scientists studying atoms and the amazingly small particles within them. He also found ways of using quantum mechanics (which describes tiny objects) together with Albert Einstein's revolutionary Theory of Relativity (which describes the vast universe). In 1928, he published calculations that explained how certain sub-atomic particles – tiny parts within atoms – behaved, and predicted the existence of new particles (which have since been discovered). He won the Nobel Prize in 1933.

31

Symbol and field of excellence
The symbol and caption indicate the person's profession or talent.

Fact panels
Novels, paintings, inventions and works are listed in panels throughout the book along with timelines to put personalities in historical context.

 *a*

◀ **ALCOCK'S FLIGHT**
Alcock and Brown made their
1919 flight in this WWI bomber.

Abbott, Diane
(born 1953)
Politician

Britain's first black woman to be elected as a Member of Parliament, Abbott is known for her forthright, sometimes controversial, views. A member of the Labour Party, she has not been afraid to criticize government policies from time to time. In Parliament, she is respected for her intelligence and her expertise in complicated matters of finance and administration.

▲ **ADAM FIREPLACE**
The Adams also designed fittings
and furniture for their houses.
This fireplace, decorated with
white stucco (carved plaster) uses
features from ancient Greek art.

 Adam, Robert
(1728–1792)
Designer

Born in Scotland, Adam travelled widely in Europe, studying ancient buildings and art. On his return to Britain in 1758, he began work as an architect, in partnership with his brother James (1730–1794). Together, they designed many great country houses. Their delicate, elegant style was based on ancient Greek and Roman designs, and on the art of Renaissance Italy. Some of their most famous buildings still survive today, including Syon House near London, Harewood House in Yorkshire, and Charlotte Square, Edinburgh.

Pope Adrian IV (Nicholas Breakspeare)
(c.1100–1159; reigned 1154–1159)
Religious leader

The only Briton ever to become pope (head of the Roman Catholic Church), Adrian studied in France, and then became head of a French monastery. A skilled administrator, he was sent to Scandinavia to reorganize the Catholic church there. As pope, he played an important part in international politics. He quarrelled with Emperor Barbarossa, who ruled Germany, Italy and Eastern Europe, and backed English King Henry II's controversial claim to rule Ireland.

Alcock, Sir John
(1892–1919)
Pilot

Alcock had a distinguished career in the Royal Flying Corps (the forerunner of the Royal Air Force) during World War I. In 1919, he made the first non-stop flight across the Atlantic Ocean, together with Sir Arthur Whitten Brown. They flew from Newfoundland, Canada, to Ireland in 16 hours 27 minutes. Alcock was killed in a flying accident soon afterwards.

FLYING FIRSTS

1783 Montgolfier brothers' hot-air balloon makes first human-carrying flight
1853 Sir George Cayley (Britain) flies first man-carrying glider
1900 Count von Zeppelin (Germany) makes first flight in dirigible (steerable) airship
1903 Wright brothers (USA) make first sustained, powered human flight in an aeroplane
1906 Airship designed by Zeppelin (above) makes first 24-hour flight
1907 Paul Cornu (France) launches first helicopter
1909 Louis Bleriot (France) makes first successful flight across English Channel
1919 Alcock and Brown (Britain) make first non-stop transatlantic flight
1927 Charles Lindbergh (USA) makes first solo, non-stop transatlantic flight
1930 Frank Whittle (Britain, see page 106) patents first jet engine
1947 Chuck Yeager (USA) makes first supersonic flight

Alcuin
(c.737–804)
Writer and scholar

Educated by monks at York, Alcuin became a greatly respected scholar. He went to work for the French king, Charlemagne, as head of the college attached to the French royal palace. Here, he taught many of the most learned men in Europe, and acted as a trusted adviser to the king.

Alexander II
(1198–1249; reigned 1214–1249)
King

Alexander lived at a time when Scotland was an independent kingdom, and often at war with England. After fighting off rivals to his Scottish throne, Alexander agreed a series of treaties with English kings. This began a period of peace that lasted for 80 years. During Alexander's reign, the boundary between England and Scotland was finally fixed, to where it still is today.

Alfred the Great
(849–899; reigned 871–899)
King

Alfred was ruler of Wessex, in southwest England. When he came to power, England was divided into several small, rival kingdoms, and a Viking army had invaded. In AD878, he was forced into hiding (in Athelney marshes), but used the time away from the royal court to plan his comeback. He defeated the Vikings at the Battle of Edington, and they agreed to leave Wessex. Alfred then gave orders for burghs (fortified towns) to be built throughout Wessex, to defend it from further attack. He also began a campaign to conquer all the other English kingdoms that were not occupied by the Vikings, and declared himself king of all England. He took control of London – then, as now, a rich and important city – and also seized land belonging to the Church.

Alfred was very interested in learning and (unusually for a warrior at that time) could read and write. He invited many scholars to live at his court, and personally translated important religious books from Latin into Anglo-Saxon (the language spoken in England) so that the people he ruled would be able to understand them.

Jewel belonging to Alfred

Anderson, Elizabeth Garrett
(1836–1917)
Doctor

Because no university or hospital would accept women as medical students, Anderson worked as a nurse and studied to be an apothecary – the old name for a pharmacist. (A loophole in the law allowed apothecaries to be named on the Medical Register, the official list of doctors.) To gain extra knowledge, she attended college lectures (where she was mocked by male students), and studied anatomy by cutting up dead bodies in her bedroom. She qualified as an apothecary in 1865, becoming the first woman to be listed as a doctor in England. Anderson used her skills to help sick women and children. In 1866, she opened a dispensary (chemist shop) for women in London, where she examined patients and gave advice, as well as selling medicines. It later became a major hospital, named in her honour.

Anderson continued to campaign for women to be allowed to train as doctors, and was appointed head of the newly-opened London School of Medicine for Women. She was elected England's first woman mayor in 1908, serving the town of Aldeburgh in Suffolk.

▶ PREHISTORIC FOSSIL
Anning sold beautiful fossils like this to tourists and scholars.

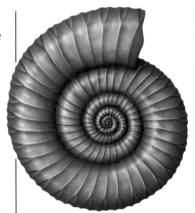

Anning, Mary
(1799–1847)
Fossil-finder

Mary Anning lived in Lyme Regis, on the south coast of England. The cliffs there are rich in prehistoric fossils, and her father, a woodworker, earned extra money by selling fossils to summer visitors. While still a child, Mary worked with him; when he died, she took over his fossil shop. Aged only 12, she discovered the fossil remains of a complete dinosaur, over 10 m (33 ft) long. She later made many other important finds and became very famous. Mary never went to school or college, but she learned a great deal about fossils by talking to experts who came to visit her shop, and by writing to scholars from Britain and overseas. Mary probably inspired the tongue-twister, 'She sells sea-shells by the sea shore'.

Appleton, Sir Edward
(1892-1963)
Scientist

Appleton investigated the layers of gas that surround planet Earth. In 1925, he discovered the top layer of the ionosphere – a blanket of gases that stretches up into space from about 50 km (31 miles) above sea level for 600 km (370 miles). Appleton found that its top layer – known today as the Appleton layer – reflected radio waves. His discovery was later used in the invention of radar.

▲ Physicist Edward Appleton photographed circa 1930

Arkwright, Sir Richard
(1732–1792)
Inventor

▲ WATER FRAME
Arkwright's water-powered spinning machine.

While apprenticed to a wig-maker, Arkwright experimented with different ways of spinning and weaving thread. In 1767 he invented a water-powered machine that could spin fine cotton thread, strong enough to be used for weaving. Arkwright's invention meant that, for the first time, pure cotton cloth could be woven by machine. This transformed the cloth-making industry in northern England. It also changed the way people dressed. Machine-made cotton cloth was cheap and washable (unlike wool) and affordable. Arkwright employed a huge workforce and was a key player in the first phase of the Industrial Revolution.

Ashley, Laura
(1925–1985)
Designer

In 1953, housewife Laura Ashley started a business at home. She printed scarves and other small items on her kitchen table, and sold them to London shops. Many of her patterns were based on costumes and furnishings she had seen in museums. The business did well, and Ashley began to design clothes, curtain fabrics and wallpapers, becoming one of Britain's most popular designers. She opened her first shop in 1967. By the 1980s, she owned 11 factories and 225 shops, in Britain, Europe, America and the Far East.

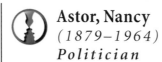

Astor, Nancy
(1879–1964)
Politician

Born in America, Astor married a wealthy newspaper owner, who was also a Member of Parliament. She helped him in his political work, and also managed his huge, luxurious home, entertaining many important businessmen, political leaders, writers and journalists there.

When her husband became a lord, he had to resign as an MP, so Astor decided to stand for election in his place. She won, and, in 1919, became the first active woman MP in Britain. (Another woman, Irish independence campaigner Countess Marciewicz, was also elected, but she refused to enter the House of Commons as a protest against the British government's policy towards Ireland.) In Parliament, Astor worked to help women and children, and campaigned for strict controls on alcoholic drinks. When Plymouth, her constituency, was bombed during World War II, she refused to stay away, risking her life to be close to the people who had elected her.

▼ NANCY ASTOR, MP
Talking to voters in Plymouth.

Attenborough, Sir David
(born 1926)
Naturalist

Throughout his career, Attenborough has campaigned to protect wildlife and the natural world. In 1954, he made the pioneering television series *Zoo Quest*, which showed wild animals in their native habitats, and explained to viewers how they lived. In the 1970s, after a time in BBC management, Attenborough returned to film-making, and became one of Britain's best-known broadcasters with *Life on Earth* and *The Living Planet*. At a time when ideas about conservation were less well known than they are today, his programmes encouraged many people to think more carefully about the natural world, and how to preserve it.

 Attlee, Clement (Earl Attlee)
(1883–1967)
Politician

From a middle-class, professional background, Attlee trained as a lawyer, and became mayor of Stepney, east London, in 1920. He was horrified at the poverty, illness and bad housing he found there, and was determined to improve it. He became a Labour MP in 1922, and held important posts in Churchill's wartime government (*see* page 24).

Attlee was elected prime minister in 1945 – the first Labour Party leader to have an absolute majority in the House of Commons. He introduced many policies to reform British society, and to shape a new role for Britain in international politics after the end of World War II. These included the welfare state (*see* Bevan and Beveridge, page 14), and state control of major industries, including coal, gas, electricity and the railways. Abroad, Attlee encouraged independence for some British colonies, and support for NATO, an alliance of western European and North American states.

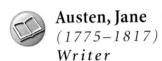 **Austen, Jane**
(1775–1817)
Writer

The youngest daughter of a country clergyman, Austen never married, and spent most of her life quietly at home with her family. She began to write while still a child. Austen completed her first full-length novel, *Pride and Prejudice*, when she was only 21. She left her sixth and last book, *Sanditon*, unfinished at her death.

One of Britain's greatest writers, Austen won little fame during her lifetime, and received hardly any money. Yet her skill at observing and describing people, her insights into character and feelings, her elegant use of language and her sharp sense of humour, have delighted readers ever since her first book appeared. In the late 20th century, her works were made into very successful films and television plays.

NOVELS BY JANE AUSTEN

Austen started writing in her teens, but waited many years before deciding to publish any of her works. She chose not to identify herself as the author. Instead, her books are described as being 'by a Lady'. Two of her best novels remained unpublished when she died in 1817. Her family sent them for publication the next year. A final novel, *Sanditon*, together with fragments of other writings, remained unfinished when Austen died.

1811 *Sense and Sensibility*
1813 *Pride and Prejudice*
1814 *Mansfield Park*
1816 *Emma*
1818 *Northanger Abbey*
1818 *Persuasion*

◀ **THE FIRST COMPUTER** Babbage's 'engine' made calculations much faster than a human brain.

 Babbage, Charles
(1792–1871)
Scientist

As a child, Babbage was brilliant at maths, and it became his life-long career. Today, he is remembered as the inventor of the world's first computer – a 'calculating engine' that he began to build in 1812. He spent the next 33 years trying to improve the design, but never completely succeeded.

 Bacon, Francis (Lord Verulam)
(1561–1626)
Politician, Scientist

After studying law, Bacon became an MP, and was appointed by King James I of England and V1 of Scotland to senior government positions. He was also a scientist and thinker, whose ideas played an important part in the 'Scientific Revolution' – a time during the 17th century when people began to study in a new, scientific way. They aimed to discover knowledge through observation, experiment and calculation, rather than through religious beliefs. Bacon died as a result of one of his scientific experiments – he caught a chill while investigating how to freeze food with snow and ice.

 Bacon, Roger
(c.1214–1294)
Scientist

A Franciscan friar, Bacon studied at the University of Oxford, and in France. He was a pioneering scientist with a very creative mind and outspoken opinions – which often got him into trouble with the Church authorities. His most important work was on optics – the science of seeing and light – but he also suggested ideas for flying machines and machine-powered carts.

 Baden-Powell, Robert
(1857–1941)
General

A professional soldier, Baden-Powell served in India and commanded British troops fighting against South Africa during the Boer War (1899–1902). He stayed in Africa to set up a police force, and was also appointed inspector of cavalry (soldiers on horseback) there.

In 1903, he returned to Britain, and began to realize that his wartime experiences could be used to train young people in fitness, community spirit and self-discipline. In 1907, he arranged the first Scout camp for boys ('scouts' were trackers and lookouts employed by the army, who knew how to survive in difficult conditions.) In 1908, a national Boy Scout organization was formed; the Girl Guides organization was founded the next year. The Scout and Guide movement soon spread to many other countries and, from the 1920s, large international 'jamborees' were held.

 Baffin, William
(c.1584–1622)
Explorer

Baffin sailed on expeditions to search for a North-West Passage – a sea route from the Atlantic to the Pacific Ocean around the top of North America. He did not find it – there is no route, because the seas are frozen in winter. Today, Baffin Island and Baffin Strait, between Canada and Greenland, are named after him.

▲ **STANLEY BALDWIN'S PROBLEMS**
Baldwin faced protests during the depression of the 1920s and '30s.

 Baird, John Logie
(1888–1946)
Electrical engineer

Born in Scotland, and trained as an electrical engineer, Baird invented the first machine to transmit live pictures, in 1922. Four years later, he built the first television set (*see* box). Baird's machines were supplied to the BBC in 1929, and used to make the first regular TV broadcasts in 1936. But in 1937, the BBC stopped using them, preferring a system which used a cathode-ray tube.

◀ **BAIRD'S TV**
Using mechanical image-scanning, Baird made the first transatlantic TV broadcast in 1928. However, a method featuring electronic scanning soon took over.

 Bakewell, Robert
(1725–1794)
Farmer

Son of a Leicestershire farmer, Bakewell pioneered the scientific breeding of farm animals, especially sheep and cows. Bakewell bred livestock that grew faster, and put on more meat, than earlier animals. He hoped that farmers would be able to make more money that way. Although Bakewell's experiments won wide publicity, most farmers did not follow his example, preferring older, tried-and-tested breeds. Scientific animal breeding did not become popular until almost 50 years after Bakewell died.

 Baldwin, Stanley (Earl Baldwin)
(1867–1947)
Politician

Three times prime minister (1923–1924; 1924–1929; 1935–1937), Conservative leader Baldwin was respected for his honesty – he liked to be known as 'the man you can trust'. He won praise for the tactful way in which he handled the Abdication Crisis – when King Edward VIII gave up the throne to marry an American woman, who had been divorced twice before. But he could also be very tough. During the General Strike of 1926 his government was able to keep essential services going. He was criticized for bad economic policies during the Great Depression of the early 1930s, when businesses collapsed and millions of people lost their jobs. Critics also said that he had failed to recognize the threat from Hitler's Germany, or to prepare Britain's defences for World War II (1939–1945).

HOW TELEVISION WORKS

Television is a way of converting visual images (the things we see) into electrical signals that can be transmitted (sent long distances) by satellite, along an electrical cable or along radio waves. Television cameras scan a moving scene, and divide it up into 300,000 or more elements. They then turn each of these into an electrical impulse, which is weaker or stronger according to the amount of light it shows.

To create a smooth picture, television cameras need to scan a scene at least 25 times per second (it is 30 times in the USA). Electrical impulses sent by cameras are picked up by household antennae (aerials or dishes) and turned back into pictures by the television receiver (the TV). This happens so quickly that the eye sees only complete pictures, one after the other

Balfour, Arthur (Earl Balfour)
(1848–1930)
Politician

Balfour came from an aristocratic family that had played a leading part in politics for many years, supporting the Conservative Party. He continued that tradition, serving as prime minister from 1902 to 1905. While in power, he introduced important laws to improve educational opportunities for all children, and made controversial plans to turn the British Empire into an international trading organization. He resigned after losing the 1906 general election, but served as foreign secretary during World War I (1914–1918). In 1917, he wrote a letter that became known as the Balfour Declaration. It promised British support for Jewish peoples' campaigns for a home of their own in the Middle East. (At that time, the state of Israel did not exist.) The Balfour Declaration caused further controversy, and tensions between different Middle Eastern nations continue today.

Bannister, Sir Roger
(born 1929)
Sportsman

Bannister became the first man to run a mile in under four minutes with a record-breaking performance of 3 minutes 59.4 seconds in 1954. He also won a gold medal at the Olympics in the same year. After retiring from athletics he worked as a surgeon, and became head of a college at Oxford University.

Barnardo, Thomas
(1845–1905)
Founder of children's homes

Barnardo came to London from Ireland to train as a medical missionary. He intended to work overseas, but was shocked by the poverty and disease of England's big cities. He set up over 90 homes to care for sick, abandoned or abused children. The organization he founded continues today.

▲ FATHER AND SONS
Thomas Barnardo shown reading with his sons.

Barry, James
See Miranda Stuart, page 97

See Miranda Stuart, page 97

Bateman, Hester
(1709–1794)
Designer

Remembered today as one of the world's great silversmiths, Bateman did not go to school or college. Instead, she learned her craft from her husband, who was a jeweller. When he died, she took over his business, helped by two of their five children. She also went to work for other silversmiths to perfect her skills. Bateman's own work soon became famous for its simple, graceful designs. She mostly made household items, such as spoons and coffee pots, for rich families to use.

▲ SILVER SEAL
A piece by Hester Bateman.

Baylis, Lilian
(1874–1937)
Theatre manager

A trained musician, Baylis worked as a music teacher until she was asked to help her aunt run a theatre in London. She soon became manager, organizing performances of operas, ballets and plays. She aimed to attract people from as many different backgrounds as possible to her theatre: young or old, educated or uneducated, rich or poor. She was also famous for inspiring and encouraging all the actors, dancers and musicians who worked for her. The theatre Baylis ran still exists; today it is known as the 'Old Vic'.

Beale, Dorothea
(1831–1906)
Campaigner

Beale wanted girls to be as well-educated as boys, so that they could lead interesting, fulfilling lives. Before around 1850, schoolgirls were not taught subjects such as maths, science or Latin. People said they were not 'suitable' for women's brains. Beale was determined to prove them wrong. Aged only 27, she became headmistress of a girls' school in the west of England. She appointed new teachers, recruited hundreds of new pupils, and built a nursery school and teachers' training college nearby.

Beale also campaigned for women's right to attend university (they were banned from most colleges until the late 1800s), and encouraged educated women to do voluntary welfare work. She was supported by many other women campaigners, especially Florence Mary Buss (1827–1894).

 ## Beatles, The
(founded late 1950s)
Musicians

A pop group, formed in Liverpool in the late 1950s, which transformed the British music industry. The Beatles owed their early success to the shrewd management of Brian Epstein (1935–1967). Later, their records achieved worldwide fame. Original members were John Lennon (1940–1980), Sir Paul McCartney (born 1942), George Harrison (1943–2002). In 1962, they were joined by Richard 'Ringo Starr' Starkey (born 1940). The Beatles wrote almost all their own songs. At first, they were based on rhythm-and-blues and rock-and-roll styles. Later, they became adventurous and experimental, using Eastern instruments and electronic techniques.

THE BEATLES' GREATEST ALBUMS

1963 *Please Please Me*	1967 *Sergeant Pepper's Lonely*
1963 *With the Beatles*	*Hearts Club Band*
1964 *A Hard Day's Night*	1967 *Magical Mystery Tour*
1964 *Beatles for Sale*	1968 *Yellow Submarine*
1964 *Help!*	1968 *The White Album*
1965 *Rubber Soul*	1969 *Abbey Road*
1966 *Revolver*	1970 *Let it Be*

Most famous singles include: 'Love Me Do'; 'She Loves You'; 'From Me to You'; 'I Want to Hold Your Hand'; 'Yesterday'; 'Day Tripper'; 'You've Got to Hide Your Love Away'; 'Penny Lane'; 'Strawberry Fields Forever'; 'Hey Jude'.

 ## Beaufort, Lady Margaret
(1443–1509)
Aristocrat

Daughter of nobles connected to the English royal family, Beaufort first married at the age of 12. (This was the custom for rich girls at that time.) She was widowed two years later and her son was born soon after her husband died. Beaufort was married twice more, to powerful noblemen, and shared in their political schemes. She also recruited a private army to help her son fight for the right to be the next king of England. In 1485, Beaufort's troops killed Richard III at the battle of Bosworth; her son became king in his place, as Henry VII.

After this, Beaufort retired from politics, and devoted the rest of her life to religion, scholarship and charity. She lived quietly, like a nun, translated many religious books, gave money to good causes, and founded colleges and professorships at Oxford and Cambridge Universities. She was also enthusiastic about new technology, and supported the first two printers to work in England.

▲ MURDER IN THE CATHEDRAL
Becket died as he sought sanctuary in Canterbury Cathedral.

 ## Becket, St Thomas (à)
(1120?–1170)
Religious leader

Becket began his career as a senior government official. King Henry II of England was so impressed by his skills that he invited him to become archbishop of Canterbury – a top political job at that time. For many years, King Henry had been quarrelling with the pope in Rome. He expected Becket to support him, and was furious when he sided with the pope.

Becket fled to France. However, when King Henry asked other bishops to perform Becket's duties, Becket returned to England to punish them for being disloyal. They complained to the king, who lost his temper and shouted, famously, 'Will no one rid me of this meddlesome priest?!' Four knights overheard him, rushed to find Becket, and murdered him in Canterbury Cathedral. The killing caused a scandal. King Henry was disgraced, and Becket became a saint.

Bede, St
(672/3–735)
Writer

Bede lived as a monk in the north-east of England. During his lifetime, he was respected as the most learned man in Europe, and his books are still read today, over 1,000 years after his death. Bede's most famous work was *The Ecclesiastical History of the English Church and People.* In it, he describes life in Anglo-Saxon England, and how the first Christian missionaries arrived there from Rome. Although it has a serious purpose (to encourage readers to live good lives) it is full of entertaining stories. Bede also wrote books about the Bible and the Latin language (to help other monks) and about how to measure time. He was the first person to divide the past into the periods 'AD' and 'BC'.

Beeton, Isabella
(1837–1865)
Writer

Beeton was married to a publisher. She worked with him on a magazine, then became editor of her own ambitious project – a cookery book published in 30 monthly instalments. This contained over 3,000 recipes, together with helpful hints on medicine, housework, good manners and the law. In 1861, the separate instalments were bound together to make one volume: *Mrs Beeton's Book of Household Management.* It became a great success, and is still in print today.

Beeton's husband, however, was no good at managing money, so she had to continue working in order to support their family. She returned to work too soon after giving birth to their fourth child, fell ill and died, aged only 28.

Behn, Aphra
(1640–1689)
Writer

Famous as the first Englishwoman to support herself entirely by writing, Behn lived an exciting, mysterious life. As a girl, she crossed the Atlantic Ocean to Surinam (in South America), and later went to the Netherlands as a British government spy. She claimed to have survived a shipwreck, and to have had many other adventures.

Returning to England, Behn began to write novels and plays. Like her, they were lively and witty, and proved very popular. Her most famous work, *Oroonoco*, tells the story of a young black prince who is transported from West Africa to the Caribbean as a slave.

Bell, Alexander Graham
(1847–1922)
Inventor

Born and educated in Scotland, Bell emigrated in 1870 to Canada, then the USA. While working as a teacher of deaf people, he experimented with different machines for transmitting sound, especially speech. He invented the telephone, which he first displayed in public in 1876. The next year, he founded a telephone company, to profit from his invention and to fund future research. In 1887, he invented the graphophone. Later, he worked on plans for travel by speedboat and aeroplane.

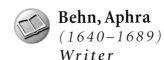

Bell Burnell, Jocelyn
(born 1943)
Scientist

Bell made an important scientific discovery while still a student. In 1967, she detected faint radio signals, and worked out that they were coming from a pulsar – a tiny but extremely dense star, formed when a larger star collapses. Earlier astronomers had suggested that pulsars might exist, but until Bell, no one had ever managed to see one or record its behaviour. Bell's observation helped prove many theories about the universe and how it was made, and allowed other astronomers to make further exciting discoveries.

▶ ISABELLA BEETON
Over 100 years after her death, recipes from Mrs Beeton's famous book are still being used by cooks.

Bentham, Jeremy
(1748–1832)
Philosopher

▲ ON DISPLAY
Bentham sits in a glass case and can be seen by appointment.

Philosopher Bentham is remembered for suggesting a new way of judging whether someone – or something – is good or bad. He suggested that if something made lots of people happy, and few people sad, then it was good. If it helped just a few people, but hurt lots of them, then it was bad. Bentham used these ideas to plan many new institutions – such as colleges and prisons – and to suggest new laws. He also helped set up London University. His mummified body is still displayed there today.

Bevan, Aneurin 'Nye'
(1897–1960)
Politician

Son of a Welsh miner, Bevan began to work as a miner himself at the age of 13. He became active in the trade union movement, and was elected as a Member of Parliament in 1929. On the left wing of the Labour Party, he was a brilliant public speaker, and campaigned passionately for workers' rights. In 1946, he was made minister of health in the new Labour government, and was responsible for setting up the National Health Service. (This was a great achievement. Before 1946, many working people could not afford medical treatment because doctors and hospitals charged fees.)

In 1951, Bevan resigned from the government when it introduced prescription charges, but in 1955 became chief Labour spokesman on foreign affairs. In 1959, he was made deputy leader of the party. He died the next year.

Beveridge, William (Lord Beveridge)
(1879–1963)
Politician

Trained as an economist, Beveridge studied poverty and unemployment. He taught in universities, and became a Liberal MP. In 1942, he wrote a report on insurance schemes and welfare benefits. From 1944 to 1946, this was used by government to plan Britain's Welfare State (*see* box) – a system of free education, health care and welfare benefits designed to support all citizens 'from the cradle to the grave'.

Bishop, Isabella
(1831–1904)
Explorer

As a young woman, Bishop was often unwell. After her family encouraged her to travel and take exercise to improve her health, she became one of England's most famous explorers, and published many books about her travels.

In 1873, Bishop began a round-the-world journey, visiting Australia, New Zealand, many Pacific islands and the USA. While exploring the Rocky Mountains of America, she became great friends with a bandit, but refused to settle down with him in his mountain hideaway. In 1878, she travelled to Japan, but returned to England to marry a doctor and train as a medical missionary. After her husband died in 1881, she went to work in India, setting up hospitals there before making a dangerous overland journey back to Europe. Her final trip was to China and Korea from 1894 to 1897; she travelled over 8,000 miles alone. In recognition of her brave travels, she became the first woman to be elected a fellow of the Royal Geographical Society.

Black, Joseph
(1728–1799)
Scientist

Scottish chemist Black studied gases and developed important new techniques for studying chemical reactions. He also formulated new scientific laws to describe how and why heat is sometimes given off when different substances combine. Black spent many years investigating the gas carbon dioxide, and how it is produced by living things. Today, his findings are still used by scientists studying atmospheric pollution and the 'greenhouse effect' (global warming).

THE WELFARE STATE

A system of health care and social welfare (education, public health, housing, pensions and benefits), funded by taxation and by National Insurance payments made by citizens. Different benefits were introduced over a number of years in Britain:
1908 Old Age Pensions
1911 National Insurance: benefits for contributors if they become unemployed, sick or injured
1925 Widows' pensions
1935 Limited help for the poor and unemployed
1942 Beveridge Report plans welfare state, helping citizens 'from the cradle to the grave'
1944 Free secondary education
1945 Family allowances for mothers with children
1946 Free health care (National Health Service); unemployment and sickness benefits

Blake, William

(1757–1827)
Writer

Artist, poet and dreamer, Blake was one of Britain's most original thinkers. He began to write verses while still a child, and illustrated them with his own designs. After training as a print-maker, he opened a shop to sell decorative prints and his own unusual books and poems.

Blake was very critical of the society he lived in, disliking its greed and hypocrisy, and calling for a return to a simpler, purer way of life. He especially hated factories, big machines, and the inhuman demands they made on ordinary people. Some of Blake's poems – most famously *Jerusalem* have been turned into rousing hymns. Since the rise of the Green movement in the late 1900s, his ideas have become increasingly popular.

Bondfield, Margaret

(1873–1953)
Politician

The first British woman cabinet minister, Bondfield began work aged 11 as a shop assistant. She went on to play an active role in trade unions and became an MP in 1923. Bondfield served in the Labour government as minister for wages and employment from 1929 to 1931. After leaving Parliament in 1931, she worked to improve training and job opportunities for women, and to encourage voluntary welfare work.

▲ **WILLIAM BLAKE**
He called for a better society.

Boniface, St

(c.675–754)
Religious leader

Around AD719, Boniface was sent as a missionary to convert the pagan peoples of Germany to Christianity. His preaching encouraged many men and women to change their beliefs. It also had important political consequences. By introducing Christian ideas to Germany, Boniface made it easier for Emperor Charlemagne of France (who saw himself as Europe's great Christian leader) to conquer German lands. This affected the way Europe was ruled for hundreds of years. Boniface also introduced writings by British monks to Germany and France, helping to create an international community of Christian scholars.

Bonny, Anne

(active 1718–1720)
Pirate

▲ **PIRATE BONNY**
Anne Bonny in mid-fight on the high seas.

Daughter of an Irish lawyer and a woman who was not his wife, Bonny was sent to America by her father so that her existence would not be discovered. There, she grew up to be wild and independent, and ran away from home with a penniless sailor.

Bonny joined a ship belonging to 'Calico Jack', one of the most famous pirates sailing around America and the Caribbean. She took part in many of his raids; on one, she became friends with another woman pirate, Mary Read. In 1720, Jack's ship was captured. Along with all the other pirates, Bonny and Read were put on trial and condemned to death. The men were hanged, but Bonny and Read were pardoned. No one knows what happened to them after this.

Booth, Catherine and William
(1829–1890) and (1829–1912)
Religious leaders

Catherine Mumford and William Booth met at a Methodist prayer meeting. They married and, working together, they founded the Salvation Army – a religious organization that aimed to teach the Christian faith to poor and outcast families. The Booths believed that the existing churches ignored these people, and that the way to reach them was by offering welfare help, and by preaching and singing hymns in the streets where they lived.

Unlike most other churches, the Salvation Army allowed women to preach in public, and to hold responsible positions. Catherine herself became a famous preacher. The Booths had eight children. All followed their parents' example and devoted their lives to Salvation Army work.

▲ **WILLIAM BOOTH**
The charity that Booth founded with his wife still helps many people in Britain, especially the homeless, today.

Boru, Brian
(reigned 975–1014)
King

Ruler of Munster (Ireland), and later Irish High King, Brian Boru fought to drive Viking invaders out of his lands. He won control of the Viking trading city of Dublin, and forced other rulers in Ireland to obey him. He was killed fighting against the Vikings and his Irish enemies at the Battle of Clontarf. Later, he was honoured as a great hero in Irish poems and songs.

▲ **BRIAN BORU**
A brave fighter against Viking invaders of his beloved Ireland.

Botham, Ian
(born 1955)
Sportsman

Cricketer Botham won fame as one of the best all-rounders ever to have played for England. In 1978, he became the first player to score 100 runs and take 8 wickets in a Test match;

later, he set many other records. He captained England from 1980 to 1981. Botham's positive, attacking play, outspoken views, and great enthusiasm made him a favourite with spectators, but his behaviour off the pitch was sometimes controversial. Towards the end of his international career, he made long-distance walks for charity, raising large sums.

Boudicca
(died AD62)
Queen

Boudicca was the wife of Prasutagus, king of the Iceni tribe of eastern England. When he died in AD60, Roman invaders put most of his family in prison, or made them slaves. Boudicca joined with another threatened tribe, the Trinobantes, to attack Roman camps and forts. In AD61, she led her army to attack London, where they destroyed buildings and killed many people. However, Boudicca's army was finally defeated by Roman soldiers, and she was trapped on the battlefield. Too proud to surrender, she killed herself by taking poison.

Boulton, Matthew
(1728–1809)
Engineer

Iron-foundry owner Boulton went into partnership with engineer James Watt (*see* page 104), to make engines for sale to industry. Boulton and Watt engines were installed mines, foundries and breweries. Without them, the Industrial Revolution of the early 19th century, when machines took over many tasks formerly done by hand, would have been much slower to start. In 1790, Boulton invented a steam-powered machine to mass-produce coins. This led to a new copper coinage being introduced in Britain in 1797.

Branson, Sir Richard
(born 1950)
Businessman

Famous for his outspoken, informal style – and his risky pastime of hot-air ballooning – Branson is one of the most successful businessmen of the late 20th century. He started his best-known company, Virgin, as a mail-order business in 1969. By 1973, it had grown to include a chain of record shops and a pop-music recording business. Branson then founded Virgin Atlantic Airlines in 1984, and launched Virgin Radio in 1993. All were designed to appeal to young people. By 1998, Branson owned over 200 businesses, including Virgin Trains and Virgin internet and banking services. In 2000, he backed a bid (as the 'People's Lottery') to run the British National Lottery.

THE ROMANS IN BRITAIN

In AD43, Roman emperor Claudius sent an army to conquer the British. Some tribal leaders fought back, but were defeated. Other leaders agreed to help the Romans in return for keeping some of their power. Boudicca's revolt was the last serious opposition to Roman rule. Across England and Wales, the Romans built splendid towns, hoping that the British would copy Roman civilization. Friendly British chiefs and Roman governors collected taxes, and made sure the British obeyed Roman laws.

NOVELS BY THE BRONTËS

The Brontës published their first works under men's names, so that the public took their work more seriously.

Charlotte:	Emily:	Anne:
1847 *Jane Eyre*	1847 *Wuthering*	1847 *Agnes Grey*
1849 *Shirley*	*Heights*	1848 *The Tenant of*
1853 *Villette*		*Wildfell Hall*

Brigid, St
(c.450–532)
Religious leader

Few facts are known for certain about St Brigid. According to legend, her father was a noble but her mother was not a free person. Brigid was sold as a slave to a druid (Celtic priest) but converted him to Christianity. She was then sold to the king of Ulster, but he was so impressed by her faith that he freed her. Later, she founded the first community of nuns in Ireland, and became its leader. Many stories tell of her courage and kindness. In people's minds, she also became linked with the earlier Celtic goddess of the same name, who was honoured for bringing fertility to families and farms.

Britten, Benjamin (Lord Britten)
(1913–1976)
Musician

Born in Suffolk, Britten began to compose tunes while still a young child. From 14 onwards, he was sent to study with well-known composers. His first major work was performed in public when he was only 19, and won great praise. In 1939, at the beginning of World War II, he left England for America. He believed strongly in peace, not war. However, he became homesick and returned. Britten began to compose operas and other works inspired by the East Anglian landscape, and by East Anglian stories and poems. With friends, he founded a yearly music festival in Aldeburgh, Suffolk, and invited the world's best musicians to perform.

Britten's most famous works include: *War Requiem*, which mourns those killed in the war; *Gloriana*, written for the coronation of Queen Elizabeth II; and *The Young Person's Guide to the Orchestra*, a witty piece in which different instruments take it in turns to perform. Britten was also an excellent pianist. He gave many concerts with his close friend, the singer Peter Pears, for whom he wrote many of his finest works.

Brontë Sisters
Charlotte (1816–1855);
Emily (1818–1848);
Anne (1820–1849)
Writers

Daughters of a clergyman, the Brontës lived in wild, remote countryside in northern England. All three worked as badly-paid schoolteachers in small schools, then returned home. From childhood, each sister wrote poems and, later, novels.

Charlotte's novel *Jane Eyre* was the first to be published. Readers were fascinated by this romantic story of a brave, strong-minded girl and a gloomy but attractive hero. Next, Emily published *Wuthering Heights*, a passionate story of doomed love between a wilful heroine (Cathy) and Heathcliffe, the man who deserted her. The public was surprised and shocked to learn that it had been written by a woman, not a man. Anne's *Agnes Grey* and *The Tenant of Wildfell Hall* were printed soon after. They were less brilliantly successful than her sisters' stories, but many people read and enjoyed them. Emily and Anne died young, of TB (the lung disease, tuberculosis). Charlotte survived a little longer, but died soon after she was married, from pregnancy complications.

▲ BRONTË SISTERS
Anne (left), Emily (centre) and Charlotte (right).

Brown, Lancelot 'Capability'
(1716–1783)
Designer

Garden designer Brown created a new form of 'landscape' garden to surround great country houses. He wanted his gardens to look natural, rather than artificial. To achieve this, he dug out irregularly-shaped lakes, planted trees in clumps, and avoided straight paths or neat beds of flowers. His nickname came from his habit of telling landowners that their gardens 'had capabilities for improvement'.

▲ LUTON HOO HOUSE, BEDFORDSHIRE
The gardens of this grand stately home are Capability Brown's work.

Bruce, Robert the (Robert I)
(1274–1329; reigned 1306–1329)
King

Famous as a Scottish patriot who fought against English armies occupying his homeland, Bruce has been celebrated in poems, novels and films for almost 600 years. He lived at a time when rival nobles and warriors were claiming the right to be king of Scotland, and when English kings Edward I and Edward II had ambitions to conquer Scotland for themselves.

▲ ROBERT THE BRUCE
Statue at Stirling Castle, Scotland.

After defeating his rivals and becoming king, Bruce led soldiers to recapture all the Scottish castles occupied by the English. He defeated Edward II at the Battle of Bannockburn (1314) and forced England to recognize Scotland as an independent nation.

BRUNEL'S ACHIEVEMENTS

1825–1831 Helped with his father's attempts to build a tunnel under the River Thames, London
1829–1831 Clifton Suspension Bridge, Bristol (completed 1864)
1835–1841 Designed and installed Great Western Railway, from London to Bristol
1838 *Great Western* – one of the first ocean-going propeller-driven steamships
1843 *Great Britain* – an iron-hulled, propeller-driven steamship
1845 Hungerford Suspension Bridge, London
1850–1854 Paddington railway terminus, London
1853–1858 *Great Eastern* – iron-hulled, paddle-driven; the world's largest ship (until 1899)

 ## Brunel, Isambard Kingdom
(1806–1859)
Engineer

Son of Sir Marc Brunel, a famous French-born engineer, Isambard Brunel also had a very successful career. He began by building bridges, including the daring Clifton Suspension Bridge at Bristol. Brunel then became chief engineer for the new Great Western Railway, surveying over 1,600 kilometres (1,000 miles) of track and designing tunnels, bridges and stations. In 1838, he designed the *Great Western*, one of the first steamships to cross the Atlantic. In 1858, he built the *Great Eastern*, the largest ship ever made (until 1899).

 ## Bunyan, John
(1628–1688)
Writer

From a humble background (he trained as a tin-smith), Bunyan fought on the side of Parliament against King Charles I during the English Civil War. He then became active in minority Christian groups – some of which held extreme views, such as believing that the world was due to end soon.

In 1660, Bunyan was sent to prison for his beliefs. When he was released, he wrote a book based on thoughts he had had while in prison. He called it *Pilgrim's Progress*, and it told the story of an ordinary man seeking to live a good life and reach heaven. Published in 1678, it immediately became popular, especially among people who did not like the organized Church, with its set services and rituals. Bunyan's book remained a favourite for the next 200 years, and is still read today.

 ## Burns, Robert
(1759–1796)
Writer

The son of a poor Scottish farmer, Burns was keen to be educated, and read all he could. He also began to write poems and songs in standard English and in the Scottish dialect he spoke at home.

Burns wrote simply and powerfully about the countryside, about friendship, and about falling in love. He also retold many traditional Scottish stories and legends. When his first book of poems was published, it became an overnight success. Rich and famous people hurried to meet 'the ploughman poet'. Burns died aged only 37, but was not forgotten. His birthday, January 25th, is still celebrated by Scots today.

 ## Butler, Josephine
(1828–1906)
Campaigner

Intelligent and strong-minded, Butler came from a wealthy family with progressive ideas. She worked hard to improve educational opportunities for women. Then, after helping women prisoners, and listening to their life stories, she began to campaign on behalf of women who were forced to earn their living from prostitution.

Butler discovered that most women became prostitutes because they were desperately poor. Often, it was the only way in which they could earn money to feed themselves and their families. Butler tried to change the laws that treated prostitutes as criminals, and demanded better wages and welfare support for all women.

Butler, Richard 'Rab' (Lord Butler) *(1902–1982) Politician*

A Conservative, Butler served in Winston Churchill's all-party wartime government (*see page 24*), where he was responsible for introducing free secondary schooling for all young people in 1944. This was tremendously important, for individual students and for the nation. It created a whole new class of well-educated young people from ordinary backgrounds, all eager to follow new careers, and to change society.

When the Conservatives won the general election in 1951, Butler became chancellor of the Exchequer. He held several other ministerial posts until he retired as an MP in 1964. Twice, in 1957 and 1963, people thought he would become prime minister. However, he was a man of moderate views who sought agreement among enemies rather than confrontation, and many Conservatives believed he was not ruthless enough to rule the country.

▼ **RICHARD 'RAB' BUTLER**
Seen soon after he had become chancellor, in 1951.

 Butler-Sloss, Dame Elizabeth *(born 1923) Judge*

The daughter of a High Court judge, and the sister of a leading lawyer, Butler-Sloss was also determined to follow a legal career. She trained as a barrister, then became a junior judge specializing in divorce and family law. In 1987, she chaired a public enquiry into controversial accusations of child abuse. Her findings were praised for their intelligence, perception and good sense. The same year, she was made a judge in the Court of Appeal – one of the highest courts in Britain. She was the first woman ever to be given such a senior and responsible legal post.

 Butt, Dame Clara *(1872–1936) Musician*

Very tall and striking, and with a deep contralto voice, Butt was one of the most famous singers of her day. Composers, including Elgar, wrote works specially for her. She was best-known for her concert tours, where she performed songs and ballads with her husband. During World War I (1914–1918), Butt gave many charity performances, especially for the Red Cross. This won her public affection and respect.

▲ **DAME CLARA BUTT**
Singing at the National Song Festival in Hyde Park, 1927.

 Byrd, William *(1543–1623) Musician*

The greatest British composer of the 16th century, Byrd wrote mostly religious music, for singers and instrumentalists. He also liked to experiment with new musical techniques. In 1588, he composed the first madrigals in English. (Madrigals are a type of song, invented in Italy, in which several vocalists sing the same words to a different tune, blending their voices together to create beautiful harmonies.)

 Byron, George (Lord Byron) *(1788–1824) Writer*

Son of an eccentric soldier from a noble family and an unhappy Scottish heiress, Byron had an unusual upbringing. As a young man, he cultivated a wild, romantic image, got into fights, ran up enormous debts, and had many risky adventures and scandalous love affairs.

Byron loved to shock, but he also had a serious side. He worked hard, was active in politics, and was the most talented writer of his day. He wrote clever, witty pieces making fun of his enemies, beautiful short poems about life and love, and exciting adventure stories in verse.

In 1816, Byron was forced to flee England, leaving his wife and young daughter, after it was reported that he had fallen in love with his own sister. He travelled to Europe, where he met other writers, and also freedom-fighters who were campaigning for independence for Italy and Greece. Byron continued to lead a scandalous life – and to write brilliant poems. In 1823, he travelled to Greece, to join the fight for independence there. He died soon afterwards, of a fever. Back in London, Church leaders refused to bury his body in Westminster Abbey, beside England's other great poets, where it belonged.

C

 ## Cameron, Julia Margaret
(1815–1879)
Artist

Pioneer of newly invented photography, Cameron took her first photograph in 1864. Later, she specialized in portraits, creating a fascinating collection of images of many of the most important men and women of her day.

 ## Campbell, Donald
(1921–1967)
Sportsman

Son of famous motor-racing driver Sir Malcolm Campbell (*see below*), Donald Campbell also drove very fast boats and cars. In 1964, he achieved a record 445 km/h (276 mph) on water, and 649 km/h (403 mph) on land. He was killed in 1967, trying to drive his boat *Bluebird* at 483 km/h (300 mph).

 ## Campbell, Sir Malcolm
(1885–1948)
Sportsman

Motor-racing driver, who broke several world speed records. In 1935, he became the first person ever to travel at 483 km/h (300 mph) on land. In 1939, he set a water-speed record of 228 km/h (142 mph).

 ## Campbell, Mrs Patrick (Beatrice Stella Tanner)
1865–1940
Actress

A famous beauty, with a quick wit, Campbell was one of the best-known actresses of her day. She performed in a wide range of classic plays, from Shakespeare to Shaw. In 1949, Shaw wrote the part of Eliza Doolittle in his celebrated play *Pygmalion* especially for her.

 ## Caractacus
(active around AD40–50)
King

Son of Cymbeline/Cunobelinus, king of a Celtic tribe, Caractacus led the fight against the Roman invasion of Britain in AD43 (*see page 16*). He was defeated and went into hiding, but in AD47 formed an alliance of other Celtic tribes to fight once more. In AD51, he was betrayed by Cartimandua, queen of a Celtic tribe that was friendly to the Romans, and was taken as a prisoner to Rome. There, Caractacus made a speech that impressed the Roman emperor Claudius so much that he set him free.

Carnegie, Andrew
(1835–1919)
Businessman

Born in Scotland, Carnegie moved to America, where he made a vast fortune by making and selling steel. In 1901, he retired from business and gave away most of his money to schools, universities, libraries and arts centres in Britain and the USA. He also set up the Carnegie Peace Fund, to encourage international peace.

▲ CARNEGIE HALL, NEW YORK
This concert hall is one of many fine public buildings paid for by Carnegie.

 ## Carroll, Lewis (Charles Dodgson)
(1832–1898)
Writer

Carroll spent most of his life as a mathematician at Oxford University, but he is remembered today as a writer of fantasy books for children. The best-known of these books is *Alice's Adventures in Wonderland*, which was published in 1865. Carroll also wrote nonsense verse for adults, and experimented with photography.

▲ THE MAD HATTER
A favourite character from Lewis Carroll's book, *Alice in Wonderland*.

Carter, Howard
(1874–1939)
Explorer

Carter won worldwide fame when he discovered the tomb of Pharaoh (King) Tutankhamun in Egypt in 1922. The wonderful treasures he found there greatly encouraged public interest in archaeology.

TUTANKHAMUN'S TOMB

Pharaoh Tutankhamun of Egypt was buried in a sealed tomb in the Valley of the Kings, Egypt, in 1327BC. His mummified (preserved) body, and all the treasures buried with him for his use in the 'afterlife' lay hidden for 32 centuries – until they were discovered by Howard Carter's team in AD1922. When Carter first peered into the tomb, he exclaimed that he could see 'wonderful things'. These included beautiful jewellery, a life-like mask of the dead pharaoh, a model boat (to transport the soul of Tutankhamun) and a golden throne.

Cartwright, Edmund
(1734–1823)
Inventor

Trained as a clergyman, Cartwright later made a career as an inventor. After visiting Arkwright's factory (*see* page 8), he became interested in power-driven machinery. In 1785, Cartwright designed the first steam-powered loom, to weave machine-spun thread into cloth. Before long, his loom was used in many British factories, and he was given a generous sum of money by Parliament as a reward.

Castle, Barbara (Baroness)
(1911–2002)
Politician

After winning a scholarship to Oxford University, Castle worked as a civil servant during World War II (1939–1945), then as a journalist. As a young woman, she was active in local politics and in socialist campaigning groups. She became an MP in 1945, and served for 34 years. During that time, Castle was a minister in several Labour governments. Her responsibilities included transport, employment and social services.

A keen supporter of equality for women, Castle introduced the Equal Pay Act to Parliament in 1970. After retiring from the House of Commons, she became a Member of the European Parliament, and a campaigner for old-age pensioners' rights.

Cavell, Edith
(1865–1915)
Nurse

A trained nurse, Cavell went to Belgium in 1907 to run a nursing college. When Germans invaded Belgium during World War I, she turned the college into a Red Cross hospital. Her staff cared for all soldiers who were brought there – whatever their nationality. Cavell was shot as a spy by the Germans because she let British and French troops shelter in her hospital and helped them escape. Her dying words became famous. She said, 'Patriotism is not enough ...'.

Caxton, William
(c.1420–1491)
Printer

The first printing press with movable type was built by Johan Gutenburg in Germany around 1455. Caxton learned the technique of printing whilst living in Bruges, Belgium and printed his first book in English there in 1474. Two years later he moved to London, where he printed about 80 further volumes, including many books of poems and romances.

◀ CAXTON'S PRESS
This was used to create the first printed books in Britain.

Cayley, Sir George
(1773–1857)
Engineer

Pioneer aircraft designer and engineer. Cayley performed many experiments aimed at discovering the laws of flight. He built several model gliders and, in 1853, achieved the world's first human-powered glider flight. A man of many ideas and great curiosity, he also designed lifeboats, railways, artificial limbs, hot-air engines and caterpillar tractors, and investigated optics (the study of sight and light) and electricity.

Cecil, William (Lord Burghley)
(1520–1598)
Politician

A lawyer, Burghley worked as an adviser to three ruling monarchs: Henry VIII, Edward VI and Elizabeth I. Wise, cautious and cunning, he helped to decide government policy. He encouraged friendship with the Netherlands and France, promoted new industries, and reformed the government's finances. At a time of great political tension, Burghley helped Queen Elizabeth stay in power and increase her own authority and England's prestige. He ordered the execution of Mary Queen of Scots (*see* page 72) because he believed – correctly – that she was a threat to peace and good government.

Chadwick, Sir James
(1891–1974)
Scientist

A specialist in nuclear research, Chadwick discovered neutrons (one of the tiny particles inside each atom of matter) in 1932. For this, he was awarded the Nobel Prize. During World War II, he helped to develop nuclear weapons.

Chamberlain, Sir Austen
(1863–1937)
Politician

Elder son of Joseph, Austen supported many of his father's policies on Ireland and Empire trade. He served as a minister in the all-party government that led Britain during World War I, and in later Conservative governments, rising to become chancellor of the Exchequer from 1930 to 1935. Unlike brother Neville (*see above right*), he called for action to deal with the threat to peace posed by German Nazi leader Adolf Hitler from the early 1930s onwards.

Chamberlain, Joseph
(1863–1937)
Politician

A Birmingham factory-owner, Joseph played a leading part in city politics, making many improvements to public health and housing. In 1876, he became a Liberal Party MP. A strong supporter of the British Empire, Joseph served as government minister responsible for British policy during the Boer War (when British troops and Dutch settlers fought for the right to rule South Africa). However, he quarrelled with other members of his party over Irish independence (which he opposed) and economic policies (he wanted to favour British colonies). This led to a political crisis. Two of his sons (*see above*) also played an important part in politics.

Chamberlain, Neville
(1869–1940)
Politician

Younger son of Joseph Chamberlain, Neville was a Conservative MP from 1918 to 1940. He served many times as a government minister, introducing important reforms in health, housing and pensions, and encouraging new industries. Today he is remembered mostly for his policy of appeasement towards German Nazi leader Hitler during the 1930s. This policy was designed to postpone war until Britain had made enough new weapons, but it also allowed Germany time to grow stronger.

By 1939, Chamberlain realized Hitler could only be stopped by fighting, and declared war (World War II) in September 1939. He served for a short while in Churchill's wartime government (see page 24), but resigned through illness in 1940.

Chaplin, Sir Charles 'Charlie'
(1889–1977)
Actor

The son of music-hall performers, Chaplin grew up in an orphanage. In 1913, he travelled with a British theatre company to America, where he was spotted by a Hollywood film director, who recognized his talent. From 1914 to 1940, Chaplin made a great many films, some featuring the character he created – a bowler-hatted tramp. Most of these films were silent (without words); Chaplin was a brilliant mime. Some of his films, like *The Kid* (1921), were purely amusing; others, like *Modern Times* (1936), commented on social conditions. In these, Chaplin sympathized with ordinary people and made fun of people with power.

After World War II, people with left-wing views were very unpopular in America. Chaplin was expelled from the country, and went to live in Switzerland.

THE ENGLISH CIVIL WAR
(1642–1649)

Battles fought between followers of King Charles I (*see* p23) and supporters of Parliament. The two sides earned the nicknames 'Roundheads' (Parliamentarians, who wore plain clothes and cropped hair) and 'Cavaliers' (from the French for 'knight'; they wore elaborate clothes and long, flowing hair). These two groups quarrelled over religion, taxes, and government policy. Parliament's army was better trained, with better leaders. It was also supported by the Scots, who disliked Charles's arrogance and religious views. Charles's army was defeated in 1645 and he was imprisoned. He refused, however, to give in to Parliament's demands, and fighting broke out again. In 1649, he was put on trial and beheaded.

Charles I
(1600–1649; reigned 1625–1649)
King of England, Scotland and Ireland

Charles I has always been a controversial figure. A charming, hard-working man, interested in the arts and his family, he was an unhappy, unsuccessful king. Stubborn and untrustworthy, he quarrelled with Parliament, mostly about religion and finance. When Parliament refused to give in, he decided to rule alone with the help of a few chosen ministers. From 1629 to 1640, he did not summon Parliament at all and many people felt that their rights had been taken away. Charles tried to impose an Anglican prayer book on the Scots and this led to the Bishops' Wars (1639–40). This caused so many financial problems that he was forced to recall Parliament in 1640, and to ask it to pass new laws so that he could collect more taxes. In 1641, he argued with Parliament again, over rebels in Ireland. This led to the outbreak of civil war in England (*see box*).

Charles II
(1630–1685; reigned 1660–1685)
King

The eldest son of King Charles I (see above), Charles spent many years in exile after his father was executed in 1649. He was welcomed back to England in 1660, when Richard Cromwell proved to be a poor leader (*see* Oliver Cromwell, page 28). Shrewd, intelligent and witty, Charles II handled the difficult situation that faced him with great tact and skill. Unlike his father, he found ways of working peacefully with Parliament, and tried to heal the divisions left by the Civil War. Even so, he still faced financial problems and religious quarrels. Famous for his love of horse-racing, pretty women and the theatre, he was also interested in the latest scientific discoveries, and encouraged new research.

Charlie – 'Bonnie Prince Charlie'
See Stewart, Charles Edward

Charlton, Sir Robert 'Bobby'
(born 1937)
Sportsman

One of England's best-known footballers, Charlton played for Manchester United from 1954 to 1973, appearing 754 times as a fast-moving striker. He was in the England team from 1957 to 1963, and scored a record 49 goals in international matches. He was also a member of the team that won the 1966 World Cup. Charlton's brother John (known as 'Jack'), a tough defender, also had a very successful international career, and played in the 1966 World Cup team.

Chaucer, Geoffrey
(c.1340–1400)
Writer

One of the first British poets to write in English as well as French and Latin, Chaucer worked as a government official and became famous for poems written to entertain members of the royal family at the courts of King Edward III and King Richard II. His best-known work is *The Canterbury Tales*. This describes a very mixed group of travellers riding on a pilgrimage to a holy site. Much of the tale is a collection of stories that Chaucer pretends were told by the pilgrims – though, of course, he wrote them himself.. Chaucer's work manages to be romantic, dramatic, very funny, sometimes rude, but deeply thought-provoking – all at the same time. He was a highly perceptive observer of people. Even today, over 600 years later, his characters still seem real and alive.

▲ CANTERBURY TALES
Some of the pilgrims from Chaucer's epic poem.

Chichester, Sir Francis
(1901–1972)
Sportsman

A daring yachtsman, Chichester made the first non-stop solo voyage around the world. He set off from Plymouth in southwest England in 1966 and returned 226 days later.

Chippendale, Thomas
(1718–1779)
Designer

Chippendale chair

P robably the greatest British furniture-maker, Chippendale made beautiful pieces from fine woods for wealthy families' stately homes. He also published a book of furniture designs – *The Gentleman and Cabinet-Maker's Director* (1754). This allowed his ideas and styles to be copied by many other craftworkers, for less wealthy people to use and enjoy. Chippendale's designs became popular throughout Britain and were also admired and copied in the USA.

Christie, Dame Agatha
(1890–1976)
Writer

A uthor of popular detective stories, Christie created some memorable characters, including Belgian detective Hercule Poirot and eccentric elderly sleuth Miss Jane Marple. Her books have complicated, clever plots and many are set in exotic, faraway lands. Christie often travelled abroad with her husband, the archaeologist Max Mallowan, and used experiences from her travels in her work.

Christie also wrote plays, including *The Mousetrap* (1952), Britain's longest-running play. Christie's work has been criticized for its narrow, cosy view of British society, but her books are still enjoyed, and have been made into many TV plays and films.

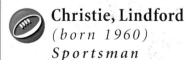

Christie, Lindford
(born 1960)
Sportsman

B orn in Jamaica, Christie moved to Britain and became one of the most successful athletes of the late 20th century. A sprinter specializing in 100-metre and relay races, he won Olympic medals in 1988, 1992 and 1996, and the world 100-metre championship in 1993.

Churchill, John, Duke of Marlborough
(1650–1722)
Soldier

A professional soldier, Churchill led British armies to many victories against rival European nations, especially against France. He pioneered new, successful battle tactics; his most famous victories were at Blenheim (1704) and Ramillies (1706). At first he was popular, but lost public support because so many men died fighting in his wars. Churchill was also involved in politics – together with his wife, Sarah Jennings. They strongly supported the Whig party, which called for civil and political freedom in place of strict rule by unreliable kings and queens.

Churchill, Sir Winston
(1874–1965)
Politician

S tubborn, independent, unpredictable and sometimes unpopular, Churchill ended his career as a national hero, admired by millions. He was born into a famous political family (he was descended from John Churchill, *see above*) and, when young, showed a talent for writing. He served as a soldier and worked as a newspaper reporter in Africa before becoming a Conservative MP in 1900. Churchill changed his views to support the Liberal Party in 1904. He served as a government minister, but resigned in 1915 after a Navy attack he had authorized went badly wrong. From 1917 to 1922, he took various junior government posts, and also wrote a history of World War I.

During the 1920s and 1930s, Churchill's views were often controversial – for example, he backed disastrous economic policies and opposed plans to give India independence from British rule. Even so, from 1924 until 1964, he was continuously elected as an MP. He rejoined the Conservative Party in 1924, served again as a government minister, then became prime minister in 1940, soon after the start of the World War II. This

war was (in words he himself made famous) 'Britain's finest hour'. Although old (almost 70) and unwell, he united the nation in a courageous war effort. His rousing speeches comforted servicemen and civilians, and made them believe they could win. He also worked very closely with Britain's allies, especially the USA, realizing that Britain could not survive without their aid.

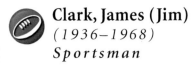

Clark, James (Jim)
(1936–1968)
Sportsman

One of the greatest racing drivers ever, farmer's son Clark won a record total of 25 Grand Prix victories before being killed in a car crash. He was world champion in both 1963 and 1965.

Clive, Kitty
(1711–1785)
Actress

Born in Ireland, Clive became an actress to help support her brothers and sisters. She performed to great applause for over 40 years, specializing in romantic, comic parts. She also wrote several humorous plays. Clive attracted many admirers, but remained single for most of her life. When she retired from the stage, she became famous as the leader of a 'salon' (group) of intelligent, interesting, entertaining friends.

Clive ('of India'), Robert (Lord Clive)
(1725–1774)
Soldier and administrator

A successful soldier, Clive conquered and ruled large parts of India on behalf of the British East India Company – a trading association of rich merchants who also had great political power. Although he committed suicide after being accused of corruption, his time in office in India prepared the way for Britain's later takeover of India as part of the British Empire in 1858.

Cobbett, William
(1763–1835)
Campaigner

Journalist and campaigner for poor people's rights, Cobbett attacked privilege and corruption among public figures. He also fiercely criticized landlords who exploited their tenants, fearing that the rapid growth of industry and big cities would ruin many ordinary people's lives.

Cockcroft, Sir John
(1897–1967)
Scientist

The first researcher to 'split' the atom (together with his colleague James Walton) in 1932. Cockcroft's experiments, using high-voltage electricity to force atoms to disintegrate, provided important information that was used by many later scientists. Cockcroft and Walton won the Nobel Prize for their work.

Cockerell, Sir Christopher
(1910–1999)
Engineer

Engineer Cockerell became famous as the inventor of the hovercraft, a vessel that can travel fast over land and sea, balanced on a cushion of air. Cockerell's first hovercraft was launched in 1959, and achieved speeds of 100 km/h (62 mph). It successfully crossed the English Channel later the same year.

▲ OVER LAND AND SEA
A modern hovercraft. Cockerell based his design on a cushion of air.

HOW A HOVERCRAFT WORKS

As its name suggests, a hovercraft hovers – or floats – above the surface over which it is travelling. It is lifted off the ground using a large aircraft propeller, powered by a gas-turbine engine. The propeller sucks air into the space under the hovercraft, forcing it to rise up. This air is kept in place by a heavy skirt of rubber that hangs down around the hovercraft's hull (body). The hovercraft then floats on this cushion of air, which supports its weight. Once launched, a hovercraft can travel over land or sea. It is pushed forward by a second propeller, at the stern (back end).

Coe, Sebastian
(born 1956)
Sportsman

Middle-distance runner Coe (*left*, number 359) won Olympic gold medals for the 1500-metre race in 1980 and 1984. In 1981, he set new world records for 800 metres, 1000 metres and a mile. When he retired from athletics, Coe became a Conservative MP.

Coke, Thomas (Lord Leicester)
(1752–1842)
Landowner and politician

A wealthy landowner and MP, Coke pioneered new ways of farming on his Norfolk estate, growing clover to increase soil fertility, and experimenting with new grasses and other crops to provide animal feed. By doing this, he made his farms ten times more profitable. He also treated the tenants unusually well. Each year, he held a meeting for other farmers, to tell them about his latest ideas and to encourage them to follow his example.

Coleridge, Samuel
(1772–1834)
Writer

The youngest of 13 children of a West Country clergyman, Coleridge wrote some of Britain's best-loved verse, including *The Rime of the Ancient Mariner* (1798), and *Kublai Khan* (1816). The young Coleridge was full of daring ideas. He planned to set up an alternative community in America, wrote political pamphlets, and became a preacher.

In 1798, Coleridge worked with poet William Wordsworth (*see* page 109) to produce a book of poems called *Lyrical Ballads*. Their simple style and plain language caused a sensation, as did their subject matter: the countryside and ordinary people's lives. Before, most poetry had been grand, complicated and difficult to understand. Coleridge later wrote about politics, literature and philosophy. He hoped that one day the world would be run by teachers, scientists, priests and philosophers, rather than soldiers and politicians.

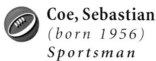 Collins, Michael ('The Big Fellow')
(1890–1922)
Politician

The son of a farmer from southern Ireland, Collins took part in the 1916 Easter Rising, when Irish nationalists rebelled against British rule. (Britain ruled Ireland from 1171 until 1921.) He was imprisoned, but soon released. In 1919 and 1920, he led guerilla attacks on British soldiers. He also took part in negotiating the treaty that set up the Irish Free State in 1921. The next year, he became Ireland's first prime minister. Some Irish Republicans, however, did not accept the Free State arrangement, which left Britain with certain powers in Ireland. A civil war broke out, and Collins was killed in an ambush by Republicans who wanted total independence.

▲ IONA ABBEY, SCOTLAND
Burial place of St Columba.

▼ THE ANCIENT MARINER
Coleridge's poem tells of a nightmare voyage after an albatross's death.

Columba, St
(c.521–597)
Religious leader

Born into a noble Irish family, Columba became a Christian and was forced to leave his homeland. He travelled to the west of Scotland, where he founded a monastery on the island of Iona, and trained missionaries to spread the Christian faith. Iona became a great centre of prayer and learning, and is still visited today.

Constable, John
(1776–1837)
Artist

Pictures of the English countryside painted by John Constable are among Britain's best-known works of art. The son of a Suffolk miller, Constable was inspired by the gentle landscape around him. He was also interested in difficult new techniques, such as painting light and shadow. His work was influenced by poets such as William Wordsworth (*see* page 109), who believed that beautiful views have powers to affect people's thoughts, feelings and ideas.

Flatford Mill, 1817

Cook, Thomas
(1808–1892)
Travel agent

Cook organized the first-ever public excursion train in England, and later set up a company arranging travel in Britain and abroad. He is said to be the inventor of mass tourism – now one of the world's biggest industries.

Cooper, Anthony Ashley (Lord Shaftesbury)
1801–1885
Campaigner

Inspired by his Christian beliefs, Cooper campaigned for shorter working hours in factories, especially for women and children. Thanks to him, new laws – known as the Factory Acts – were introduced between 1833 and 1850. He also introduced laws protecting boys and girls from being sent underground to work in mines.

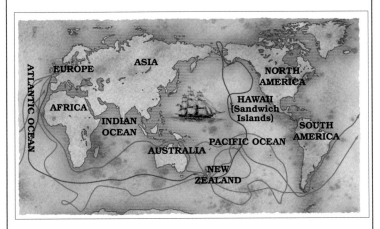

Cook, Captain James
(1728–1779)
Explorer

▲ COOK'S MAP
Captain Cook was one of the world's greatest explorers and navigators.

Cook joined the navy as an ordinary seaman, but was promoted to officer because of his navigation skills. He was also expert at surveying, and recording information. Cook was chosen to command the ship *Endeavour* on a round-the-world voyage to collect scientific and geographic data. Between 1768 and 1771, he made the first scientific maps of the coasts of New Zealand, eastern Australia and Hawaii. He also proved that there was no vast 'Southern Continent', as earlier sailors had claimed. Cook made further voyages to explore the Pacific (1772–1775 and 1776–1779). He was killed by local people in Hawaii.

Cornwallis, Charles
(1738–1805)
Soldier

▲ US VICTORY
After losing to US forces at Yorktown, in 1781, Cornwallis (centre) was forced to surrender.

A professional soldier, Cornwallis led British troops against American colonists in the US War of Independence, in 1780–1781. Later, he was governor-general of India and lord lieutenant of Ireland, where he defeated Irish independence campaigners fighting against British rule in 1798.

Cranmer, Thomas
(1489–1556)
Religious leader

A priest and scholar with firm but moderate Protestant views, Cranmer played an important part in arranging for King Henry VIII to divorce Catherine of Aragon, his first wife. (*See* Henry VIII, page 51.) As a reward, Henry made Cranmer archbishop of Canterbury in 1533.

▲ THOMAS CRANMER
A leading reformer of the English Church.

As archbishop, Cranmer wrote new prayer books, for use in English churches, devised new kinds of church service, and drew up a list of core beliefs (known as the 'Thirty-Nine Articles') for a reorganized, Protestant Church of England. When Roman Catholic Mary I became queen in 1553, Cranmer was put in prison. He was burned to death as a heretic (person whose beliefs are thought to be wrong) in 1556.

 ## Crick, Francis
(born 1916)
Scientist

Together with American James Watson, Crick made one of the most important discoveries in biology of the 20th century. They discovered the 'double-helix' structure of DNA, the basic building block from which all living cells are made.

Crick and Watson's work allowed other scientists to make great advances in understanding genetics (the study of inherited biological features) and led to hopes of finding a cure for many serious diseases.

THE DOUBLE HELIX

DNA is an acid – DeoxyriboNucleic Acid in full. This occurs in every living cell (except in a few viruses). It enables inherited characteristics to be passed on from parents to their children. DNA's structure was first discovered in 1953, by Briton Francis Crick and American James Watson.

Watson and Crick found that DNA was made of long strands, twisted together like a spiral staircase. They called this a 'double helix'. When cells divide, the two strands within the DNA separate,

and are used to make fresh copies of themselves. In this way, DNA passes from old cells to new cells, all the time, making new cells just like the old ones. The modern science of genetics (the study of inherited characteristics) could not exist without knowledge of DNA.

 ## Crompton, Samuel
(1753–1827)
Inventor

Son of a weaver, Crompton was put to work spinning thread as a boy. He found old-fashioned hand-spinning so slow, and early spinning machines so inefficient, that he invented a new machine of his own. It became known as a 'mule', and produced fine, strong cotton thread. It was copied and used in many factories, but Crompton got little payment from factory owners, and died poor.

 ## Cromwell, Oliver
(1599–1658)
Politician

A devout Puritan (Christian with strict, simple beliefs), Cromwell became an MP, and supported Parliament against King Charles I during the English Civil War (1639–1660). When the king was defeated in 1649, Cromwell helped arrange his trial and execution.

Cromwell was an excellent army commander. In 1649, he was sent to Ireland, to lead Parliament's soldiers against rebels there. He became hated and feared for his brutal tactics, but he believed he was doing God's work. In 1653, he was appointed 'Lord Protector' of Britain – head of the government that Parliament set up to replace the dead king. He ruled sensibly and tolerantly, and refused to be called 'king'. His son, Richard, ruled after him, but was not a success. When King Charles II came to power in 1660, Oliver Cromwell's body was dug up and cut to pieces.

 ## Cromwell, Thomas
(c.1485–1540)
Politician

Son of a tradesman, Cromwell was a merchant before going to work for Cardinal Wolsey – one of the top politicians of his day – and then for King Henry VIII (see page 51). He helped Henry during his quarrel with the pope, and in re-organizing the Church of England. Throughout his career, Cromwell's actions were inspired by a mixture of religious belief, political cunning and personal ambition. He is most famous for his attacks on nunneries and monasteries (from 1536 onwards), in which he took away their property and closed them down. He also introduced many reforms in the way English government was run. He was executed after Catholic priests and nobles plotted against him.

Dalton, John
(1766–1844)
Scientist

A teacher at first, Dalton spent his later career as a scientist, investigating gases and how they behave. He discovered how gases expand when heated and his findings became known as Dalton's Law. His researches into clouds and air helped other scientists who were studying the weather. He also investigated atoms – the smallest particles of matter that had been discovered at that time.

ATOMS

Atoms are the smallest particles of matter that can be detected by chemical tests. Until the 20th century, scientists believed that nothing smaller than an atom could exist. Today, we know that atoms are made of many much smaller particles, or 'sub-atomic' particles. These include hadrons, muons, leptons, neutrinos and quarks. Some sub-atomic particles are so rare, and behave so strangely, that no one has seen them. But scientists have calculated that they must exist.

Darby, Abraham
(1667–1717)
Iron master

After a visit to study brass-working in the Netherlands, Darby set up a new metal-works in Bristol. There, he invented new ways of casting iron, which allowed goods to be made more quickly and cheaply, so ordinary people could afford them. He moved to Coalbrookdale in Shropshire, where he pioneered a new technique for smelting iron, using coke. His work was continued by his son (also Abraham Darby: 1711–1763), who built the world's first cast-iron bridge at the Coalbrookdale works between 1776 and 1779.

Darling, Grace
(1815–1842)
Heroine

Grace lived on the wild, rocky Farne Islands, off the northeast coast of England. Her father was lighthouse keeper there. In 1838, Grace and her father risked their lives by rowing through raging seas to rescue five survivors from a wrecked steamboat. Grace's bravery caused a sensation. She was given gold medals and a large reward. But in spite of public attention, Grace refused to leave her island home. She died there suddenly, of the lung disease TB (tuberculosis), at only 27.

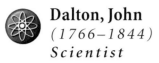

Darwin, Charles Robert
(1809–1882)
Naturalist

After completing his university education, Darwin was appointed naturalist (biologist) on *HMS Beagle*, a ship making a pioneering voyage to South America from 1831 to 1836. On this voyage, Darwin saw and reported on many new species of plants and animals. His findings led him to work out a new theory of 'evolution', in which he described how all life on Earth has developed and changed over millions of years.

In 1859, Darwin published his ideas in a book, *On the Origin of Species by Means of Natural Selection*. This was followed by *The Descent of Man* in 1871. Darwin's theories caused great controversy. Many people were shocked by the thought that humans might be descended from apes, and religious leaders said Darwin's ideas were blasphemous (going against sacred beliefs). But today, most scientists think that he was correct.

▲ DARWIN'S ISLANDS
Travels in the Pacific Galapagos Islands helped Darwin form his theories.

David I
(c.1082–1153; reigned 1124–1153)
King

Scottish king David I aimed to introduce French and English cultures to Scotland, as he considered these more civilized than Scottish ways. Some Scottish nobles did not agree. David was the first Scottish king to issue his own coins. He also reformed government and the legal system, encouraged trade and built many new towns. He invited educated monks from France to settle in Scotland, and promised to reduce taxes for Scots who lived peaceful lives. He claimed – and won – the right to rule northern England from English kings.

 Davies, Emily
(1830–1921)
Campaigner

▲ GATEWAY TO GIRTON
The entrance to Girton, the
women's college founded by
Emily Davies.

A clergyman's daughter, Davies worked to reform society and win rights for women, especially rights to education, and to vote on equal terms with men. She trained as a teacher and in 1866 set up the London Schoolmistresses' Association, so that women could work together to improve schooling for girls.

In 1869, Davies founded a college for young women, which later became Girton College at Cambridge University – the first women's college at Oxbridge (Oxford and Cambridge universities). At that time most jobs were held by men and this proved to be a great breakthrough in helping women achieve high-powered careers.

 Davison, Emily Wilding
(1872–1913)
Campaigner

E mily Davison was a member of the Suffragettes, a group who used violent tactics to campaign for votes for women. She studied at Oxford University, and worked as a teacher. Between 1906 and 1913 she was imprisoned eight times for her Suffragette activities (which included stone-throwing and setting fire to post-boxes), and went on hunger strike. In 1913, wrapped in a Suffragette banner, she threw herself under the feet of the king's racehorse as it ran in the Derby – a very famous race. She died four days later.

 Davy, Sir Humphry
(1778–1829)
Scientist

B orn in Cornwall, the son of a wood-carver, Davy conducted pioneering experiments to investigate chemistry and electricity.

In 1815, Davy invented a safety lamp, which was carried by coal miners working deep underground. Unlike earlier miners' lamps, it did not set fire to mine gases and cause dangerous explosions. Davy's invention saved many lives. He also worked to make science useful for industry, and to help ordinary people understand the latest scientific ideas.

Davy lamp

 Defoe, Daniel
(c.1660–1731)
Writer

D efoe fought as a soldier, set up in business as a merchant, and then became a journalist and novelist. Today, his most famous book is *The Life and Surprising Adventures of Robinson Crusoe*, which he based on the story of a real-life castaway.

 de Havilland, Sir Geoffrey
(1892–1965)
Designer

▲ WARPLANE
De Havilland's famous
Mosquito fighter.

O ne of the world's greatest aircraft designers, de Havilland built his first planes, which were designed as fighters, during World War I (1914–1918). He set up his own company in 1920, to produce planes that he had designed. These included some of the best-known and most trusted early aircraft, such as the *Gypsy Moth*. He also designed the *Mosquito* fighter plane, flown by the RAF in World War II, and some of the earliest jet-powered aircraft.

Delius, Frederick
(1862–1934)
Musician

Born in Yorkshire of German descent, Delius composed music based on traditional English tunes, in a graceful, romantic style. He continued to compose, with the help of a devoted friend, even after he lost the ability to see and speak.

▲ ROYAL BALLET
Dancers from the company founded by Ninette de Valois.

 ### de Valois, Dame Ninette (Edris Stannus)
(1898–2001)
Dancer

Born in Ireland, de Valois danced in France before settling in London to found her own ballet school. She began to create very successful new ballets of her own, and to direct dancers in new productions of existing ballets. In 1931, she founded her own ballet company, which later became the Sadlers Wells Ballet and then, in 1956, the Royal Ballet.

A woman of great imagination, skill and determination, de Valois worked closely with choreographer Sir Frederick Ashton to promote British ballet and to make her company one of the best in the world. She also founded the Royal Ballet School, to train dancers from a very young age.

 ### Dewar, Sir James
(1842–1923)
Scientist

Inventor of the vacuum flask, which keeps contents warm or cold, Dewar worked in cryogenics – the science of freezing. He was the first to discover how to produce large quantities of liquid oxygen and liquid hydrogen (both are now used in space rockets), and to cool substances down to almost absolute zero (-459.67 °F/-273.15 °C).

 ### Dickens, Charles
(1812–1870)
Writer

Born into a poor family, 12-year-old Dickens was sent to work in a factory and was determined to make a better life for himself. After starting as a solicitor's clerk he worked at different reporting jobs. His first novel, *The Pickwick Papers*, was published in instalments in a popular magazine when Dickens was only 24. It was a great success, and he became famous.

Dickens produced many more novels and short stories. All combine dramatic plots, vivid character sketches, humour, and social criticism. Dickens was shocked by the miserable conditions in which many ordinary people had to live and work. He also used his skill as a popular writer to campaign for many causes.

NOVELS BY CHARLES DICKENS

1836 *The Pickwick Papers*	1854 *Hard Times*
1839 *Oliver Twist*	1857 *Little Dorrit*
1839 *Nicholas Nickleby*	1859 *A Tale of Two Cities*
1841 *The Old Curiosity Shop*	1861 *Great Expectations*
1841 *Barnaby Rudge*	1865 *Our Mutual Friend*
1843 *Martin Chuzzlewit*	1870 *Edwin Drood**
1848 *Dombey and Son*	
1850 *David Copperfield*	*unfinished when
1853 *Bleak House*	Dickens died

 ### Dirac, Paul
(1902–1984)
Scientist

Son of a Swiss father and a British mother, Dirac worked in a new and exciting form of mathematics known as quantum mechanics. This is used by scientists studying atoms and the amazingly small particles within them. He also found ways of using quantum mechanics (which describes tiny objects) together with Albert Einstein's revolutionary Theory of Relativity (which describes the vast universe). In 1928, he published calculations that explained how certain sub-atomic particles – tiny parts within atoms – behaved, and predicted the existence of new particles (which have since been discovered). He won the Nobel Prize in 1933.

Disraeli, Benjamin
(1809–1882)
Politician

Disraeli trained as a lawyer and worked as a journalist, but soon became active in politics. He was a keen, ambitious Tory (Conservative) Member of Parliament. In 1852, he became chancellor of the exchequer, and was prime minister in 1868 and from 1874 to 1880.

Disraeli believed in the idea of 'one nation', in which rich and poor worked together for the country's good. His government won praise for its policies to improve housing, make factories safer, and ban the sale of harmful food and drugs. Disraeli also negotiated important treaties between Britain and other nations. He strongly supported Britain's claims to rule an Empire, and arranged for Queen Victoria (who admired him greatly) to become empress of India. His great rival was Gladstone (*see* page 43).

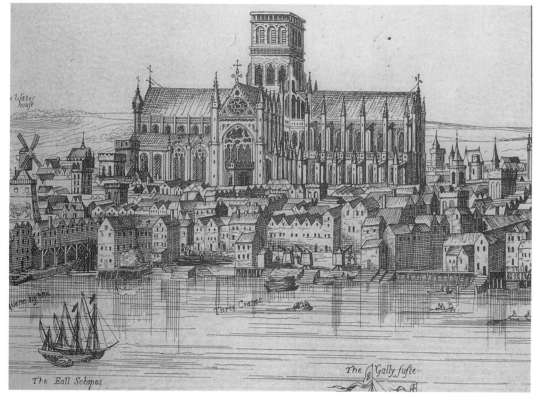

▲ ST PAUL'S CATHEDRAL, LONDON
Where preacher and writer John Donne gave his popular sermons.

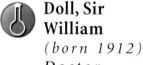

Doll, Sir William
(born 1912)
Doctor

A doctor specializing in research, Doll was the first to prove the link between smoking and lung cancer, together with his colleague Sir A. Bradford Hill. Their findings led to government campaigns to teach people about the dangers of cigarettes, and to limit smoking in public places.

Donald II
(?–900; reigned 889–900)
King

The first Scottish ruler to be called 'king of the Scots'. King Donald completed the task that many earlier Scottish leaders had failed to achieve. He succeeded in uniting almost the whole country – and its many very different peoples (including the Picts, Scots and Vikings) – under one single rule.

Donne, John
(1571?–1631)
Writer

A scholar, soldier, and then clergyman, Donne wrote some of the best-loved poems in the English language. Some of his lines, such as 'no man is an island' are still often quoted today. He was also a famous preacher, attracting many people to hear him at St Paul's Cathedral in London.

Doyle, Sir Arthur Conan
(1859–1930)
Writer

Doyle trained as a doctor in Edinburgh, but is famous today as the writer of stories featuring the brilliant, eccentric detective, Sherlock Holmes. When Doyle started writing, detective stories were a new and unusual type of fiction. His work did much to make them highly popular with readers round the world.

Drake, Sir Francis
(c.1542–1596)
Explorer

Born in Devon to a sea-faring family, Drake sailed with his cousin, Sir John Hawkins, to West Africa and the Caribbean. Fiercely Protestant, he regarded the Spaniards as his enemies. (They were Roman Catholics, and England's rivals at sea.) His pirate raids on Spanish ships off the coast of America were encouraged by Queen Elizabeth I. He also claimed California as a British colony.

Drake's raids made him very wealthy, and annoyed Spain. As a reward, Elizabeth knighted him on board his ship, *The Golden Hind*. From 1577 to 1580, Drake sailed round the world; only one ship had achieved this before. The peak of his career came in 1588, when he led English ships to fight against the Spanish Armada (armed fleet) and helped defeat it.

▶ THE GOLDEN HIND
Sir Francis Drake took three years to sail around the world in his favourite ship – *The Golden Hind*.

Dunlop, John
(1840–1921)
Inventor

Dunlop worked for most of his life as a vet, but was also a keen inventor. In 1888, he made the first-ever pneumatic (air-filled) tyre, which transformed 20th-century transport. Without it, bicycles (*right*), cars and lorries would not have been able to travel so safely or comfortably, or so fast.

Dunstan, St
(c.909–988)
Archbishop and Saint

Born to a noble family, Dunstan was brought up to be a monk. He was shrewd and scholarly, and soon became a leading adviser to King Edgar (*see* page 34). Dunstan also reformed the way the English Church was run.

du Pré, Jacqueline
(1945–1987)
Musician

From a musical family, du Pré's outstanding talent – as a cello-player – was clear even while she was a child. She gave her first solo performance aged 16, and was immediately in demand all round the world. She was forced by illness to retire from public performance in 1972, but continued to teach.

▶ MUSIC-MAKER
Cellist Jacqueline du Pré at the height of her fame.

THE STORY OF BICYCLES

*c.*1800 'Hobby-horse' – seat on two wheels ('bicycle' means 'two wheels'), pushed along by feet
1839 Scotsman Kirkpatrick Macmillan builds first pedal-powered bicycle
1863 French Michaux brothers invent bicycle with pedals fixed to front wheel
1870s Bicycle front wheel is made larger, to go faster
1879 H. J. Lawson invents chain mechanism to link pedals to wheels
*c.*1880 British engineer James Starley invents 'Penny-farthing' (huge front wheel and tiny rear wheel)
1885 John Starley invents 'Rover' safety bike, forerunner of modern bicycles
1889 Bicycles first fitted with pneumatic (air-filled) tyres (*see* Dunlop, left)
*c.*1900–1940 Bicycles now a cheap, popular form of mass transport
1960s First mountain bikes made in California, USA

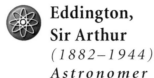

Eddington, Sir Arthur
(1882–1944)
Astronomer

Based at the Royal Observatory and the University of Cambridge, Eddington devoted his life to studying the composition and life-cycle of stars. He was one of the first people to understand the importance of scientist Albert Einstein's Theory of Relativity – a famous joke told how he and Einstein were the only people really to understand it. Eddington also wrote books, on the nature of the universe and on the scientific laws that rule its behaviour.

Edgar
(943–975; reigned 959–975)
King

Edgar lived at a time when Britain was divided into several separate kingdoms. It was also under attack from Viking raiders. By fighting and by peaceful negotiation, he tried to bring many parts of England under his control. He also reformed the coinage, made many new laws, and tried to limit the power of the Church.

Edward I
(1239–1307; reigned 1272–1307)
King

A famous warrior, Edward I earned the nickname 'Hammer of the Scots' for his wars against Scotland. He won many battles, but his armies were eventually driven back by Sir William Wallace (*see* page 103). Edward was more successful in his attacks on Wales. He defeated Welsh prince Llywelyn (*see* page 65) and took control of Wales in 1284. Many of the massive castles he built to control his newly-conquered lands still survive today. In England, Edward was best-known as a strong law-maker, who reformed the way English government was run.

◄ EDWARD III
One of England's longest-reigning monarchs.

Edward III
(1312–1377; reigned 1327–1377)
King

Grandson of Edward I (*see* left), Edward III came to power at a difficult time. His father, Edward II, had been put in prison, then murdered, by English nobles, because of his bad government. His mother, Isabella of France, was ruling the country with her lover, Mortimer. While still a teenager, Edward took control of the government, sent Isabella back to France, and gave orders for Mortimer to be killed.

Edward's strong government brought peace and prosperity to England for the rest of his reign. Handsome, brave and popular, he encouraged chivalry (noble, romantic fighting) among his supporters, and staged many lavish tournaments (mock battles, fought to win prizes). In 1337, he claimed the right to rule France, starting a long series of battles that became known as the Hundred Years War (1337–1453).

From 1348, outbreaks of plague (the 'Black Death') killed millions of people in England. This led to demands for better wages and conditions among ordinary people who survived, but Edward passed new laws to limit these demands. The laws pleased noble landowners, but made working people very angry. As Edward grew older, he handed over power to his son, the Black Prince (*see* page 35) and to his younger brother, John of Gaunt.

Edward IV

(1422–1483; reigned 1461–1483)
King

Edward ruled at a time when there was civil war in England. These battles – the Wars of the Roses (1455–1485) – were fought between rival nobles. All claimed the right to be the next king. Edward became king after his father, the Duke of York, was killed at the Battle of Wakefield. He was immediately challenged by the Earl of Lancaster's army, but defeated them at Towton.

A brave army leader, Edward was also a clever politician, famous for his intelligence and charm. He used these to help win over enemies and bring peace, though he could also be ruthless. His rule was constantly threatened by plots and rebellions, all of which he survived. His was criticized, however, for his pleasure-seeking lifestyle, and for his marriage (for love) to a widow from a non-noble family. Her scheming, ambitious relatives angered many of Edward's supporters, and turned them against him.

Edward VII

(1841–1910; reigned 1901–1910)
King

Son of Queen Victoria, Britain's longest-reigning ruler (*see* page 102), Edward did not became king until he was 60 years old. He spent his early years enjoying life – he was famously fond of good food, lively music and pretty women, and a keen sportsman – but he also helped and supported his mother after his father died.

Skilled at foreign languages, especially French, he took a keen interest in overseas affairs, before and after he became king. He supported the elected government's plans to make peaceful alliances with many European countries, hoping this would help to prevent future wars, and performed many public duties, at home and abroad, with good humour. He gave his name to a period of British history – the 'Edwardian Age' (*c.*1900–1914) – when Britain was at its richest, most powerful and most confident.

Edward, the Black Prince

(1330–1376)
Prince

Eldest son of Edward III (*see* page 34), Prince Edward was his father's top army commander. He fought many battles against France during the Hundred Years' War, and also in Spain. There, he caught a disease that killed him young, so he never became king. Famous and very popular in his own time, his wartime adventures were recorded by Flemish historian Froissart, who portrayed him as the perfect noble knight (*see* box). He has been remembered in this way for over 600 years.

Edward, the Confessor

(c.1005–1066; reigned 1042–1066)
King and Christian Saint

Eldest son of King Ethelred II ('the Unready') and his wife, Emma. When a child, Edward had to flee to Normandy (northern France) to escape the Vikings. He lived there for many years. He returned to England in 1041, and became king in 1042. He ruled well, but faced problems. Rival nobles were quarrelling, the Vikings threatened to invade, and he had no son to inherit his kingdom. Foolishly, he promised two ambitious young men that they could rule after him. The first was Duke William of Normandy, who had helped him in France; the second was Harold, Earl of Wessex, who was the brother of Edward's wife.

When Edward died, in 1066, Harold declared himself king. He was attacked by Vikings from the north, then Duke William invaded from the south. Harold was killed by William's soldiers at the Battle of Hastings in 1066. William (now known as 'the Conqueror') became king.

KNIGHTS AND CHIVALRY

Knights were expert fighting men who came from high-ranking families. They were trained from boyhood to handle deadly weapons and spirited war-horses. Knights were bound by a code of honour to be loyal to the king and to treat women and the Church with respect. Ordinary people called them 'sir'. Some knights owned castles and rich estates. Others, who were less wealthy, served in the private armies of great lords. Being a knight was difficult and dangerous, but it could bring rich rewards of treasure captured in war – and the chance to win fame that might last for hundreds of years. The brave deeds of noble knights were praised in minstrels' poems and songs.

 ## Elgar, Sir Edward
(1857–1934)
Musician

One of the most important English composers, Elgar wrote many works for orchestras, choirs and solo instruments that are still popular today. His music blended the rich 'romantic' style of great European classical composers with gentler English themes. Many of Elgar's works were inspired by the beautiful countryside of the Malvern Hills, where he lived. One of his tunes was later turned into the famous song 'Land of Hope and Glory'.

 ## Eliot, George
(pen-name of Mary Ann Evans)
(1819–1880)
Writer

Daughter of a wealthy landowner, Evans was a very clever child. She was also a talented musician, and deeply religious. When her mother died, she took over the running of their large household, but religious doubts led to quarrels with her father, so she left and spent years studying philosophy and writing for serious magazines.

From 1854, Evans lived with scholar G. H. Lewes, who encouraged her to write fiction. As she doubted her skills and wanted no publicity, she published under a man's name. However, her books won great praise and popularity for their intelligence, skilful story-telling, understanding of how people think and feel, and perceptive comments about 19th-century life. Her major novels include *The Mill on the Floss* (1860) and *Middlemarch* (1871–1872).

THE GOLDEN AGE OF ELIZABETHAN ENGLAND

The years 1558-1603, when Queen Elizabeth ruled England and Wales, are sometimes called 'a golden age'. Her cautious policies brought peace after years of religious quarrels, and her courage and determination helped fight off attacks from rival nations, especially France and Spain.

Elizabeth's reign saw tremendous achievements in English culture, including poems and plays by writers such as Shakespeare, Marlowe and Spenser. Elizabeth also encouraged voyages of exploration to North and South America, and round the world.

 ## Elizabeth I
(1533–1603;
reigned 1558–1603)
Queen

Elizabeth came to power at a time when the country faced many problems. At home, there were serious quarrels between Catholics and Protestants. Abroad, there were threats from rival nations Spain and France, and from rival claimants to her throne, especially Mary Queen of Scots (*see* page 72).

A clever, well-educated, very cautious politician, Elizabeth arranged a moderate settlement to the religious quarrels, and worked with trusted advisers and army commanders to defend England from foreign attack. Where possible, she made peace treaties, but, when war could not be avoided, she encouraged English troops with rousing speeches. She became tremendously popular after English sailors stopped the Spanish Armada (fleet of ships) from invading in 1588.

During Elizabeth's reign, great achievements were seen in music, art and especially literature. She paid for many poets and writers – including Shakespeare – to perform their works at her court. She also encouraged explorers like Sir Francis Drake (*see* page 33) and Sir Walter Raleigh (*see* page 87) to seek treasure and claim new lands for England overseas.

Elizabeth's private life was always unhappy. Her mother, Anne Bolyen, was executed by her father, Henry VIII (*see* page 51). Her older sister, Mary I (*see* page 71), died bitter and disappointed, hated by many of the people she ruled. Her only surviving brother, Edward VI, was sickly and died in his teens. As a young woman, Elizabeth survived various plots against her life. Early in her reign, she decided to remain single and did so. This was the only way that she could be sure of staying in power. As a result it seems that she often felt extremely lonely, especially in older age.

▲ ELIZABETH I
One of England's most successful rulers.

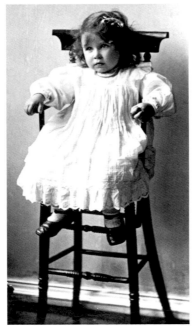

▶ BRITAIN'S
FUTURE QUEEN
Elizabeth, the Queen
Mother, photographed at
about three years of age.
She went on to become one
of her country's best-loved
royal figures.

 ## Elizabeth II
*(born 1926; started reign 1952,
crowned 1953)*
Queen

When Elizabeth was born, her parents, the Duke and
Duchess of York (*see* right), did not expect to become
king and queen. She was educated at their home in London
and at Windsor Castle, and was a bright student, especially in
history, music and languages. During World War II, she
volunteered to work as a driver for the ATS (the women's
branch of the army). In 1947, she married a distant cousin,
Prince Philip of Greece, and from 1951 began to undertake
royal duties on behalf of her father, who was unwell. He died
in 1952, and she was crowned queen the following year.

Although she has no say in government policy, Elizabeth is
admired by politicians for her knowledge and judgement. She
performs many royal
duties and has travelled
more than any previous
British ruler. She is
particularly interested in
the Commonwealth – a
worldwide group of
nations, all of which were
once part of the British
Empire. Some younger
members of her family
were criticized in the late
20th century, but
Elizabeth is still widely
respected for her hard
work and devotion to
duty. In private, her great
enthusiasm is for
horse-racing, and she
owns some of the best
racehorses in Britain.

 ## Elizabeth, the Queen Mother
(1900–2002)
Queen and Queen Mother

The ninth child of an aristocratic family, Elizabeth Bowes-
Lyon was brought up in Glamis Castle, Scotland. She liked
the countryside and country sports, especially horse-racing and
fishing. Petite and pretty, she became celebrated as one of the
most charming young women in London 'high society', and in
1923 she married Prince Albert, Duke of York.

The couple performed many royal duties, including long trips
to Africa and Australia, although they preferred a quiet life at
home with their children. Their lives changed dramatically in
1936, when Albert's brother, Edward VIII, decided to abdicate
(stop being king). Albert was crowned George VI, and Elizabeth
became queen. She was now a public figure, and soon became
well-loved, especially after she refused to leave London during
World War II. She faced dangerous bombing raids and spent
much time encouraging war-workers and comforting survivors.

King George died in 1952, and Elizabeth and Albert's
daughter became queen (as Elizabeth II, *see* left). Elizabeth
chose the title 'Queen Mother' and continued to make many
public appearances. There were national celebrations when she
reached her one-hundredth birthday, in 2000.

 ## Evans, Sir Arthur
(1851–1941)
Explorer

Evans pioneered many modern archaeological techniques,
and became famous for his excavations of the royal palace
at Knossos, on the Greek island of Crete. His work added a
great deal to people's knowledge of early Greek history and art.

 ## Evans, Dame Edith
(1888–1976)
Actress

One of Britain's
best-known and
best-loved actresses,
Evans could use her
unmistakable voice to
express a wide range of
deep thoughts and feelings.
During a very long and
successful career, on stage and in
films, Evans played many different
roles, from Shakespeare to 20th-century drama. She was most
famous as Lady Bracknell – uttering the words, 'a handbag?' –
in the play *The Importance of Being Earnest*, written by Oscar
Wilde (*see* page 107).

Faraday, Michael

(1791–1867)
Scientist

Faraday began his career as assistant to Humphry Davy (*see* page 30), then started his own investigations. He won great respect among other scientists for the brilliant experiments he designed. Faraday made many important discoveries about electricity and magnetism, and also investigated the electrical properties of atoms. A unit of electrical measurement, the farad, is named after him.

Fawcett, Dame Millicent Garrett

(1847–1929)
Campaigner

Fawcett spent most of her adult life campaigning peacefully for women's right to vote, and for laws that treated women equally with men. In 1897, she became president of the National Union of Women's Suffrage Societies – a nationwide federation of groups campaigning for women's rights. Fawcett also worked as assistant to her politician husband, who was blind, and wrote books about famous women, and about women and the law. She lived just long enough to see the law passed, in 1928, that gave votes to all women over 21.

Fawkes, Guy

(1570–1606)
Activist

One of the leaders of the Gunpowder Plot, 1605. This was a conspiracy to murder the Protestant king, James I of England, by blowing him up with gunpowder, and to replace him with a Roman Catholic ruler. The plotters believed this was the only way to win religious freedom for Catholics in England. However, most Catholics did not support the plot, and disliked the violence involved. The plotters were betrayed, and Fawkes was discovered on November 5th, hiding with barrels of gunpowder under the Houses of Parliament. With seven others, he was hanged for treason. Fawkes' plot is still remembered today, when people burn 'guys' on bonfires on November 5th.

Ferrier, Kathleen

(1912–1953)
Musician

Born in Lancashire, Ferrier worked as a telephone operator until she won a singing competition in 1940, soon after the start of World War II. In wartime, she gave many concerts to troops and factory workers. Her mellow voice, skilled musicianship and warm personality attracted many fans. After the war was over, Ferrier established a very successful career singing in concerts and operas; she was greatly missed when she died, aged only 41.

Fielding, Henry

(1705–1754)
Writer

Playwright and novelist Fielding produced many satirical books, mocking other writers and criticizing the way some people lived. His most famous novel was *Tom Jones*. Fielding was friends with many politicians and lawyers, and, in 1748, was appointed a magistrate (junior judge). Until his early death, he worked hard to reform law and order in London.

Fiennes, Celia
(1662–1741)
Explorer

Between 1662 and 1702, Fiennes made many journeys on horseback around England. At that time, it was extremely unusual for a woman to travel without her husband or father to protect her, but Fiennes took just one or two servants for company. She travelled (as she herself said) 'in a spirit of pure curiosity', keeping diaries and noting all the interesting or unusual things that she had seen. Today, her diaries are a highly valuable source of information about daily life in 17th-century England.

Flamsteed, John
(1646–1719)
Astronomer

In 1675, Flamsteed was appointed England's first astronomer royal, based at the Royal Greenwich Observatory in London. He was asked to help draw up accurate star-charts, to guide sailors at sea. In fact, he produced the world's first star atlas, describing the carefully observed positions of almost 3,000 stars. Flamsteed also observed the changing position of the Sun and Moon in the sky, and calculated tables showing the changing tides.

Fleming, Alexander
(1881–1955)
Doctor

Born in Scotland, Fleming worked as a medical researcher. In 1928, he noticed that green mould growing on a dish in his laboratory was killing bacteria nearby. From this discovery, he helped create penicillin, one of the world's first antibiotic drugs (*see* box). Penicillin was not widely available until 1940, when Sir Howard Florey found ways of mass-producing it. Since then, it has saved many lives. Fleming and Florey were jointly awarded the Nobel Prize for medicine in 1945.

Fonteyn, Margot (Peggy Hookham)
(1919–1991)
Dancer

Fonteyn was the first internationally acclaimed ballerina to be trained in England. (Before her, most ballet dancers came from Russia, Italy or France.) She gave her first performance in 1935, and continued to dance – and win great applause – for many years.

Fonteyn was famous for her elegance, sensitivity and charm. She performed many well-established roles, but also created new ones. In 1962, she formed one of the most famous dancing partnerships in the history of ballet, with Russian superstar Rudolf Nureyev. Fonteyn also worked to popularize ballet, by appearing on television and writing books.

ANTIBIOTICS

An antibiotic is any substance that can destroy, or weaken, the growth of harmful bacteria, or 'germs' (tiny micro-organisms, or life-forms, found all around us). Many antibiotics occur naturally; for example, they are made by fungi in the soil. Others are made by humans in laboratories. Penicillin, the first antibiotic to be used as a drug, is based on a naturally occurring mould. It was discovered by Alexander Fleming (*see* Fleming entry) in 1928. Since then, many more antibiotic drugs have been created. They have had a major impact on human health, dramatically reducing the death rate from diseases caused by bacterial infection.

Foster, Sir Norman

(born 1935)
Designer

Architect Foster is famous for dramatic buildings made of glass and steel. He uses the latest engineering technology to create exciting new shapes. Well-known buildings include: head-quarters of the Hongkong and Shanghai Banking Corporation, Hong Kong (completed 1986), Stansted Airport, Essex (comp. 1991), Canary Wharf underground station, London (comp. 1999), the new German Reichstag (Parliament building), Berlin (comp. 1999) and the Millennium Bridge in London, across the river Thames (comp. 2000, but general opening delayed due to technical problems).

▲ GLASS AND STEEL
Passenger buildings at Stansted Airport, Essex, England, designed by Sir Norman Foster.

Fox, Charles James

(1749–1806)
Politician

Fox became an MP aged only 19, as a member of the Whig (Liberal) Party. He was soon famous for his revolutionary views. He supported the American colonists who were rebelling against British rule in the late 1700s, and French citizens who rebelled against their king in 1789. In 1806, he helped to get a law banning slavery passed by Parliament.

Fox, George

(1624–1691)
Religious leader

Christian preacher Fox disagreed with the way the Church in England was run. He disliked elaborate ritual, and distrusted the power of priests. From 1647, he spent many years travelling the countryside, speaking to ordinary people about his religious views. He taught that God speaks directly to people's souls, and that God should be worshipped simply and straightforwardly. Around 1650, Fox founded a religious society called 'Friends of the Truth'. It later became known as the 'Society of Friends', or the 'Quakers'. Fox was put in prison many times for his views, but continued to preach.

Foxe, John

(1516–1587)
Religious writer

Christian priest Foxe lived during the Reformation - a time when people in Europe held very strong views about religion, and were prepared to fight over them. On one side, reformers known as Protestants criticized the beliefs and practices of the Roman Catholic Church. On the other side, Catholics thought that Protestants were dangerous, and wrong. Foxe was a Protestant. He fled from England during the reign of Catholic queen Mary I, who executed many Protestants for refusing to give up their beliefs. He recorded details of the executions in a book (later known as *Foxe's Book of Martyrs*), published in England in 1563. Many people were so shocked by reading it that they stopped being Catholics and supported the Protestant cause.

▶ GEORGE FOX
Preacher and founder of the Quaker movement.

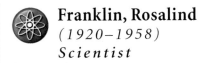 ## Franklin, Rosalind
(1920–1958)
Scientist

Franklin was one of the first scientists to use X-rays to study how matter is made. She began her work by investigating coal, and then started to explore living substances, including viruses and DNA – the basic 'building block' of life that is found in all human cells. Discovering how this was made was tremendously important, and laid the foundations for all future work in genetics.

Franklin died aged only 38, of cancer – probably caused by the X-rays she used in her work. Some people believe that she should have been given greater credit for her discoveries, but in fact fame and praise for investigating DNA went to American James Watson and Briton Francis Crick (*see* page 28).

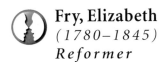 ## Fry, Elizabeth
(1780–1845)
Reformer

Married to a wealthy banker, Fry could have had a comfortable, sheltered life. But she believed it was her duty to help others. She began to visit women in prison, and was shocked at the conditions she found. The women were in crowded, dirty cells, often without any food. Their children had to go to prison with them, even though they had not committed any crime. Fry organized clean clothes and water and fresh food. She set up prison schools and found work, such as sewing, that the women could do to earn a little money. She also spent hours talking or reading to them, believing that most prisoners could be helped to live honest, useful lives.

Frobisher, Sir Martin
(1539–1594)
Explorer

Aged 14, Frobisher left his respectable, wealthy family for a risky, adventurous life at sea. He took part in pirate raids off Africa, and against Spain, but later decided to search for the North-West Passage (*see* Baffin, page 10). In 1576, he reached the Arctic Circle, but was forced to retreat by ice. He tried again in 1577 and 1578, but failed, and people mocked him. He won back his good name by fighting bravely against the Spanish Armada (invasion fleet) in 1588.

▼ FROBISHER'S JOURNEYS

Fuchs, Sir Vivian
(born 1908)
Explorer

Trained as a geologist, Fuchs (*see* below) led the Commonwealth Trans-Antarctic expedition of 1955 to 1958. His team made the first-ever crossing of Antarctica.

▲ SIR VIVIAN FUCHS
Arriving at the South Pole in 1958.

ARCTIC AND ANTARCTIC EXPLORATION

ARCTIC (NORTH POLE):
1878–1879 Nils Nordenskjold (Norway) is first to sail along Northeast Passage
1883–1885 Fridtjof Nansen (Norway) gets closer to North Pole than anyone before, after daring expedition via frozen sea
1903–1906 Roald Amundsen (Norway) is first to sail along North-West Passage
1909 Robert E. Peary (USA) claims to be first to reach North Pole
1926 Richard Byrd (USA) flies over North Pole
1958–1959 US submarine *Nautilus* makes first crossing of Arctic Ocean underneath polar ice-cap
1969 Wally Herbert (UK) leads first surface crossing of Arctic Ocean

ANTARCTIC (SOUTH POLE):
1820-1840 Various US and UK ships explore Antarctic coast
1900–1904 Robert Scott (UK) leads National Antarctic Expedition; travels inland in Antarctica
1908–1909 Sir Ernest Shackleton (UK) gets within 155 km (96 miles) of South Pole, closer than anyone before
1911 Roald Amundsen (Norway) is first to reach South Pole
1912 Sir Robert Scott (UK) reaches South Pole; dies on return journey
1914–1916 Sir Ernest Shackleton (UK) and crew are trapped in frozen sea; make daring escape to South Georgia
1929 Richard Byrd (USA) flies over South Pole
1955–1958 Sir Vivian Fuchs (UK) makes first crossing of Antarctica

Gainsborough, Thomas
(1727–1788)
Artist

 ▲ VIEW OF DEDHAM
Gainsborough painted many genteel scenes of the English countryside.

The most famous and popular artist of his time, most of Gainsborough's works portray fashionable people, in beautiful landscape settings. Towards the end of his career, he turned to painting dramatic scenery and ordinary people's lives.

Gaskell, Elizabeth (known as 'Mrs Gaskell')
(1810–1865)
Writer

After marrying a clergyman, Gaskell devoted her life to caring for her children and sharing her husband's welfare work. She began to write to help cope with her grief at the death of her baby son. Her novels, such as *North and South* (1854–1855), paint a vivid picture of life among ordinary people, and show a deep sympathy with their troubles, hopes and fears. Gaskell also supported many campaigns to improve working and housing conditions in big factory towns.

George I
(1660–1727; reigned 1714–1727)
King

Great-grandson of King James VI and I (*see* page 55), George was born in Germany, and became ruler of the German state of Hanover in 1698. He inherited the right to be king of Great Britain and Ireland after Queen Anne, last ruler of the Stuart dynasty, died without children. He never learned English, and relied heavily on government ministers to help him rule. He was very unpopular throughout Britain, but is remembered today as the founder of a new dynasty (ruling family) – the Hanoverians.

George III
(1738–1820; reigned 1760–1820)
King

Grandson of George I, George III was a very different character. Hard-working, religious, and devoted to his family, he played an important part in politics, supporting the Tory Party and strengthening royal control of the government.

However, George faced many problems that he was unable to solve. There were riots by political reformers, a long war with France, quarrels with India and Ireland, and demands for independence by Britain's colonies in America. George refused to compromise with any of them, and this led to further protests at home, and the formation of a new, independent nation in America. George also suffered from mental illness, and in 1811 was declared unfit to rule. His son, the Prince Regent (later George IV) ruled for him until he died.

George V
(1865–1936; reigned 1910–1936)
King

Son of Edward VII (*see* page 35), George V served in the Navy as a young man. He did not expect to rule, but became heir to the British throne in 1901, when his older brother died. He won respect for his hard work and devotion to duty, especially during World War I. He also tried to solve political problems in Ireland (the southern part of the country was demanding independence), and worked closely with top politicians during the economic crisis of the 1930s. He was the first British ruler ever to make a broadcast to the nation.

George VI

(1895–1952; reigned 1936–1952)
King

The second son of George V, he became a naval officer, taking part in battles at sea during World War I. He also served in the Royal Air Force. By nature shy and quiet, he became king (and the centre of public attention) when his elder brother Edward VIII scandalously decided to give up the throne. His personal courage and sincerity helped to improve the image of the royal family, as did his happy family life with his wife (Elizabeth, now the Queen Mother) and his daughters, Elizabeth (now Queen) and Margaret.

▲ **GEORGE VI**
King Edward VIII (second from left) and his brothers. The future George VI is second from right.

Gerard, John

(1545–1612)
Doctor

Trained as a barber-surgeon (a doctor who performed rough-and-ready operations), Gerard also studied plants. In 1597, he published a picture book (known today as *Gerard's Herbal*) listing hundreds of medicinal plants. It was used by doctors and ordinary people for over 100 years, and is still consulted today.

Gibbon, Edward

(1737–1794)
Writer

Writer and Member of Parliament, Gibbon won fame for his massive book, in five volumes: *The History of the Decline and Fall of the Roman Empire*. In it, he described the way in which powerful nations – such as Rome – eventually weaken and collapse, and tried to explain the reasons why. He also criticized the effects of Christianity throughout Europe. This won him many enemies.

Gielgud, Sir John

(1904–2000)
Actor

Famous for his beautiful speaking voice, and intelligent, sensitive performances, Gielgud won praise for acting classic roles such as Shakespeare's Hamlet, and for taking part in daring modern plays. He also directed various stage productions, appeared on radio and television, and starred in many films. He won an Oscar in 1980.

▲ **SIR JOHN GIELGUD**
One of Britain's finest actors, with an unforgettable voice.

Gladstone, William Ewart

(1809–1898)
Politician

After serving as a Conservative government minister, Gladstone changed his political views and joined the Liberal Party. He campaigned for better working conditions in factories, religious tolerance, and a ban on slavery. He was prime minister four times between 1868 and 1894.

While in office, Gladstone reorganized government finances, the armed forces and the civil service. He also introduced many reforms. The most important were designed to improve education, make Parliament closer to the people, and remove unfairness in Irish land-owning law. He believed strongly that Ireland should have the right to rule itself (*see* box). This led to a major split within the Liberal Party.

▲ **GLADSTONE, PM**
Gladstone making a rousing speech in Parliament.

HOME RULE

Many people in Ireland opposed the 1801 Act of Union, which made Ireland a part of Britain. In 1886 and 1893, Gladstone's Liberal Party put 'Home Rule' bills before Parliament, asking for the Union to be abolished. They were defeated. In 1916, Irish independence supporters began a series of violent rebellions. A fourth Home Rule bill came before Parliament in 1920. Ireland (apart from Ulster) finally won independence in 1921.

Glendower, Owen
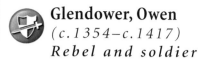
(c.1354–c.1417)
Rebel and soldier

Descended from Welsh princes, Glendower began his political career working for the English government. However, his failure to win promotion, and his disgust with brutal and arrogant English rule in Wales turned him into a rebel, fighting for independence.

Glendower won many Welsh supporters, and in 1400 they declared him 'Prince of Wales' – a title claimed by the sons of English kings. For the rest of his life, Glendower led armies to attack English soldiers and capture English castles in Wales. This was the last Welsh revolt against English rule, and it failed. By around 1416, English troops controlled all of Wales. Glendower was killed in the fighting, but no one knows exactly where or when. Legend says he will return to fight again.

Godiva, Lady
(died 1080)
Noblewoman

Godiva was the wife of Leofric, Earl of Mercia (in the English Midlands). Legends told how she promised to ride naked through Coventry market-place if her husband abolished an unfair and unpopular tax on ordinary people. He agreed, not thinking that she would keep her promise – but Godiva did. Out of respect, all the citizens stayed indoors, looking the other way, except for one man – 'Peeping Tom'. It is said that he was punished by going blind.

Goodall, Jane
(born 1934)
Naturalist

Even as a child, Goodall was fascinated by animals. In 1957, she went to Tanzania, Africa, to work with pioneer archaeologist Louis Leakey, who was investigating ape-like ancestors of modern human beings. In 1970, Goodall moved to study living apes at the Gombe Reserve, where she has been based ever since.

Goodall's methods were at first criticized for treating animals like people, but she has since won admiration for her discoveries about animal behaviour. She has also become an active campaigner for wildlife and environmental conservation.

Gordon, Charles George

(1833–1885)
General

A soldier, explorer and administrator, Gordon fought bravely in the Crimean War. In 1860, he went to China with British army engineers. While there, he led troops that crushed the Taiping Rebellion (1863–1864), which was threatening to overturn the Chinese government and attack its foreign allies.

In 1874, Gordon joined the staff of the Khedive (ruler) of Egypt as an expert administrator, and worked to end the slave trade there. In 1884, he was ordered by the British government to go to the Sudan, further south in Africa, to rescue British soldiers surrounded by rebel armies. However, he became trapped in the Sudanese city of Khartoum, where he died after a siege lasting 10 months. His death aroused public anger in Britain, and he was honoured as a hero of the British Empire.

Grace, W. G. (William Gilbert)
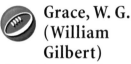
(1848–1915)
Sportsman

One of the most famous sportsmen of the 19th century, batsman Grace played cricket for Gloucestershire and England, finally retiring aged 50. During his long career, he scored over 50,000 runs and made 126 centuries. He captained the English side twice, in 1880 and 1882.

▲ W. G. GRACE
Scored 54,896 runs and took 2,864 wickets during a long career.

CRICKET

Cricket has probably been played in England since the 16th century, or earlier. Today, the sport is popular worldwide, especially in countries that were once part of the British Empire. (During the late 20th century, non-British teams were much more successful than the English side.) The first recorded game between rival English counties was in 1719. By 1744, elaborate laws governing the game had been drawn up. From 1787, they were administered by the MCC (Marylebone Cricket Club, in London). The first test match (international challenge contest) was held between England and Australia, in Melbourne, in 1877.

Grade, Lord (Lew) (originally Louis Winogradsky)

(1906–1991)
Entertainer

Born to a Jewish family in Russia, Grade moved to London aged 12, to escape religious persecution. At first he worked in the clothing industry, then became a professional dancer. With his brother Leslie, he opened a theatrical agency in 1934. It soon became the largest in Europe. When independent television broadcasting began in the 1950s, Grade recognized its great potential as a new form of entertainment. He set up Associated Television (ATV) to provide popular comedy and variety programmes, and ran the (highly profitable) programming for the London and Midlands regions from 1954 until 1968.

▲ Lady Jane Grey

Grattan, Henry

(1746–1820)
Politician

Born and educated in Dublin, at a time when all Ireland was ruled from England, Grattan campaigned for Irish independence. He trained as a lawyer, then entered the Irish Parliament, where he won fame as a brilliant speaker. He campaigned, successfully, to repeal (cancel) the rule by which all laws made in Ireland also had to be approved by the English Parliament. This made him a national hero. He also opposed the union of the English and Irish Parliaments in 1801, but agreed to represent an Irish constituency in the new united Parliament. Once there, he campaigned strongly for equal rights for Roman Catholics.

Greene, Graham

(1904–1991)
Writer

One of the most famous writers of the 20th century, Greene's novels combine exciting storylines with the discussion of important moral questions of sin and forgiveness, right and wrong. All Greene's work was strongly influenced by his Roman Catholic faith. His best known works include *Brighton Rock* (1938), *The Power and the Glory* (1940), *The Third Man* (1950), and *Travels with My Aunt* (1969). Many were made into successful films.

Grey, Lady Jane

(1537–1554)
Noblewoman

Great-niece of King Henry VIII, Lady Jane Grey was used by her powerful relatives to try and win power. Well-educated, and a keen supporter of the reformed Protestant Church, she was married to the son of a top politician, the Duke of Northumberland, who hoped that his family would one day rule England. When sickly boy-king Edward VI died in 1553, Northumberland and his supporters declared that Jane was queen. But they were challenged by other nobles, loyal to Henry VIII's daughters Mary and Elizabeth. Jane was forced to give up the throne after only nine days, and Mary came to power. Jane was imprisoned and executed the next year.

Gryffud ap Llewellyn

(1039–1063)
King

King of Gwynedd (southern Wales), Gryffud was the first and only Welsh king to unite all Wales as one nation. He spent most of his life fighting, against Welsh rivals and English invaders. He also fought against the Vikings and, for a while, drove them from his lands. He was defeated in battle after the English and Vikings united against him, then killed by his own men. After his death, Wales split up again into several small kingdoms.

▲ Gryffud ap Llewellyn

Gwynn, Nell

(1650–1687)
Actress

From a poor background, Gwynn started her career selling oranges to audiences in London theatres. She then became an actress, and her beauty, good humour and wit attracted many noblemen. Her most famous lover was King Charles II, and their children were given noble titles. On his deathbed, Charles was reported to have asked his servants to make sure that Nell was well looked after. He said, 'Let not poor Nelly starve.'

h

Hallowes, Odette
(1912–1995)
Secret agent

French-born Hallowes was recruited by the British army to serve as a secret agent during World War II. She entered German-occupied France in disguise in 1942, and worked with members of the French Resistance (anti-German spies) there, until she was captured by German troops in 1943. She was imprisoned and tortured, but refused to betray her colleagues or reveal British secrets. She was set free at the end of the war, and was awarded the George Cross medal for her courage.

▲ FLOWER OF WAR

The poppy is a symbol of World War I (*see* Haig), because many soldiers died in French poppy fields.

Haig, Douglas (Earl Haig)
(1861–1928)
Army Field Marshal

From a wealthy family, Haig went to university then joined the army as a career officer. He fought in the Sudan with Gordon (*see* page 44), and in the second Boer War (1889–1902, against Dutch settlers in South Africa).

Appointed commander of British troops in France during World War I (1914–1918), Haig's tactics caused great controversy – and enormous loss of life. He was convinced that Germany could only be defeated by sending huge armies to fight along the Western Front (the boundary between the enemies, in Belgium and northern France). Millions of men suffered and died there, trapped in muddy trenches, caught on barbed wire, suffocated by poisoned gas or killed by machine-gun bullets and shells. After the war was over, Haig worked for ex-soldiers' welfare. He set up the Haig Fund, which sold red poppies once a year to raise money for injured men and their families. Historians still cannot agree on whether Haig's battle plans were justified.

Hanway, Jonas
(1712–1786)
Campaigner

Businessman Hanway made adventurous journeys to Europe and the Middle East, but is today remembered for his work to help poor people – especially children – in Britain.

Hanway used the money he made from trade to set up schemes to train boys to become sailors, to care for abandoned babies, and to bring up orphaned children. He campaigned for laws to stop boys being forced to work as chimney-sweeps (hundreds died this way) and encouraged prison reform. He set up Sunday schools, where children could learn to read, write and study the Bible. He hoped this would help them find work, and free them from a life of poverty.

Halley, Edmond
(1656–1742)
Astronomer

Oxford mathematics professor, astronomer and friend of brilliant astronomer Isaac Newton (*see* page 77), Halley was one of the first scientists to study nebulae – mysterious clouds of glowing gas that appear in the night sky. He is best-known today for his observations of a bright comet, now named after him, that travels at regular intervals (every 76 years) across the sky. (*See* box p47.)

▶ HALLEY'S COMET
The comet glows brightly in the night sky as it passes Earth.

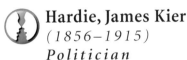

Hardie, James Kier
(1856–1915)
Politician

Born to a poor, unwed mother in Scotland, Hardie went out to work aged only 8 years old, to help his family survive. He became a coal-miner aged 10. As a young man, he began to campaign for improvements in miners' pay and conditions; he also studied at night school. He found work as a journalist, then became an MP. In 1893, he was a founder member of the Independent Labour Party. This later joined with other working people's organizations to form the Labour Party, and Hardie served as Party Chairman from 1905–6. Although Hardie never held government office, he was an important political figure. He was respected for his firm Christian faith and his strong belief in trade unions, worldwide peace and co-operation, women's rights and social reform.

HALLEY'S COMET

A bright comet, with a distinctive fiery tail, that is visible from Earth about once every 76 years as it orbits the Sun. Its first recorded sighting was 240BC, although it has probably been travelling along its present orbit for the past 200,000 years. It was first recognized to be a regular visitor to the skies above Earth by astronomer Edmond Halley, and bears his name. Like other comets, it is a ball of ice and dust with a tail of dust and gas, and it is getting smaller. Astronomers calculate that it will disappear completely around 300,000 years from now.

Hardwick, Elizabeth (Bess of Hardwick)
(c.1520–1608)
Noblewoman

Famous for her energy, determination, artistic flair – and fiery temper – Bess made marriage her career. She had four husbands; each was very wealthy, and left her vast estates and large sums of money when they died. She spent this on building magnificent country houses, employing the leading architects and craftworkers of her time. Her most famous house, Hardwick Hall (in Derbyshire), survives almost unchanged today.

Bess was a shrewd businesswoman who invested in land and industry. She also made money from lending to other people. Her last husband, the Earl of Shrewsbury, was from one of the grandest noble families in the land. Bess arranged a politically useful marriage for their son, and plotted to make their daughter-in-law queen – but failed.

Hardy, Thomas
(1840–1928)
Writer

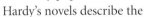

Son of a stone-mason from Dorset, in south-west England, Hardy trained as an architect but became a writer. He published a series of novels set in Dorset and the counties nearby, which he called Wessex. They became very popular.

Hardy's novels describe the lives of ordinary people and their struggles against injustice, bad luck and misunderstandings. He also painted vivid pictures of the Wessex countryside, in which the weather and scenery often seem to mirror his characters' feelings. His most famous works include *Tess of the D'Urbervilles* (1891), *Far From the Madding Crowd* (1874), and *Jude the Obscure* (1896). Towards the end of his life, Hardy wrote poetry, which also won great praise.

Hargreaves, James
(c.1720–1778)
Inventor

Trained as a woodworker and maker of weaving-looms, Hargreaves invented a new machine that could spin several strands of thread at once. It became known as a 'Spinning Jenny', and played a great part in the Industrial Revolution that transformed the British economy during the early 19th century. Using machines like Hargreaves' 'Jenny', goods could be made much more quickly and cheaply than in the old-fashioned way, by hand.

 Harold II
(1019–1066; reigned 1066)
King

▲ **HAROLD'S DEFEAT**
A scene from the Bayeux tapestry (c.1100), showing the king's death.

The last Anglo-Saxon king of England, Harold reigned for less than one year. Son of Earl Godwin of Wessex, the most powerful nobleman in the country, Harold was sent to France by English king Edward the Confessor (*see* page 35) in 1064. There, he promised loyalty to Duke William of Normandy, who wanted to be king of England after Edward died. Edward, however, wanted Harold to be king instead, and publicly named him as his heir. He was crowned the day after Edward died.

Harold soon faced problems. Many noble families would not support him; his own brother (Tostig), and Viking king Harald Hardrada invaded northern England. Harold led an army to meet them, and defeated them at Stamford Bridge. Meanwhile, however, William was also planning an invasion. Harold hurried south to fight bravely against William at Hastings, but was killed. William became king.

THE NORMANS IN ENGLAND

After Harold II died at the Battle of Hastings, a new dynasty ruled England. They became known as the Normans, after their homeland in Normandy, northern France. The first, most famous, Norman king was William I (William the Conqueror). The Normans helped to make many major changes in England:

• they strengthened and reformed many government departments, including local government and law-enforcement
• they introduced new, and heavier, taxes
• French replaced English as the language spoken at the royal court and by noble families and government officials
• a new style of architecture developed, with massive pillars and rounded arches
• the government of the English Church was reorganized

 Harrison, John
(1693–1776)
Clock-maker

Harrison originally trained as a carpenter but taught himself mathematics and from there soon became interested in the whole field of time and clocks. He invented several devices to improve the time-keeping of clocks, but is most famous for his 'chronometer'. This was a small, portable clock, powered by a spring, that kept extremely accurate time for long distances. Harrison received half the prize of £20,000 for his invention – still a huge sum for the 1700s.

For the first time ever, Harrison's chronometer enabled sailors who were out of sight of land to calculate their precise position at sea. This greatly improved safety – sailors could avoid dangers such as reefs and whirlpools and ran less risk of getting lost. It also helped shipping companies to plan and develop new trade routes round the world.

Harrison quarrelled with many rivals, who said that his ideas would simply not work. However, after his death, his system was taken up and praised by Captain Cook (*see* page 27), which helped it to become widespread and well-accepted.

◀ **HARRISON'S CHRONOMETER**
Invented in 1735 it revolutionised maritime travel.

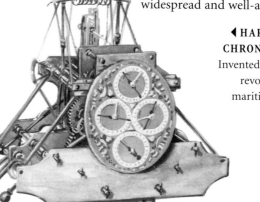

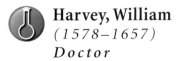

Harvey, William
(1578–1657)
Doctor

Court physician (doctor) to kings James I and Charles I, Harvey was the first European to discover how the blood circulates round the body through veins and arteries, and how the heart works as a pump. He also studied how babies grow and develop in the womb, and how animals move.

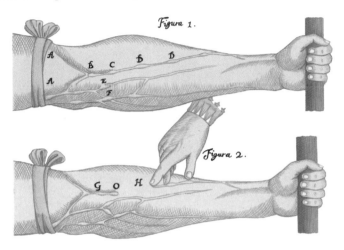

▲ SIR WILLIAM HARVEY
His diagram of how blood flows.

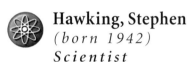

Hawking, Stephen
(born 1942)
Scientist

One of the youngest people ever elected to membership of Britain's prestigious Royal Society (an association of top scientists). Hawking has investigated the structure and origins of the universe by combining the two most important – and challenging – theories of 20th-century mathematics and physics: relativity and quantum mechanics. He also studied mysterious space objects such as black holes. His book on the universe, *A Brief History of Time*, became a best-seller when it was published in 1988.

◄ STEPHEN HAWKING
One of the greatest, and most famous, late 20th-century scientists.

BRITAIN IN EUROPE

The European Economic Community (or 'EEC', the forerunner of today's European Union) was set up in 1957 by France, Belgium, Luxembourg, the Netherlands, Italy and the Federal Republic of Germany. Members hoped to work together to boost economic development, encourage trade, and plan joint policies for farming, transport, financial services and employment. Some members also hoped for political union.

Britain applied to join the EEC in 1961 and 1967. Both times, the application was vetoed (turned down) by France. Many British people, however, including Edward Heath (*see* below) believed that Britain should join. Heath began discussions with the EEC in 1971, and signed a treaty agreeing membership the next year. After Heath left office, the new Labour government, led by Harold Wilson (*see* page 108) held a 'referendum' – a vote to see whether the British people might want to change the situation and leave the EEC. However, in 1975, British citizens voted to stay in the EEC by a large majority. Ever since then, Britain has remained a member, but many British politicians, and ordinary people, still do not think that close ties with Europe are a good idea.

Heath, Sir Edward
(born 1916)
Politician

▲ SIR EDWARD HEATH
Led Britain into Europe.

Conservative prime minister from 1970 to 1974, Heath is remembered today for his lifelong wish to bring the British closer to the rest of Europe. While he was in power, Britain finally joined the European Economic Community (today known as the EU, or European Union), after many years of negotiations and uncertainty (*see* box above). At home, Heath was less successful. His government faced serious economic problems, and he was forced to resign after a series of major strikes by coal-miners.

Henry I
(1068–1135; reigned 1100–1135)
King

Third son of William the Conqueror (see page 107), Henry was a well-educated man and a skilful politician and negotiator. When his eldest brother, King William II (William Rufus), died in an accident, Henry seized power, even though his older brother, Robert, was the rightful heir. This led to war, which Henry won in 1106. Henry worked hard to strengthen royal power, and to reorganize government finances. However, he did not leave a male heir and his death caused quarrels that led to civil war.

Henry II
(1133–1189; reigned 1154–1189)
King

Founder of the Plantagenet dynasty (line of rulers), Henry came to power as king of England after years of civil war fought between his mother, Matilda, and her rival, King Stephen. He conquered lands in Ireland and France, and forced the king of Scotland to recognize him as overlord. He also tried to reduce the power of the Church in England, but less successfully. He had to make a public apology after the murder of Archbishop Thomas Becket (*see* page 12).

Henry II

Henry IV
(1367–1413; reigned 1399–1413)
King

Grandson of Edward III (*see* page 34), and son of John of Gaunt, Henry (*above*) married a noble heiress and became the richest man in England. Henry also had political ambitions and wanted to be king. He won fame fighting in Germany, but was accused of plotting against King Richard II of England, and was exiled (sent away). His lands in northern England – the source of his wealth – were taken away from him.

In 1399, Henry returned to England, took back his lands, and forced Richard to give up the throne. He became king in Richard's place, founding a new dynasty – the Lancastrians. At first, his rule was successful and he defeated various riots and rebellions. However, he clashed with Members of Parliament, who accused him of extravagance. Henry was ill for most of his final years, and died at 46. He was succeeded by his son, Henry V (reigned 1413–1422), who won great fame fighting in the Hundred Years' War – a major dispute that had also been running throughout his father's reign (*see* box below).

THE HUNDRED YEARS' WAR

This was a long and damaging war between England and France, and one that England eventually lost. The conflict continued for so long (1340s–1450s) that it became known as the Hundred Years' War.

Fighting began in 1337, when the French king took control of English-ruled lands in southern France. At the same time, King Edward III of England claimed the right to inherit the French throne. It ended in 1453, when the English lost control of all their lands in France, except for the port of Calais.

Henry VII
(1457–1509; reigned 1485–1509)
King

Born in Wales, Henry went to live in France in 1471, partly to escape the civil war that was raging in England at that time. He was descended from the Lancastrian dynasty of kings, but did not have a strong claim to the throne. However, after King Edward V was murdered, and England became more and more lawless, Henry saw his chance to seize power.

Henry invaded England in 1485, fought against, and killed, King Richard III, and married the daughter of king Edward IV. He realized that their children and grandchildren – known as the Tudor dynasty – would have a strong claim to be rightful kings or queens.

Henry spent the early years of his reign restoring law and order and putting down rebellions. He ruled with a small group of close, efficient friends and began to repair the damage to England's economy caused by years of war. He also made peace treaties with France and Spain. Henry's style of government was cold, stern and calculating, but in private he was a loving husband and devoted son. (You can read about his remarkable mother, Lady Margaret Beaufort, on page 12.)

▶ HENRY VII
Founder of the powerful Tudor dynasty of rulers.

Henry VIII
(1491-1547; reigned 1509-1547)
King

Henry was the second son of Henry VII; his older brother, Arthur, died as a teenager. Famous for his good looks when young, skill at sports, love of music and dancing, and interest in new ideas, Henry VIII was very different from his father, and seemed the ideal man to be king of England. Today, however, he is mostly remembered for disastrous circumstances surrounding his six wives. This is not a fair judgement on his reign. While Henry was in power, the navy was rebuilt and strengthened, new law courts were set up, and new officials were appointed to help the government in London keep close control of outlying regions of the country – and of the powerful noble families who lived there.

Henry hated the day-to-day business of government, but cleverly chose very capable ministers, including Thomas Cromwell (*see* page 28) and Thomas Wolsey (*see* page 109), to help him rule. Henry and his ministers also had plans to reform religion. At first, they had no quarrel with the head of the worldwide Catholic Church, the Pope in Rome. Like many other people at the time, they wanted church organization to be less corrupt. However, when the Pope refused to allow Henry to divorce his first wife, Spanish princess Catherine of Aragon, because she had not produced an heir, Henry took control of the church himself. As a result, a new Church of England was formed.

When Henry's second wife, Anne Boleyn, also failed to produce a son, she was accused of unfaithfulness, and beheaded. His third wife, Jane Seymour, did give birth to a boy, but she died a few days later from disease. Henry then married Anne of Cleves, a German princess, because he supported her family politically. The couple did not get along, however, and separated. Henry's fifth wife was Catherine Howard. She bore no children, was unfaithful to him, and was executed. His final wife, Catherine Parr, also had no children, but they lived contentedly together until Henry's death.

Hepworth, Dame Barbara
(1903- 1975)
Artist

A pioneer of abstract art (art that does not aim to create a recognizable picture of a person, object or place), Hepworth created sculptures in metal, wood and stone. Her work was inspired by the textures and colours of the materials she worked with, and by the natural environment. It is famous for its smooth, flowing shapes, and for often being pierced with holes.

▶ NATURAL FORMS
Sculpture by artist Barbara Hepworth, in the garden of her home in St Ives, Cornwall.

Herschel, Sir William *(1738–1822)*
Astronomer

Born in Hanover, Herschel moved to Britain, where he worked as an astronomer. Using a telescope of his own design he discovered the planet Uranus, situated between Saturn and Neptune, in 1781. His observations helped to double the known size of the solar system. He was made King's Astronomer by George III and went on to become first president of the Royal Astronomical Society. His son John (1792–1822) was also a notable astronomer.

▲ ST HILDA'S MONASTERY
The ruined monastery at Whitby where St Hilda was abbess.

 ## Hilda, St
(614–680)
Religious leader

A member of the Northumbrian royal family, Hilda became a nun and then abbess (head) of a large monastery at Whitby, on the northeast coast of England. There, she was in charge of a community of men and women and won their respect for her wise rule. She also played a part in Church politics and attended synods (meetings about Church government) that made important decisions about the organization and services of the early Church.

 ## Hill, Octavia
(1838–1912)
Campaigner

Inspired by her strong Christian faith, Hill aimed to reform the morals of ordinary people and to improve the conditions in which they lived. She believed that by working to help themselves, they would learn to become better people.

Hill set up many new housing schemes, where homeless families and people from miserable slums could make a fresh start in life. She also believed that gardens and open spaces were important for health and happiness, and was one of the founders of the National Trust.

 ## Hill, Sir Rowland
(1795–1879)
Campaigner and inventor

Trained as a teacher, Hill pioneered new educational methods, and campaigned to end physical punishments in schools. He was also a keen inventor, and in 1835 planned a new postal service, to be paid for by glue-backed stamps. Each stamp cost one penny, so the scheme became known as the 'Penny Post'. It was introduced in Britain in 1840, and continues today – although stamps cost much more now! Hill was made secretary to the postmaster-general in 1846, working on improvements to postal services until he retired.

 ## Hitchcock, Alfred
(1889–1980)
Film director

One of Britain's most successful film directors, Hitchcock worked in Hollywood – the centre of the 20th-century film industry – as well as in the UK. He became famous for a series of horror films, including *Psycho* (1960) and *The Birds* (1963). Hitchcock's film work combines excitement, fear, and chilling thoughts about why some people's minds become twisted or evil.

▲ MASTER OF SUSPENSE
In thoughtful mood, Hitchcock poses in a deserted studio.

Hobbes, Thomas
(1588–1679)
Philosopher

Political philosopher Hobbes is remembered today for his book, *Leviathan*, published in 1651. In it, he put forward his views on how society works. He believed that people were selfish by nature, and that they would only work to benefit themselves – or to escape death and danger. This led him to suggest that strict laws and powerful rulers were necessary to run society. Without them, Hobbes believed, people could not be trusted to behave well towards others and would just please themselves.

 ## Hockney, David
(born 1937)
Artist

Famous for large paintings in bright colours, and for small but powerful drawings, Hockney was one of the most popular artists in late 20th-century Britain and America. His work appealed to ordinary people as well as to art experts. His much-loved works are dramatic, full of strong feelings, sometimes humorous, and brilliantly portray effects of light and shade. Hockney's designs for the theatre are also highly praised.

 ## Hodgkin, Dorothy
(1910–1994)
Scientist

▲ DOROTHY HODGKIN
Nobel Prize-winning scientist.

Using newly invented X-ray techniques (*see* box below), Hodgkin studied the way crystals were made. She then used this information to find out more about how chemicals combine to form new compounds, making important discoveries that helped doctors and chemists formulate new drugs. Hodgkin was awarded the Nobel Prize for Chemistry in 1964.

 ## Hooke, Robert
(1635–1703)
Scientist

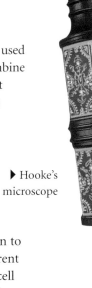

▶ Hooke's microscope

After working as assistant to Robert Boyle, Hooke began to make experiments of his own. He studied many different topics, including astronomy, optics (the science of light), cell biology and the science of materials. He discovered a law (now named after him) that describes how materials bend and stretch. Hooke also invented new scientific machines, and suggested improvements to microscopes and telescopes.

X-RAYS

X-rays were discovered by Wilhelm Röntgen – in Germany, in 1895. Later, scientists like Hodgkin (*see* above), found that X-rays could also be used to investigate the arrangement of atoms within a wide range of crystalline materials (substances in crystal form). These materials ranged from rocks and metals to tiny parts of the human body such as blood cells and genes. When X-rays are passed through crystals containing different chemicals, they create different patterns of dots. By comparing patterns from known and unknown crystals, researchers can find out which chemicals the unknown crystals contain.

'Hotspur'
See Percy, Henry

Hugh of Lincoln, St
c.1135–1200
Religious leader

Born in France, Hugh was sent to England to be bishop of Lincoln. He became famous for his devotion to helping sick people, and for his personal good humour and charm. Like another medieval saint, Francis of Assisi, Hugh honoured nature and befriended animals. He was also a skilled politician, defending the Church against attack from nobles and kings.

Hughes, Ted
(1930–1999)
Writer

In his poems, Hughes used powerful, direct language to communicate his vision of the world as a beautiful but cruel and savage place. Most of his works are about animals, fish or birds. Towards the end of his life, when Hughes knew he was dying, he also wrote about his feelings for his wife, the poet Sylvia Plath, who committed suicide in 1963. Some people think that this was his finest work. He won many awards and was made poet laureate in 1984.

WORKS BY TED HUGHES

1957 *Hawk in the Rain*
1960 *Lupercal*
1961 *Meet My Folks* (for children)
1963 *Earth Owl* (for children)
1968 *The Iron Man* (for children)
1970 *Crow*
1982 *The Rattle-Bag* (for children)
1997 *The School Bag* (for children)
1998 *Birthday Letters*
1998 *Tales from Ovid*

Hume, David
(1711–1776)
Philosopher

Born in Edinburgh, Hume worked as a government official. However, he is remembered today for his books on politics and philosophy. In them, he described his theories about how people think and learn, how society should be governed, and how the economy should be run. At a time when almost everyone believed in God, he shocked many people by refusing to do so. Instead, he argued that people – and governments – should be guided by reason, intelligence and experience.

Huntingdon, Countess of (Selina Hastings)
(1707–1791)
Religious leader

The daughter of one leading nobleman, and the wife of another, Hastings could have led a quiet, easy life. However, she became converted to Methodism – a branch of the Christian faith preached by John Wesley (*see* page 105). She devoted her time and energy to helping other Methodists, and to winning new converts for her beliefs among her noble friends.

The countess supported many Methodist preachers, and protected them from prosecution – at that time, Methodists were thought to be breaking Church law. She founded many chapels, and a college in Wales where preachers could train. Her network of friends and fellow Methodists became known as 'The Countess of Huntingdon's Connection', and grew into an independent church. This still exists today.

James IV
(1473–1513; reigned 1488–1513)
King

After years of civil war in Scotland, James won back control of the whole country, including the wild, lawless highlands. He also played a leading part in European politics, making alliances with France and marrying a daughter of King Henry VII of England (*see* page 51). When England and France went to war in 1513, however, he supported France. This led England to attack, and James was killed, along with many Scots nobles, at the Battle of Flodden.

UNITING ENGLAND, SCOTLAND, IRELAND AND WALES

For many centuries, England, Scotland, Ireland and Wales were separate nations. However, England was larger, richer and stronger, and English kings sent armies to invade and conquer the other areas. In Wales, they succeeded. In Ireland, there were many centuries of conflict. England and Scotland were eventually united.

WALES:
1284 Statute of Rhuddlan. King Edward I of England claims Welsh lands belong to English crown. Builds castles to control conquered Wales
1536 and 1543 Acts of Parliament unite English and Welsh laws and local government

SCOTLAND:
1603 James VI of Scotland inherits English throne from Elizabeth I; rules England as King James I. England and Scotland remain separate nations, with separate parliaments, Churches, and laws
1707 Act of Union. Joins crowns of England and Scotland. Abolishes Scottish Parliament; Scots send MPs and Peers to London Parliament instead. Scottish Church and laws remain separate

IRELAND:
1171 King Henry II of England invades Ireland. Most Irish kings accept him as overlord. Other Irish people do not, and fight against English settlers and rulers for the next 600 years
1800 Act of Union. British Parliament declares that England and Ireland are united
1921 Irish Free State formed. Ireland (except Ulster) becomes independent

James VI and I
(1566–1625;
reigned Scotland 1567–1625;
England and Ireland 1603–1625)
King

Son of Mary Queen of Scots (*see* page 72), he became king of Scotland while still a child. When Queen Elizabeth I of England died, in 1603, he also inherited her throne. James became the first king ever to rule England, Scotland and Ireland, although the nations were not legally united.

Intelligent, yet quarrelsome and stubborn, James believed strongly that God had given kings a 'Divine Right' to rule, and that they should therefore be obeyed without question. This angered many nobles and Members of Parliament. His favouritism towards certain people also made him unpopular, as did his friendship with England's traditional enemy, Spain.

Jebb, Eglantyne
(1876–1928)
Campaigner

At first a teacher and social worker, Jebb devoted most of her life to charity work. After working with refugee children during World War I, she became convinced that an international organization was needed to help children worldwide.

In 1919, she founded the Save the Children Fund. Many people were hostile (they did not like Jebb's pacifist, or anti-war, views) but she was a determined campaigner, and excellent fund-raiser. The fund still continues with its work today. Jebb fought on for a Children's Charter, guaranteeing children's rights to housing, health care and education. She died, exhausted by her efforts, aged 52.

Jekyll, Gertrude
(1843–1932)
Designer

Jekyll trained as a painter, but had to abandon this career when her eyesight began to fail. She turned to gardening instead, and designed over 300 gardens for wealthy clients. Her designs make clever use of colours and shapes, and were based on detailed knowledge of trees, shrubs and plants. She worked closely with famous architect Edwin Lutyens (*see* page 66). They planned houses and gardens that fitted together to create beautiful places to live.

▲ Jenner vaccinates a patient.

Jenner, Edward
(1749–1832)
Doctor

Country doctor Jenner pioneered the medical technique of vaccination. This places dead or weakened germs inside a person's body, so that it will learn to fight against them and protect them from future disease.

Jenner discovered that dairymaids, who often caught a rash called cowpox from the animals they milked, never got smallpox, a similar but much more deadly human disease. So he deliberately infected patients with cowpox, by rubbing pus from a cowpox blister into a scratch on their skin. Although people said this was very dangerous, Jenner's patients did not catch smallpox. He had proved that vaccination worked. Today, vaccinations protect millions of people from many different dangerous diseases.

John
(1165–1216; reigned 1199–1216)
King

Nicknamed 'Lackland', because as the youngest of Henry 11's sons there had been nothing left over to give him, John was not a very successful king. His reign is remembered today for a very important document that he was forced (by angry nobles) to seal in 1215. Its name was Magna Carta ('big charter'), and, for the first time ever, it introduced laws limiting the king of England's powers and guaranteeing rights to his subjects. When John broke these laws, the English nobles rebelled against him.

John, Augustus
(1878–1961)
Artist

Born in Wales, the brother of Gwen John (*see* below), Augustus was also a successful painter. He was famous for his portraits, mostly of beautiful women and famous people, painted in a bold, dramatic, colourful style.

▲ AUGUSTUS JOHN
An unconventional and bohemian figure throughout his life.

John, Gwen
(1876–1939)
Artist

Born in Wales, John studied in London and then moved to live and work in Paris – the art centre of Europe in the early 20th century. There, she became close to many great artists, notably Rodin, and writers, while producing important paintings of her own..

Unlike much modern art, which was lively, bold and colourful, John's work was calm, quiet and often grey-toned. Usually, it showed women or girls in peaceful rooms.

Towards the end of her life, John's art was strongly influenced by her religious beliefs. She became a Roman Catholic, and moved to live close to a community of nuns..

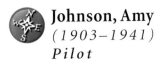

Johnson, Amy
(1903–1941)
Pilot

One of the first women to gain a pilot's licence, Johnson won worldwide fame when she flew solo from Britain to Australia in 1930. Her flight took 17 days, and was very dangerous.

Later, Johnson flew solo to India and Japan, and became the first-ever woman to fly across the Atlantic from East to West. In 1932, she broke the record (previously held by her husband) for the fastest flight from London to Cape Town, in South Africa. She volunteered to fly for the Women's Auxiliary Air Force during World War II, but her plane was shot down over the river Thames, and she was killed.

WOMEN AIR PIONEERS

1927 Lady Mary Bailey (UK) is first woman to fly across the Irish Sea
1928 Sophia Heath (USA/UK) is first woman to fly solo from South Africa to England
1930 Amy Johnson (UK) is first woman to fly solo from England to Australia
1931 Beryl Markham (Kenya) is first woman to work as a commercial pilot, in Africa
1932 Amelia Earhart (USA) makes first solo transatlantic flight by a woman
1935 Jean Gardner Batten (New Zealand) is first woman to fly across South Atlantic, from England to Brazil. Also set speed record for solo flight from England to New Zealand
1936 Beryl Markham is first person to fly solo across Atlantic from East to West
1939–1945 Jacqueline Cochran (USA) becomes director of Women Auxiliary Service Pilots – team of over 1,000 women pilots who flew transport planes, freeing men for active service in warplanes
1950 Jacqueline Auriol (France) becomes first woman test pilot

▼ Amy Johnson

1953 Jacqueline Cochran (USA) is first woman to break sound barrier (fly faster than the speed of sound)
1963 Valentina Tereshkova (USSR) is first woman in space
1965 Sheila Scott (UK) makes longest-ever solo flight round the world
1983 Sally Ride (USA) is first American woman in space
1986 Teacher Christa MacAuliffe dies in Space Shuttle accident; was first civilian woman in space
1986 Jeana Yeager (USA) (with male co-pilot) makes first-ever non-stop flight round the world without refuelling

◄ SAMUEL JOHNSON
Compiler of the first true dictionary of the English language.

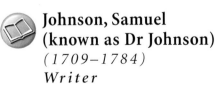

Johnson, Samuel
(known as Dr Johnson)
(1709–1784)
Writer

Son of a bookseller in Lichfield, Staffordshire, Johnson began his career as a schoolmaster, but left to live and work in London. At first, he wrote reports of debates in Parliament for newspapers, but in 1747 was commissioned to produce an English dictionary. This was a great success when it was published in 1755, and Johnson became respected for his scholarship, outspoken opinions and wit. (He was also well-known for his eccentric personal behaviour.)

Johnson also wrote essays, novels and biographies, and founded a Literary Club. Members included some of the leading writers of his day.

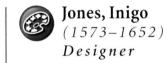

Jones, Inigo
(1573–1652)
Designer

After travelling in Europe to study art and architecture, Jones returned to England, where he introduced many new, Italian-style designs. He admired and copied the Italian architect Palladio, who based his own work on ancient Greek and Roman styles. Jones was employed by King James I and his family to create costumes and scenery for masques (plays with music) at the royal court. The king also asked him to design houses and palaces. The most important of these, the Banqueting House in Whitehall, London, still survives.

▲ BANQUETING HOUSE, WHITEHALL, LONDON By Inigo Jones.

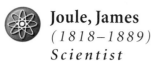

Joule, James
(1818–1889)
Scientist

Joule's family were brewers who had a private laboratory where they tested the beers they produced. Joule used this laboratory for his own experiments into how heat works, and how electricity is conducted (travels along wires). Working with William Thomson (*see* page 99), Joule discovered the law that describes how the temperature of a gas changes when its volume expands. This discovery was later used by the inventors of refrigerators, and other cooling devices.

Joyce, James
(1882–1941)
Writer

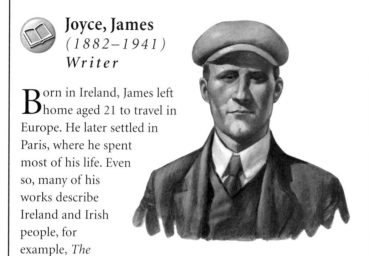

Born in Ireland, James left home aged 21 to travel in Europe. He later settled in Paris, where he spent most of his life. Even so, many of his works describe Ireland and Irish people, for example, *The Dubliners* (1914) and *Finnegan's Wake* (1939).

In his novels and short stories, Joyce experimented with many new ways of writing. He broke away from traditional rules of grammar, choosing instead to use words in long strings, or short busts, or to imitate the jumble of thoughts and feelings experienced by the characters in his books. He saw no need for neat chapters or paragraphs, 'proper' punctuation – or even standard spelling. His writing created startling, sometimes shocking, pictures in readers' minds, and is still greatly praised and admired for its creative power today.

THE CHURCH IN MEDIEVAL ENGLAND

Today, people in Britain follow a wide range of different faiths, and some people have no faith at all. Church leaders are often listened to respectfully when they make comments on public issues, but they have no real power. However, it was a very different situation in the Middle Ages (roughly, the years from around ad1000 to 1500). In medieval times, there was only one organized Church in Britain - the Roman Catholic Church. In some cities, there were also small communities of Jews.

Everyone in medieval Britain believed in God, although many ordinary people mingled Church teachings with old, pagan (non-religious) superstitions. The Church had great power and wealth. Clergymen were the best-educated people in society, and Church leaders played an important part in government. The Church was very influential in other areas of people's lives, too.

Many men and women at this time were so deeply committed to their faith that, like Julian of Norwich (see below), they shut themselves away from the world to devote their lives to God.

▼ JULIAN OF NORWICH
A religious woman whose wisdom helped many people.

Julian of Norwich
(c.1342–c.1413)
Wise woman

Julian was an anchoress – a religious woman who decides to live shut away from the rest of the world to devote her life to God. She spent most of her life in a small room attached to a church in Norwich, in eastern England.

During an illness, Julian reported seeing visions from God. She described these to priests at the church, along with the thoughts and feelings they had inspired in her. Julian's words were later written down in a book. During her life, Julian became well known for her wise advice and spiritual counselling. After her death, her book gave comfort and hope to many readers.

SAINT JULIAN of NORWICH

Kay, John
(1704–c.1764)
Inventor

Son of a factory owner, Kay invented machines to replace traditional methods of producing cloth by hand. In 1730, he made a hand-operated twisting machine that produced yarn that was stronger and smoother than hand-spun thread. In 1733, he invented a weaving machine that made wide cloth much more quickly and cheaply than hand-workers could. It became known as 'the flying shuttle', and was used in many factories during the Industrial Revolution.

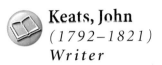

Keats, John
(1792–1821)
Writer

One of Britain's best-loved poets, Keats was born to a poor family in London, and trained as an apothecary. (Apothecaries made and sold medicines, and offered simple medical treatment to people who could not afford to pay for a doctor.) Keats, however, was determined to be a writer, and in 1816 gave up his medical work.

In 1818 and 1819 – often called his 'wonderful years' – he produced a series of brilliant poems, including 'Ode to a Nightingale', 'To Autumn', 'The Eve of St Agnes', and 'Ode to a Grecian Urn'. However, he was already seriously ill with TB. Keats left England in 1820, to escape the cold winter weather. He died in Italy, aged only 25, the next year. Keats's work was – and still is – admired for its rich language, which he used to create vivid pictures and to conjure up powerful feelings. He was inspired by the sights and sounds of nature, by traditional stories, and by ancient Greek myths and legends.

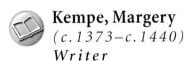

Kempe, Margery
(c.1373–c.1440)
Writer

Remembered today as the author of the first-known autobiography (personal life story) written in English, Kempe was famous in her own time for her extreme devotion to the Christian faith. She spent hours saying prayers, claimed to see visions of heaven, and wept loudly in public when she attended church services or saw anything that reminded her of Jesus Christ's life and death.

Kempe was born into a wealthy merchant family in eastern England, married, brought up 14 children, and ran a business of her own, brewing ale. When she was around 40, she decided to live separately from her husband, and devote the rest of her life to religion. She went on many pilgrimages (visits to holy places) in Europe and the Middle East. At that time, it was most unusual and very dangerous for a woman to travel alone. In old age, she dictated her extraordinary life-story to priests.

Kenneth I (Kenneth MacAlpine)
(died c.859; reigned c.843–858)
King

Kenneth lived at a time when Scotland was divided into several different kingdoms. A famous warrior, he became ruler of Dalriada, in the Highlands, around 841. Two years later, he conquered the other Scottish kingdoms and declared himself the first-ever king to rule all Scotland. Kenneth may have been helped by the Vikings, who attacked the other kingdoms, and weakened them. Around 848, Kenneth moved the remains of St Columba (*see page 26*) to a church at Scone, in central Scotland. This then became the place where Scottish kings were crowned.

Kent, William
(c.1685–1748)
Designer

Kent worked as an architect, and as a landscape gardener. He was responsible for introducing many new ideas in art and architecture into England, especially those based on ancient Greek and Roman styles, and on 16th-century Italian fashions. He designed many important government buildings in London (which are still used today), including the Treasury and offices in Whitehall. He also designed stately homes, including Holkham Hall in Norfolk.

Kent's buildings were grand and formal, but his garden design was very different. He aimed to recreate natural-looking landscapes by sowing acres of rolling grassland, digging streams and lakes, and planting little woods and clumps of trees. He removed the neat, tidy flower-beds, low hedges and gravel pathways that had been fashionable before.

▲ HORSE GUARDS PARADE. LONDON
One of Kent's many grand London buildings

Kidd, William
(c.1645–1701)
Pirate

Born in Scotland, Kidd worked as a sea-captain, commanding a merchant ship that sailed between ports on the northeast coast of America and the Caribbean. He became a privateer (a raider licensed by a government) and attacked French ships sailing in the same waters. He was also employed by the government to fight against pirates in the Caribbean. But Kidd became a pirate himself – claiming that his mutinous crew had forced him to attack other ships. He was arrested in 1699, sent to England for trial in 1701, and executed. Many people have searched for the treasure that Kidd claimed to have buried on the Caribbean island of Haiti, but it has never been found.

 ## Kingsley, Mary
(1862–1900)
Explorer

Kingsley spent the first 30 years of her life quietly at home with her parents. When they died, she decided to travel. At first, she simply hoped to gain information to help complete a book that her father had left unfinished when he died. However, she soon began to enjoy travel for her own sake, and became a daring, adventurous explorer. She made two long journeys through West Africa, travelling along rivers by canoe, and meeting dangerous animals along the way. She also climbed to the top of Mount Cameroon, the highest point in West Africa – becoming only the second-known climber to do so.

Mary collected examples of West African wildlife on her journeys, and presented them, for study, to London museums. Unlike many Europeans, she was sensitive to the cultures and traditions of African people, and did not try to force her beliefs on them. Back home in Britain, she campaigned on behalf of Africans who were unhappy with British rule, and demanded that their way of life be treated with respect. She died of fever, aged only 38, in South Africa, while working as a volunteer nurse.

 ## Kipling, J. Rudyard
(1865–1936)
Writer

Born in India, Kipling worked as a journalist in Lahore (now in Pakistan) and published many poems and stories there. His books described everyday life in the sub-continent, and among members of the British Raj (ruling class). From 1889, Kipling lived in Britain and earned his living as a full-time writer. His most successful works were for children, and included *The Jungle Book* (1894) and *Just So Stories* (1902).

Kipling's work was remarkable for including ordinary speech and soldiers' slang. He had a gift for creating memorable phrases, which were widely copied in Britain, India and elsewhere. In 1907, Kipling became the first British writer to win the Nobel Prize for literature. More recently, his works have been criticized for his support for the British Empire and his attitude to non-white people. Even so, his poem 'If' was voted the most popular poem in Britain at the end of the 20th century.

 ## Kitchener, H. Herbert (Lord Kitchener)
(1850–1916)
Soldier

▲ LORD KITCHENER
In full military dress at an army parade.

A professional soldier, Kitchener fought against rebels in Sudan, as chief of staff in the Second Boer War (1900–1902) in South Africa, and as commander-in-chief of British troops in India.

At the start of World War I, he was made government minister responsible for war. He organized a massive recruiting campaign, calling on young men to volunteer as soldiers. His stern, commanding face became famous after it appeared on thousand of posters, with the slogan 'Your Country Needs You!'. He was killed on his way to talks with Britain's allies in Russia, when the battleship he was travelling in hit a German mine.

Knox, John

(c.1513–1572)
Religious leader

Scholar and church lawyer Knox was a leading Protestant during the early years of the Reformation (a reform movement that divided the Christian Church in the 16th century; *see* box). As a young man in Scotland, he was captured by the French (who wrongly suspected that he had been involved in murdering a Roman Catholic cardinal) and sent to work as a slave, rowing galleys.

Knox was set free in 1549, travelled to England, and then studied with Protestant scholars in Switzerland. In 1559, he returned to Scotland. There, he became a famous preacher, encouraging Protestant reforms. He also protested against his country being ruled by a woman, Mary Queen of Scots. His book, *First Blast of the Trumpet Against the Monstrous Regiment* [rule] *of Women* infuriated Mary, and her cousin, Queen Elizabeth I.

▶ JOHN KNOX
Famed for his powerful preaching.

Krebs, Sir Hans Adolf

(1900–1981)
Scientist

Born in Germany, biology expert Krebs moved to Britain in the 1930s, to escape the Nazis. He became famous for his work in understanding how carbohydrates (starchy foods such as bread, potatoes and rice) are broken down by the body and used to give us energy. He discovered a complicated set of chemical processes (now known as the 'Krebs cycle') that occur inside cells, and are essential to human life. In 1953, Krebs won the Nobel Prize for medicine.

THE REFORMATION

During the 15th and 16th centuries, many people in Britain and Europe, from scholars and priests to ordinary men and women, disagreed with the teachings of the Roman Catholic Church. They wanted to worship in their own way, and to read the Bible in their own language. They also complained about Church involvement in politics, and the way the Catholic Church was run. As a result of their protests, the Catholic church was divided, and new, 'Protestant' churches were formed.

Lanchester, Frederick

(1868–1946)
Engineer

Designer of some of the world's earliest motor-cars, Lanchester built his first automobile in 1896. He founded his own car-making company two years later. His inventions included a starter for engines, and disc brakes for car wheels.

Langland, William

(c.1330–c.1400)
Writer

Langland is remembered today for only one poem, a long story in verse about an 'ordinary man' – the man and the poem are called *Piers Plowman*. In the poem, Piers travels through 'a fair field full of folk', observing and reacting to all he sees. Langland had a clear purpose when writing this. He used his poem to criticize the society he lived in for its foolishness, vanity and greed. In so doing, he created many memorable characters (including Piers and his bossy wife, Rose) and painted a lively picture of the late medieval world.

Larkin, Philip
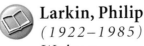
(1922–1985)
Writer

Larkin made his career as a librarian, but today he is remembered as one of Britain's most uncomfortable poets. Many of his works describe lonely individuals, or empty lives in bleak cities and boring suburbs. Larkin often does not like – or treat as equals – the people he describes. Although simple on the surface, Larkin's poems often contain deeper meanings, full of bitterness or regret. They can also be very witty, sharply observant and sometimes cruel.

Lawrence, D. H.
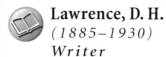
(1885–1930)
Writer

One of the most important writers of the 20th century, Lawrence was born in the English Midlands. Its mines, factories, busy cities and wooded countryside form the setting for several of his books. Encouraged by his protective, ambitious mother, Lawrence trained as a teacher. In 1912, just a few years after he started work, he eloped (ran away) with Frieda von Richtoven, the headstrong, aristocratic, German wife of one of his college professors. Lawrence spent the rest of his life travelling with Frieda, and writing. His novels are mostly about people, and how they relate to one another. In them, he deliberately used plain, simple language, and sometimes local dialect words. He wanted to show that ordinary people's lives and thoughts were important.

Many of Lawrence's novels are based on his own feelings or experiences. In *Sons and Lovers* (1913), he explored his love-hate relationship with his mother. In *Women in Love* (1921), he described the uncertain, confused feelings of many young people after the end of World War I. His last novel, *Lady Chatterley's Lover* (1928), was banned in Britain until 1960, because it described sex, and used swear words. Lawrence did intend it to shock, but he also wanted to break down old rules that stopped people from different classes and different backgrounds living happily together. For many years of his adult life, Lawrence was ill with the lung disease, TB. He died in Italy aged 45.

Lawrence, T. E. ('Lawrence of Arabia')

(1888–1935)
Soldier

After working as an archaeologist in the Middle East, Lawrence volunteered to help the British government's allies there during World War I. He was employed by Prince Faisal, leader of an Arab rebellion against the Turks. (Turkey was an ally of Germany, Britain's chief enemy in the war.) Lawrence helped train Arab soldiers to fight against Turkey; later, he described (and perhaps exaggerated) his desert adventures in a book.

After the war was over, Lawrence helped Arabs who were campaigning for independence, but the British government did not agree with his views. Unable to settle in peacetime, Lawrence joined the RAF (Royal Air Force) in 1922, under a false name. He also began to write. He was killed, rather mysteriously, in a motorbike accident near his home in 1935.

▲ **LAWRENCE OF ARABIA**
The campaigner for Arab rights, dressed as an Arab sheikh.

Leakey, Louis

(1903–1972)
Anthropologist
(studies different peoples)

Leakey was born in Tanzania to British parents, who were missionaries. After education in England, he returned to Africa to study Stone Age remains. In 1948, he discovered the skull of an early ancestor of modern apes, from 25-40 million years ago. In 1959, his wife, Mary (*see right*), discovered another ancient skull, this time from a creature half-way between apes and humans (now known as *Australopithecus boiseii*). Leakey used this skull to prove that human beings had evolved from apes about a million years earlier than anyone had previously thought.

The Leakeys found many other important remains, mostly in Olduvai Gorge, Tanzania. Today, all archaeologists do not accept the theories Leakey based on these finds, but they agree that their discoveries were very important.

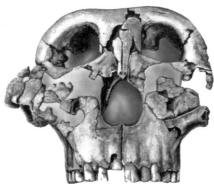
◀ **HUMAN ANCESTOR**
Skull of *Australopithecus boiseii*

Leakey, Mary
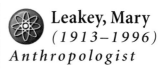
(1913–1996)
Anthropologist

Wife of Louis Leakey (*below left*), Mary helped her husband, and later her son, Richard, excavate very ancient sites at Olduvai Gorge, Tanzania. After her husband's death, Mary continued his work. She also published many books and papers on her own special interests. She was a respected expert on prehistoric rock paintings and ancient technology.

Lean, David

(1908–1991)
Film director

One of the most highly respected British film directors, Lean began his career as a junior assistant in film studios, and learned how to make films by watching older, more experienced people.

Lean's first success came with the World War II film, *In Which We Serve* (1942), which he co-directed with the famous songwriter and playwright, Noel Coward. His next movie, *Brief Encounter* (1946), became one of the best-known British films of all time. Other highly successful films include *Bridge Over the River Kwai* (1948), *Lawrence of Arabia* (1962), *Doctor Zhivago* (1965) and *A Passage to India* (1984).

Lee, Baroness Jennie
(1904–1988)
Politician

Daughter of a poor Scottish miner, Lee won scholarships to school and university, then became a schoolteacher and volunteer trade union organizer. In 1929, aged 24, she was elected as a Labour MP, but served for only two years, preferring to work as a lecturer and organizer for the Labour Party. Lee returned to Parliament from 1945 to 1970, and held many government posts. Today, she is remembered for her work in setting up the Open University, which allows any student who may have missed earlier chances of education to study part-time for a degree and other qualifications.

 ## Lessing, Doris
(born 1919)
Writer

Lessing spent her childhood in Rhodesia (now Zimbabwe). In 1949, she moved to live in England, and to write. For many years, Lessing was active in politics, at first as a Communist, later as a feminist and supporter of human rights. Her novels deal with important political issues in a thoughtful, perceptive way. (*The Grass is Singing* is about racial prejudice in southern Africa; *The Golden Notebook* explores women's hopes for independence.) Her later stories have many different themes, but all deal with the problems of how to live, and how to take political action, honestly and responsibly.

 ## Leverhulme, Lord William
(1851–1925)
Social and business pioneer

Factory-owner Leverhulme won fame in two separate ways. With his brother, he began to make soap from vegetable oil, rather than tallow (sheep's-fat). To sell this new product, he gave it an attractive brand-name, 'Sunlight', and launched an advertising campaign. Today, this is commonplace, but it was new and unusual at the time. Leverhulme also pioneered ways of providing good housing and welfare benefits for his employees. Close to his factory on Merseyside, he built a new town (called Port Sunlight; *see* box on New Towns), with pleasant homes for workers, and arranged medical care, pensions, and profit-sharing schemes for his staff.

 ## Linacre, Thomas
(c.1460–1524)
Doctor

A scholar and doctor, Linacre founded the Royal College of Physicians in London in 1518. Its aim was to make sure that doctors were properly qualified before they treated patients. It still exists, and performs the same task today. Linacre also translated books on medicine from ancient Greek, and used them to teach his students. In this way, he introduced important 'lost' knowledge about medicine into England, greatly improving English doctors' understanding of how the body works, and practical skills.

▲ THOMAS LINACRE
Pioneer of professional standards for doctors and founder of The Royal College of Physicians, in London.

 ## Lind, James
(1716–1794)
Doctor

Born in Scotland, Lind worked as a doctor on board Royal Navy ships. At that time, many sailors died, or became seriously ill, from scurvy, a disease caused by shortage of vitamin C. All vitamins were unknown in Lind's time, but he observed that scurvy could be prevented and cured by giving sailors citrus fruit, especially lemons and limes. (Today, we know that they are rich in vitamin C.)

Lind set up a series of experiments to check his observations, then reported his findings to Navy chiefs. They took a little while to accept what he said, but eventually issued all Navy personnel with an official daily ration of lime juice. Scurvy was no longer a problem and British sailors were given a new nickname: 'limeys'!

NEW TOWNS

Port Sunlight, built by Lord Leverhulme, was one of several 'company towns' planned by factory-owners for their workers. These towns were important for the people who lived there, but also had a much wider effect. They influenced governments, landowners, architects and designers for the next 100 years. They were studied by pioneers like Ebenezer Howard, who built Britain's first 'Garden Cities' at Letchworth (1903) and Welwyn (1920) in Hertfordshire, and by the planners of 1960s new towns, such as Milton Keynes. They all wanted to create pleasant, healthy, well-organized environments, because they believed this would help people lead better, happier, more productive lives.

Lister, Lord Joseph
(1827–1912)
Doctor

Lister was a surgeon, who pioneered a new technique that saved countless lives. In the past, many patients died from infections after operations. In 1865, Lister read that French chemist Pasteur had discovered that infection was caused by bacteria (germs). So he decided to try to kill any germs before they could infect his patients. He covered wounds with dressings soaked in strong disinfectant, and sterilized his operating theatre with a fine mist of disinfectant sprayed in the air.

Lister's technique – which he called 'antisepsis' – worked well. Most of his patients' wounds did not get infected. Later, Lister also helped introduce 'aseptic' operating procedures, which aimed to stop germs getting into wounds by keeping surgeons' hands, clothes and instruments, and patients' skin, as clean as possible. This technique is still used today.

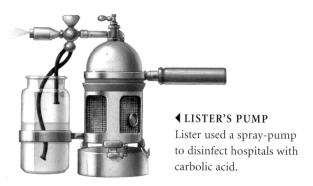

◄ LISTER'S PUMP
Lister used a spray-pump to disinfect hospitals with carbolic acid.

Livingstone, David
(1813–1873)
Explorer and missionary

Born in southern Scotland, Livingstone worked in a cotton mill until he had saved enough money to study medicine. As soon as he qualified as a doctor (in 1840), he sailed for southern Africa. Here, he worked as a medical missionary, set up schools and simple hospitals, and earned the respect and affection of many of the African people he worked with and trained.

Livingstone also made several long journeys of exploration. He explored the Zambezi River, and became the first European to see Lake Nyasa and the Victoria Falls. In 1865, he set off to search for the source of the river Nile. Nothing was heard of him for over five years, until American journalist H. M. Stanley went in search of the explorer, finding him in 1871 and greeting him with the now-famous words, 'Dr Livingstone, I presume?'

Lloyd, Marie
(Matilda Alice Victoria Wood)
(1870–1922)
Entertainer

Daughter of a waiter with 11 children, Marie Lloyd was born in poverty. While still a child, she began performing in London music-halls (popular theatres where comedians, singers and dancers entertained crowds of workers). She also played leading parts in pantomimes.

Lloyd became famous for her outspoken stage personality and for her witty songs, which she performed with great style and skill. Some of these are still well known today, such as 'My Old Man Said Follow The Van', and 'Oh Mister Porter'. Bolder and much funnier than other female performers of her day, Lloyd was extremely popular, and was known as 'the Queen of the Music Hall'.

Lloyd George, Lord David
(1863–1945)
Politician

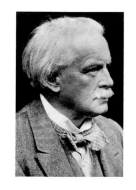

Trained as a solicitor, Lloyd George aimed for a political career. He became Liberal Party MP, and was soon appointed to government posts. From 1908 to 1915, he was chancellor of the exchequer, and introduced many important social reforms. He provided government money to pay the first Old Age Pensions, and started a National Insurance scheme (where working people contributed a share of their wages to pay for welfare benefits.) In 1916, Lloyd George challenged his fellow Liberal, Herbert Asquith, for power, and became prime minister.

Lloyd George proved a strong, capable leader during World War I. But his decision to work closely with Conservative politicians angered many Liberal supporters, and left the Liberal party weakened and divided. After the war was over, he planned large government housing schemes, to provide 'homes fit for heroes' – the soldiers returning from battle. However, his government ran short of money in 1921, and many of the schemes were halted. He was forced to resign in 1923. Lloyd George continued as leader of the Liberal Party until 1931. He never again took part in government, although he drew up schemes to help unemployed people during the severe economic crisis of the 1930s.

WALES

For many centuries, Wales was independent of Britain. Its first inhabitants were Celtic tribes, ruled by chieftains. In the first century AD, the Romans invaded. Although the Celts fought back, Roman soldiers occupied the land until the 4th century AD. From around AD400, Celtic peoples from farther east settled in Wales, to escape from Saxon invaders who had arrived from Germany and the nearby lands. Wales remained independent, but divided into many chiefdoms and kingdoms, until the 11th century AD.

After this, the Norman rulers of England encouraged their supporters to settle in Wales, and tried to take control. Again, the Welsh fought back, but were finally defeated by King Edward I, in a series of battles from 1277 to 1301. By that year, Edward controlled a large part of Wales, and made his oldest son prince of Wales. This linked Wales with other parts of Britain ruled by English kings. During the 14th and 15th centuries, Welsh leaders continued to rebel against British rule, but were unsuccessful. Wales became permanently linked with the rest of England in 1536, when King Henry VIII (whose father, Henry VII, was of Welsh ancestry) passed laws uniting the English and Welsh systems of law and government.

Llywelyn the Great (Llywelyn ap Iorwerth)
(died 1240)
Prince

Prince of Gwynedd (north Wales), Llywelyn became the most powerful ruler in Wales, and was accepted as leader by all the other rulers of Welsh kingdoms, although he never claimed the title 'Prince of Wales'. In 1211–1212, he successfully led the fight against an invasion by English King John (*see* page 56), and kept English troops out of Wales for the next 20 years. His own homeland, Gwynedd, became the most powerful among all the Welsh kingdoms. He also made alliance with powerful marcher lords, who owned vast estates on the Welsh-English boundaries, and were often hostile to English kings.

Locke, John
(1632–1704)
Philosopher and politician

Locke lived during a time of political unrest and civil war in England. In his writings, he discussed the nature of political power. Locke argued that kings and governments had no absolute right to power. Instead, it was given to them by the citizens they ruled, because citizens needed someone to make laws and enforce public order. If a king or government made bad laws or failed to protect citizens from war and crime, they lost the right to rule, and should be replaced.

Locke also wrote about how humans gather knowledge. He believed that we are born knowing nothing, and have to learn everything though our five senses, or by experience. Locke's ideas about government, and about human learning, were seen as dangerous and revolutionary.

Lockyer, Sir J. Norman
(1836–1920)
Astronomer

Astronomer Lockyer studied the Sun, and the glowing gases it sent out into space. In this way, he discovered a new element (naturally-occurring chemical that cannot be broken down into separate substances), which he named helium, after the ancient Greek god of the Sun. He also studied ancient monuments, such as Stonehenge, in southwest England, to find out whether they had been used as places for studying the stars. He was the founder of the great Science Museum in London, and edited the very important scientific journal *Nature* (where scientists report new discoveries) for 50 years.

Lonsdale, Dame Kathleen
(1903–1971)
Scientist

Born in Ireland, Lonsdale moved to England with her family as a child. She trained as a research scientist, and spent her career using newly-developed X-ray technology to investigate the composition of chemical compounds and to explore the structure of crystals. She became the first-ever woman 'fellow' of the prestigious Royal Society (a group of top scientists) in 1945, and received many other honours for her scientific work.

A sincere Quaker (*see* George Fox, page 40), Lonsdale refused to register for war work during World War II, because she believed that fighting and killing was wrong. As a result, she was sent to prison. Many people admired her courage and commitment to her beliefs, even if they did not share her views.

Lovelace, Countess Ada
(1815–1852)
Mathematician

The only daughter born in wedlock to wild poet Lord Byron (*see* page 19), Ada Lovelace inherited her father's title – and considerable intelligence from both her parents. Encouraged by her mother, she studied mathematics and logic, and, from 1833, worked closely with Charles Babbage (*see* page 9) to develop a 'difference engine' – a forerunner of modern computers. She published a description of how this worked, and also suggested that it might have revolutionary uses in the future. In recognition of her work, American computer programmers named an advanced computer language (ADA) after her in 1977.

 ### Lovell, Sir (A. C.) Bernard
(born 1913)
Astronomer

Lovell is a pioneer of radio astronomy (the study of stars and other heavenly bodies using the faint radio waves they give off; *see* box). He spent many years raising funds to build the world's first large steerable radio telescope, at Jodrell Bank, in northwest England. It was completed in 1955, and demonstrated its power and usefulness by tracking *Sputnik*, the first-ever satellite launched into space in 1957. The telescope was later named after Lovell, who remained head of the Jodrell Bank Observatory for a remarkable 30 years (1951-1981).

▼ **JODRELL BANK**
Lovell's radio telescope.

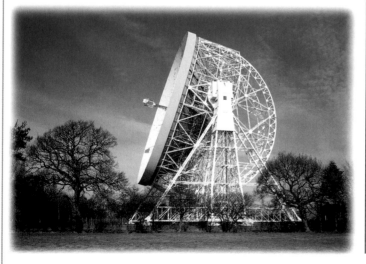

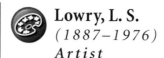 ### Lowry, L. S.
(1887–1976)
Artist

Born in Manchester, Lowry worked as a clerk and studied art at night school. His paintings – in a deliberately childish, 'matchstick-figure' style – portray people and their everyday activities in the industrial city of Salford, where Lowry spent most of his life. Opinions are divided on Lowry's work. Some see him as a shrewd, amused observer of life in industrial northern England; others see his paintings as decorative, but without deep meanings.

 ### Lutyens, Sir Edwin
(1869–1944)
Designer

Architect Lutyens began his career designing country houses for wealthy clients in fashionable 'Arts and Crafts' (mock-cottage) style. He worked closely with garden designer Gertrude Jekyll (*see* page 56) to create many beautiful, comfortable homes where privileged people could live.

In 1912, he was asked to advise on the design for a whole new city – New Delhi, the capital of British-ruled India. He planned it as a 'garden city', where each block of big buildings was surrounded by its own spacious grounds. He admired Indian architecture, and used many Indian designs to decorate his buildings. Lutyens was also asked to design the Cenotaph in London (the national memorial to solders killed during World War I, built 1919–1921) and many other war memorials.

 ### Lynn, Dame Vera (born Vera Margaret Lewis)
(born 1917)
Entertainer

With a charming smile, warm personality and soft, attractive singing voice, Lynn became known as 'the Forces' Sweetheart' during World War II. She gave many concerts and broadcasts for troops, and also recorded patriotic songs such as 'The White Cliffs of Dover'. Lynn began her career early, first singing in public aged 7, and working as a dancer from age 11.

After the war, Lynn appeared on television and in variety shows, in Europe, Australia and America. Throughout her career, Lynn continued to support charities that offered help to former servicemen and their families.

RADIO ASTRONOMY

Radio telescopes collect rays of energy (radio waves) given off by objects in space. They are used to observe stars and other bodies that cannot be seen using visible light, even with large optical telescopes. Radio waves were first detected in 1931, by Karl Jansky in the USA. The first radio telescope was built by Grote Reber in 1937, also in America. Today, clusters of radio telescopes, called arrays, are linked together by computers to create massive systems for collecting radio waves. The biggest is the Very Large Array (VLA) in Socorro, New Mexico. This array is a staggering 8,000 km (5,000 miles) wide.

MacAdam, John
(1756–1836)
Engineer

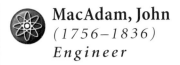

Scottish engineer MacAdam moved to America, where he worked in business, and became very rich. In 1783, he returned to Scotland, and used some of his money to pay for experiments in road design. Five years later he moved to Cornwall and continued his road research; this time it was paid for by the government.

MacAdam's experiments showed that several things were needed to create a smooth, long-lasting road. It needed to be well-drained, waterproof, and laid on top of layers of well-packed soil. MacAdam also developed a new, long-lasting road surface, made of small rocks and stone chips, bound together with gravel or slag (waste from iron-smelting factories).

MacAlpine, Kenneth
See Kenneth I

▲ Macbeth

Macbeth
(c.1005–1057; reigned 1040–1057)
King

Today, Macbeth is remembered as the hero – or villain – of one of Shakespeare's most dramatic plays, *Macbeth*. The real Macbeth was a nobleman who became king of Scotland after killing his cousin Duncan I; King Duncan had attacked him, as part of a long-standing feud. Macbeth was accepted as king by the Scots, and ruled peacefully until Scotland was attacked by the earl of Northumberland, who wanted to help Duncan's son (Malcolm III, *see* page 69) seize the throne. Macbeth was defeated, but survived for a further three years. He was killed in another battle against members of Duncan's family, who were determined to continue their feud.

MacDonald, Flora
(1722–1790)
Heroine

Flora MacDonald was born on the island of South Uist, in the Hebrides. She was adopted by a Scottish noblewoman, travelled to Edinburgh to be educated, then went to live in Skye, winning praise for her beauty and calm, gentle manner.

In 1746, Flora was asked to help Jacobite leader Charles Edward Stewart (*see* page 96), who was trying to escape from English soldiers. She disguised him as her Irish woman servant, 'Betty Burke', and smuggled him to safety on a waiting French warship. Later, the English government found out what she had done, and put her in prison. Within a year, she was set free. She married, then, in 1774, went with her husband to live in America. After five years, she returned to Scotland, and lived peacefully there until she died.

MacDonald, J. Ramsay
(1866–1937)
Politician

Born to a very poor unwed mother who was a servant on a Scottish farm, MacDonald worked hard at school, found a job as a Labour Party official, then became a Labour MP in 1906. Chosen as leader of the Labour Members of Parliament due to his party loyalty and experience, he resigned this post in 1914. He was a pacifist (someone who believes that all war is wrong), and could not support Britain fighting in World War I. His views angered many voters, and he lost his seat in Parliament in 1918.

He was re-elected in 1922, and again became head of his party in Parliament. A moderate, he aimed to make Labour 'responsible' and fit for government. He was prime minister for a few months in 1924, and from 1929 to 1931. During the economic crisis of the early 1930s, MacDonald headed a national government (from 1931 to 1935), with members from Labour, Conservative and Liberal Parties. He believed that this would be best for the country, but many Labour Party supporters saw him as a traitor, and he was expelled from the party. To them, his career ended in disgrace.

MacKenzie, Sir Alexander
(1764–1820)
Explorer

Born in Scotland, MacKenzie moved to Canada, where he worked for the North-West Company, exploring rivers and lakes, and looking for good hunting grounds. He travelled vast distances along icy rivers (including the Mackenzie River, which is named after him) and became the first European to cross Canada and reach the Pacific Coast, in 1793.

Mackintosh, Charles
(1766–1843)
Chemist

Remembered today for coats made of waterproof fabric, named after him, Scottish chemist Mackintosh studied dyestuffs and other chemicals used in industry. In 1823, he invented a way of coating cloth with rubber solution. Later, he also developed a vulcanization (strengthening) process for rubber tyres.

Mackintosh, Charles Rennie
(1868–1928)
Designer

Creator of a distinctive new style, based on flowing lines and tall, slender shapes. He was one of the main exponents of the Art Nouveau style in Scotland. Mackintosh is seen today as one of the first truly modern artists in Britain. He trained as an architect, and designed many buildings in and around Glasgow, including a dramatic and stylish new School of Art. There is still widespread interest in Mackintosh's work today.

He married another artist, Margaret Mackintosh who was well-known for her watercolours and stained glass. They often collaborated in their work.

However, he failed to make enough money to survive, and left Scotland to live abroad and work as an artist, where his paintings were greatly admired.

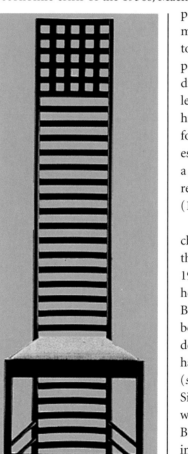

▸ **MACKINTOSH STYLE**
Mackintosh also designed distinctive furniture.

Macmillan, Harold
(1894–1986)
Politician

Grandson of a Scottish crofter, and son of a successful publisher, Macmillian came from a family that had moved rapidly from poverty to wealth. Educated as a 'gentleman', he fought bravely during World War I, then went into politics, as a Conservative. He was first elected MP in 1924. During the economic crisis of the 1930s, Macmillian was shocked by the poverty and hardship that many of his constituents had to suffer. He believed that people with money had a duty to help those who were less fortunate, and worked hard to improve conditions for ordinary people, especially when he became a government minister, responsible for housing (1951-1954).

He later served as chancellor of the exchequer, then prime minister (from 1957 to 1963). Macmillan held power at a time when Britain's economy was booming, and he proudly declared, 'Most of our people have never had it so good!' (*see* box on the 'Swinging Sixties'). In foreign affairs, he worked with leaders in many British colonies who wanted independence from British rule. He also tried to arrange Britain's entry to the European Common Market, but this was vetoed (turned down) by France. Macmillan was a skilled politician, and good at creating favourable publicity for himself and his party.

Since he left office, historians have questioned just how much he really achieved. During Macmillan's time in power, Britain missed important chances to rebuild its economy, and have a real influence on world politics.

THE 'SWINGING SIXTIES'

During the late 1950s and early 1960s, Britain was prosperous and seemed confident. At the same time, there was also rapid social change. A new generation was growing up that, unlike their parents, had no experience of war. They expected to spend their teenage years having fun, or else campaigning to change the world, and to 'ban the [nuclear] bomb'. Welfare State reforms meant that intelligent young people from ordinary families could go to university to train for well-paid, high-status jobs. The old class system no longer seemed to matter, and

was mocked by many thinkers, writers – and also by teenagers.

New clothes fashions (such as mini-skirts) and popular music (such as the Beatles) were designed to appeal only to the young; they shocked many older people. The contraceptive pill (introduced in the 1960s) led to new sexual freedom, especially for women. The late 1960s saw an increase in the experimental use of drugs and a growing tendency to challenge the establishment. Protesters chanted 'make love not war.'

Macmillan, Kirkpatrick
(1813–1878)
Inventor

Scottish blacksmith Macmillan invented the world's first pedal-driven bicycle (*above*) in 1839. The pedals were very hard to use, putting great strain on the knees. However, when copies of Macmillan's invention were made by another Scot, Gavin Dalzell, in 1846, cycling began to grow more popular.

Macmillan, Margaret
(1860–1931)
Campaigner

Together with her sister Rachel, Macmillan worked to improve education for young children from ordinary families. She trained as a governess, and worked in London. At the same time, she joined socialist political groups and took part in suffragette campaigns. After several years in Bradford, a northern industrial town, Margaret returned to London, where she joined in Rachel's campaigns for better health care for mothers and young children.

The Macmillans organized clinics in poor parts of London, took children from poor, dirty homes to spend time outside, in fresh country air, and set up an infant school with a garden, where city children could play. These ideas were revolutionary at the time, but they were later copied by teachers worldwide.

▲ BETTER SCHOOLS
Children in a schoolroom in 1925.

Makin, Bathshua
(1608–1675)
Teacher

A clergyman's daughter, Makin came from a scholarly family. Her brother was a well-known mathematician, who also had connections with the royal court. Around 1640, Makin was appointed tutor to the daughters of King Charles I. She taught them many subjects that were, at that time, believed to be too 'difficult' for girls, including Greek, Latin, Hebrew, mathematics, French, Italian and Spanish. Later, Makin opened a school for girls, to teach them similar subjects, as well as many practical and technical skills. Although she was criticized, she believed firmly that women had a right to receive as good an education as men.

Malcolm III 'Canmore'
(c.1031–1093; reigned 1058–1093)
King

Malcolm became king after killing Macbeth (*see* page 67) in battle. He worked to try and unite the different peoples of Scotland into a single kingdom, but had to spend much of his reign defending Scotland against English attack. He was killed in battle in Northumberland.

Malthus, Thomas Robert
(1766–1834)
Scholar

A clergyman and scholar, Malthus investigated the way that a population (the number of people in a country) grows. He believed that each population would naturally go on increasing until it grew too big for its local food supply. Then there would be famine, people would die and the population would fall. There would be enough for everyone to eat until the population grew too big again.

Malthus argued that it was possible to stop this miserable cycle of events. If people had fewer children, populations would remain the same size, and might even fall. Then there would be no danger of famine. Malthus believed that people could be encouraged to have fewer children by stopping charity and welfare payments. His ideas were taken up by politicians who wanted to cut back on government help for poor families.

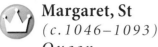 ## Margaret, St
(c.1046–1093)
Queen

A member of the Anglo-Saxon royal family, Margaret was married to King Malcolm III (*see* page 69) as a way of making peace between two countries, England and Scotland, who were often at war. She introduced many English words and customs to Scotland – for example, she gave all eight of her children non-Scottish names (many were taken from the Bible, instead).

Margaret was reported to be very religious, kind, and charitable. She also encouraged leaders of the Church in Scotland to obey international Church laws. She collapsed and died when she heard the news that her husband and eldest son had been killed in battle. Margaret was buried in a beautiful church at Dunfermline, and made a saint in 1250.

 ## Markova, Dame Alicia (Lilian Marks)
(born 1910)
Dancer

Born in London, Marks studied with leading French and Russian ballet teachers before going to dance with a famous international company (the Ballets Russes) aged only 14. There, her name was changed to 'Markova', since almost all other top dancers had Russian names. When the Ballets Russes company closed, in 1929, Markova returned to England, becoming a prima (leading) ballerina at 19. She performed many star parts, becoming the first English ballerina to dance difficult roles in famous classical ballets, such as *Swan Lake*. She also danced with companies in America and France, and made guest appearances worldwide. Markova was a great success everywhere, her delicate appearance combined with brilliant technical skill.

In 1935, Markova founded her own ballet company, with male dancer Anton Dolin, which later became the London Festival Ballet. It was the only major company to perform outside London, giving many people a chance to see ballet for the first time. Markova was also a dedicated teacher. For many years after she retired from the stage in 1963, she taught in America, and at London's Royal Ballet School.

Marlborough, Duke of
See Churchill, John

▲ Christopher Marlowe

 ## Marlowe, Christopher (Kit)
(1564–1593)
Writer

Creator of several successful plays in blank (non-rhyming) verse, such as *Dr Faustus* and *Tamburlaine the Great*, Marlowe's lines are often still quoted today. He also wrote many poems, mostly about love. He died young, in a tavern brawl, so we do not know how his writing skills would have developed. Shakespeare himself borrowed ideas from Marlowe's work to use in his own early plays!

Martineau, Harriet
(1802–1876)
Writer

Brought up in a very religious family, Martineau was unexpectedly left to earn her own living after her father died. She decided to become a writer, and published a series of short stories based on controversial political and economic issues of her time. They became very popular. She also wrote newspaper articles supporting progressive causes (such as ending slavery and fair treatment for women at work), stories for children, and novels for adults.

When told by her doctors that she was dying, Martineau wrote her own life story. In it, she discussed her past with great openness and courage – something that was unusual, and shocking, for a woman at that time. She described her unhappy childhood, her search for political ideas and a new religious faith, and her determination to live independently in a man's world.

 ## Marx, Karl Heinrich
(1818–1883)
Political thinker

Born in Prussia, north Germany, writer and thinker Marx spent most of his adult life in England. After working as a radical journalist, he was expelled from Germany for his revolutionary ideas. He moved to live in England in 1849. Working closely with his friend and supporter, sociologist Friedrich Engels, Marx began to write a series of books and pamphlets setting out his political views. He believed that ordinary working people were oppressed (badly treated) and exploited by governments and big businesses, and called for worldwide revolution.

His most famous texts were *The Communist Manifesto* (*see* box) and *Das Kapital* (about economics and the power of money). During his lifetime, and after his death, Marx's ideas inspired many revolutions and protest movements, notably in Russia (1917) and China (1948).

MARX AND COMMUNISM

In 1848, Karl Marx (with his colleague, Friedrich Engels) published a book setting out his political ideas. He called it *The Communist Manifesto*. In it, he described his hopes for the way society would be run in future. He wanted power and property to belong to the whole community, not just a privileged few, and for people to work to benefit society as a whole, not just to earn money or power for themselves. In return, he expected that all workers would be rewarded fairly, according to their needs. Marx hoped that the new working class, living in big cities and working in industry, would lead a revolution to overthrow the old ruling class and set up a communist society.

Mary I

 ## Mary I
(1516–1558; reigned 1553–1558)
Queen

Daughter of Henry VIII (*see* page 51) and his first wife, Catherine of Aragon, Mary was intelligent and very well educated. As her parents' only child, she was brought up to expect that she would one day rule England. In 1527, however, when she was 11 years old, her life changed completely. Henry VIII demanded a divorce from Mary's mother, so that he could marry his new love, Anne Boleyn. Henry hoped that Anne would bear him a male child, to be his heir. Mary sided with her mother, and remained loyal to her mother's Roman Catholic faith. Henry, and especially Anne, however, favoured Protestant reformers, who wanted to break away from Rome.

In 1534, Henry declared that his marriage to Catherine had not been lawful, and that Mary was illegitimate. Henry took Mary away from Catherine, and they never saw each other again. After Henry died, Edward VI, his child by his third wife, became king. But Edward was sickly, and died in his teens. Ambitious nobles then declared that Lady Jane Grey (*see* page 45) was queen. Mary's supporters fought against this, and she was proclaimed queen in 1553.

Aged 37, and needing an heir, Mary arranged a marriage with King Phillip II of Spain. Like her, he was Catholic. However, his country was one of England's enemies, so the marriage was very unpopular. Mary became hated still further after she began to persecute Protestants who refused to accept her Catholic faith. Countless ordinary people were hanged as rebels, and over 300 well-known figures were burnt as heretics. People called her 'Bloody Mary'. She died in 1558 of cancer, hoping that her swollen stomach was the sign of a longed-for baby, not disease.

Mary, Queen of Scots
(1542–1587; reigned 1542–1567)
Queen

Daughter of Scottish King James V, and a French princess, Mary of Guise, Mary became queen of Scotland aged just six days old. She was sent to France to be educated, while her mother ruled Scotland on her behalf. As a child, Mary married the French crown prince. He became King Francois II in 1559, but died one year later, and Mary was sent back to Scotland in 1561. She faced a difficult situation. She was young, in an unknown country, at a time when many people thought that women were unfit to rule. She was a Roman Catholic, but most Scots were Protestants. She also had to find a suitable husband, so that she could produce an heir.

Mary was pretty, elegant and intelligent, and many men wanted to marry her. However, she ignored all advice, and wed her cousin, English nobleman Henry Darnley. It was an unwise choice. Darnley was ambitious, but very stupid, and jealous of Mary's power. He was accused of planning the murder of her friend, musician David Rizzio. Soon afterwards, Darnley was found dead, in mysterious circumstances. Mary then scandalized Europe by eloping with one of the chief suspects – a violent Scots noble named Bothwell.

After this, the Scottish people no longer wanted Mary as queen. They locked her up in a castle, but she escaped, and fled to England in 1558. There, she became a serious problem for Queen Elizabeth, because England's enemies in Spain and France wanted Mary to be queen. Some Roman Catholics in England wanted this, too. For almost 20 years, Elizabeth kept Mary shut up in remote country houses, as it was too risky to set her free. Finally, she accepted senior ministers' advice and had Mary executed, after Mary was accused of taking part in several plots.

 ## Matthews, Sir Stanley
(1915–1999)
Sportsman

A professional footballer since the age of 17, Matthews played in 886 first-class matches, and in 54 internationals for England. Usually playing at right wing, he became known as 'the wizard of the dribble'. Few players before or since have shown such balance or control. His career lasted for a remarkable 33 years, until he was 50.

 ## Maudslay, Henry
(1771–1831)
Engineer

Engineer Maudslay invented many machine tools (machines that work as tools) that helped British industry develop quickly during the Industrial Revolution. His most important inventions included slide rules, micrometers (machines for measuring tiny, precise distances), and lathes for cutting screws.

 ## Maxwell, James Clerk
(1831–1879)
Scientist

A physicist, Maxwell studied electricity and magnetism. He was the first to realize that electromagnetic radiation existed, and to realize that light is a form of electromagnetic energy. He worked out mathematical equations to describe how electromagnetic forces work. He was also a capable administrator, setting up and running the Cavendish research laboratory at Cambridge University for many years.

Mill, J. S. (1806–1873)
Philosopher

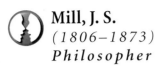

A civil servant and later an MP, philosopher Mill is remembered today for his writings on liberty, justice, women's rights and economics. He supported individual freedom, and was suspicious of state control and of 'free market' forces. He believed that neither would create a good environment for all citizens.

Mill campaigned for ordinary men and women to get the vote, and for workers to have the right to help run factories. He believed that everyone should be taught about politics, so that they could make well-informed decisions about how their society should be run.

Milton, John (1608–1674)
Writer

Milton lived at a time when England was divided by religious disputes and civil war. Both these are reflected in his writings. During the civil war, he wrote poems and pamphlets calling for England to become a republic, and defending the right to express an opinion in print without fear of prosecution.

Milton's greatest work, *Paradise Lost* (1667), is a long epic that re-tells the Bible story of Adam and Eve. Milton went blind in middle age, but this did not stop him writing or studying as his wife and daughters read to him.

▼ Illustration from Milton's *Paradise Lost*, showing Satan (the Devil).

THE STORY OF PARLIAMENT

1200s Parliament begins as formal meetings of king and his officials (mostly nobles)

1265 After defeating Henry III, Simon de Montfort (*below*) summons a parliament. It includes nobles, knights, clergymen, and two citizens elected from every large town in England

1295 Edward I summons 'Model Parliament'. It also contains nobles, clergy, and elected people's representatives. Nobles meet in House of Lords, non-nobles in House of Commons

*c.*1300–*c.*1500 Parliament slowly grows more powerful; from now on, kings and queens need its approval before collecting taxes

1529–1536 Reformation Parliament passes laws allowing Henry VIII to split Church of England from Roman Catholic Church

1629 Charles I quarrels with Parliament, and refuses to summon it. Needing money from taxes, he is finally forced to do so in 1640

1642–1649 Parliament's army beats Charles's in English Civil War

1660 Parliament invites Charles II to become king

1688–1689 Glorious Revolution. Parliament removes James II as king and decides who will be next rulers (James's daughter Mary and her husband William of Orange, William III)

1701 Act of Settlement. From now on, Parliament and the legal system no longer controlled by royalty. Parliament must agree to all declarations of war; only British people can be government ministers; only Parliament can remove judges from office

Montfort, Simon de (c.1208–1265)
Nobleman

Born into a noble family in Leicester, and married to the sister of Henry III, de Montfort won fame as a soldier. Brave, energetic and clever, but also greedy, ruthless and self-satisfied, he won both admirers and enemies. He quarrelled with Henry over the running of royal government and in 1263 started a civil war. In 1264, de Montfort captured the king and his eldest son, Prince Edward, on the battlefield. He forced Henry to summon parliament, which had not assembled for many years, believing that its members would help the king rule. However, Edward escaped from prison, de Montfort's enemies attacked, and he was killed at the Battle of Evesham, in 1265.

Montgomery, Lord Bernard
(1887–1976)
Soldier

A professional soldier, 'Monty' (as he was known) fought and was wounded during World War I. He stayed in the army, training soldiers for future wars. He returned to active service during World War II, commanding British troops during the dangerous retreat from Dunkirk, on the French coast, in 1940. His senior officers were so impressed that they offered him command of the Eighth Army, a British force that fought against the Italians in North Africa, largely defeating them by 1941. Monty's battle plan was simple, but it usually worked. He built up the morale of his men, and made sure they had more weapons than their enemies.

After the defeat of Rommel's Afrika Korps in 1942, Monty went on to help plan the D-Day Landings – an invasion of German-occupied Europe by combined British and American troops. It succeeded, but over 10,000 invading soldiers died. Monty's only great failure was at Arnhem in 1944, when a force of British paratroops and gliders tried to cross the river Rhine into Germany and seize key buildings and bridges. Even today, Monty remains controversial. Some of the men he commanded became very loyal, while others disliked him. Senior army colleagues respected his achievements, but found him vain and quarrelsome, and a very difficult character to work with.

Moore, Henry
(1898–1986)
Artist

Sculptor Moore created massive single figures and family groups, mostly of stone. His work stands in front of many important public buildings, in Britain and around the world. Unlike earlier sculptors, Moore did not make small-scale models of his designs. Instead, he carved straight into wood or stone, believing that he would create a more truthful image that way. Moore was also a skilled draughtsman (someone who draws). During World War II, he worked as an official war artist, creating many memorable drawings of ordinary people, sheltering from bomb attacks.

More, Sir (or St) Thomas
(1478–1535)
Politician

A famous scholar and government minister at the court of King Henry VIII (see page 51), More was a Roman Catholic, who opposed Protestant church reforms. He resigned as chancellor when Henry announced his decision to seek a divorce from Catherine of Aragon, and was put in prison in 1534 for refusing to accept Henry's marriage to Anne Boleyn. Henry gave orders for More to be executed the next year. More's writings ensured that his fame survived his death. He is still remembered for his book *Utopia*, in which he discussed the best way of running society, and criticized the governments of his own day.

Morris, William
(1834–1896)
Designer

Morris planned a career as a clergyman, but gave up religion to devote his life to arts and crafts. He believed that hand-made, individually designed goods were better than items mass-produced in factories. (To him, such goods were more individual, more solidly made, did not rely on poor workers being exploited, and contained the spirit of the worker who made them.)

Morris was a brilliant designer, especially of fabrics and printed books. He also wrote many stories, poems and political works, putting forward his socialist and sometimes communist ideas. He greatly admired medieval art and architecture, and helped found the Society for the Protection of Ancient Buildings, to preserve Britain's heritage.

▼ Decorated panels by William Morris

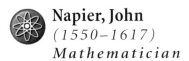

Napier, John
(1550–1617)
Mathematician

Scottish mathematician Napier is remembered today as the inventor of logarithms – sets of tables where numbers are shown as functions (forms) of different bases (number used as units for multiplying or dividing). For example, 2 is the logarithm of 100 to base 10, because 100 = 10 x 10. Before calculators or computers were invented, logarithms were used by mathematicians to perform complicated calculations quickly and accurately. Today they are still used to measure and describe natural phenomena (for example, the way our ears respond to sound) in precise mathematical ways.

▼ BRIGHTON
PAVILION
Originally designed by Henry Holland, Nash re-created the pavilion into an eastern-style building. (*below*).

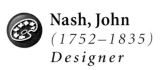

Nash, John
(1752–1835)
Designer

One of the earliest architects to plan whole streets and towns, Nash worked for the Prince Regent (later King George IV) to design elegant new buildings, especially in London. He planned Regent Street and Trafalgar Square (both 1826–1835), rebuilt Buckingham Palace and designed Marble Arch (both 1821–1830). In Brighton, he created a fantastic, Eastern-style pavilion for the Prince Regent.

Nasmyth, James
(1818–1890)
Engineer

Designer of several experimental steam-powered machines and railway locomotives, engineer Nasmyth was most famous for the huge, steam-powered hammer that he invented in 1839. It became widely used in metal-working factories and iron forges. Towards the end of his life, Nasmyth became interested in astronomy, producing one of the first detailed maps of the Moon.

Neill, Alexander Sutherland
(1883–1973)
Teacher

After a bitterly unhappy time at school, Scottish teacher Neill pioneered a new kind of education, based on encouraging, rather than forcing, children to learn. In 1924, he founded a 'progressive' school, Summerhill, where children chose whether to attend lessons or not, and made many of the decisions about how the school was to be run. Neill's school has been praised for its 'child-centred' approach to education, and also criticized for its lack of discipline and for its failure to teach some pupils even basic skills.

THE REGENCY ERA

From 1811 to 1820, King George III was too ill to rule; his eldest son, the Prince of Wales (later George IV) became regent (temporary ruler) in his place. The years he was in power are known as 'the Regency'. Politically, they were mixed. Britain was unable to win a war against newly independent America, but did play an important part in defeating France, and in negotiating the European treaties that followed. During wartime, the economy boomed, but slumped when peace began in 1815.

In his private life, the Prince of Wales was keenly interested in the arts. Today, his regency is remembered for the grand yet graceful buildings that were constructed in many British towns (especially London, Brighton and Bath), for elegant fashions, and for the witty novels of Jane Austen (who he admired; *see* page 9).

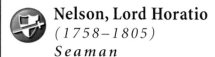

Nelson, Lord Horatio
(1758–1805)
Seaman

Nelson joined the Navy aged 12, and served on ships sailing to the Arctic and the Caribbean. His skill as a seaman and leader was soon recognized, and he was given his first ship to command while still in his twenties. Although small and slight, he showed great physical courage. He lost his right eye fighting against the French in the Mediterranean Sea in 1793, and his right arm in 1797. The following year, he commanded British ships against the French at the Battle of the Nile. He won a great victory, and became a national hero. He also became friends with beautiful, scandalous Lady Emma Hamilton, whose husband was British ambassador in southern Italy. They had a daughter, Horatia, and remained deeply in love for the rest of Nelson's life.

Promoted to admiral in 1801, Nelson ignored orders given by a cautious senior officer to win a daring victory at the Battle of Copenhagen. (It was said that he held his telescope to his blind eye, and so could not see the flags sending messages from the senior officer's ship.) His greatest success came at the Battle of Trafalgar (*see* box) in 1805, where his ships destroyed the French fleet. Nelson was killed in the fighting, but his victory made Britain the greatest sea power in the world. Without control of the seas, the British Empire, which grew rapidly in the 19th century, could never have developed.

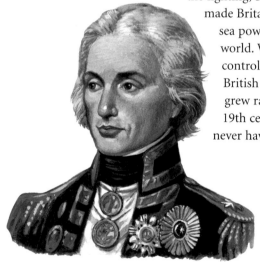

THE BATTLE OF TRAFALGAR

Nelson and his sailors won this battle by risky, daring tactics. At that time, ships taking part in sea-warfare usually arranged themselves in long rows, firing cannon at each other. They hoped the cannon balls would smash the hulls of enemy ships, setting them on fire or sinking them. Nelson, however, decided to fight in a different way. He gave orders for his ships to sail towards the French fleet, at right angles. This broke through their defensive line, and scattered them. It also gave Nelson's ships the chance to sail much closer to the French, and launch a more deadly attack.

Newcomen, Thomas
(1663–1729)
Engineer

Engineer Newcomen invented the first steam-powered engine that was strong and reliable enough for industrial use. Made to pump water out of deep coal mines, it was first installed in 1712. Newcomen's design was later adapted and improved by famous inventor James Watt (*see* page 104).

▼ PUMPING ENGINE
Newcomen's steam pump was highly successful, and prevented many mines from flooding.

Newman, J. H.
(1801–1890)
Religious leader

Newman was one of the senior figures in the Oxford Movement, a group of church leaders and others who aimed to bring the Church of England closer to the Roman Catholic Church. They faced strong opposition, partly from people with moderate views on religion, but chiefly from Evangelicals, a rival group within the Church who firmly believed that it should keep well clear of Rome, and base all its teachings on the words of the Bible.

Newman left the Church of England to become a Roman Catholic in 1845. He published many writings on religious politics, and also many hymns and poems. They became well-loved for their beautiful words and deep feelings. In the late 20th century, the Roman Catholic Church announced that it was considering making Newman a saint.

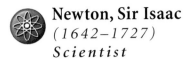

Newton, Sir Isaac
(1642–1727)
Scientist

Said by some to be the greatest British scientist of all time, Cambridge professor Newton was a mathematician and physicist. He made many key mathematical discoveries. He also discovered, and explained in mathematical terms, the natural laws that rule the Universe. Newton's 'Laws of Motion' describe the forces at work when movement happens. His 'Law of Gravitation' describes terms such as weight and mass, and explains why objects fall to Earth, and why the Earth orbits (moves around) the Sun.

Newton also studied optics (the science of light and vision) and was the first to show that white light is made up of many different colours (*see* box). In 1703, he was elected president of the Royal Society, the highest scientific honour of his day. Later scientists, such as Einstein, have suggested new theories about how the universe works, but these have not replaced Newton's laws. Instead, old and new theories are seen as different ways of explaining the same things.

LIGHT

Light is a form of electro-magnetic radiation that can be detected by human eyes. (Other 'invisible' forms of radiation include radio waves and microwaves.) Scientists describe light as either a stream of particles or as waves of energy.

The colour of light changes according to the length of each wave. Newton discovered that white light – daylight – is a mixture of different-coloured light waves, and that it can be split by passing it through a glass prism. It splits into a rainbow spectrum of colour: red, orange, yellow, green, blue, indigo, violet.

Nightingale, Florence
(1820–1910)
Nurse

Born in Florence, Italy, while her wealthy British parents were travelling there, Nightingale received a strict academic education from her father, and accompanied her mother on visits to sick and poor people. She wanted to become a nurse, but her parents would not allow it – nursing was not a well-trained or respectable career at that time. So Nightingale used some money she had set up to found a nursing home for 'gentlewomen', making all important decisions herself, but employing other women to work there.

In 1854, British troops were sent to fight in the Crimea (southern Russia). Nightingale volunteered to lead a group of nurses there, and a family friend (who was a government minister) obtained official permission for her to go. Nightingale and her nurses found that conditions in army hospitals were dreadful, and set about improving them, with great success. Nightingale proved to be a brilliant, formidable organizer, who cared deeply about the wounded men in her charge. She became known as 'the Lady with the Lamp' (because of her habit of checking the wards every evening), and was honoured as a heroine back in Britain. To thank her, the British public raised large sums of money to set up a school of nursing at a top London hospital, where Nightingale taught other capable women to care for patients and to manage hospitals and nursing homes of their own. She also advised the government on army nursing services, and on public health schemes for lands in the British Empire.

▼ LADY WITH THE LAMP
Florence Nightingale checking on her patients.

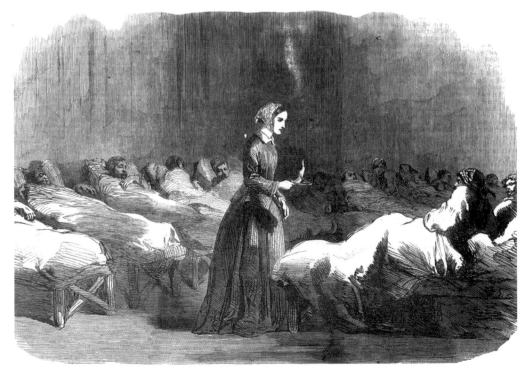

North, Lord Frederick
(1732–1792)
Politician

A Tory MP, North became chancellor of the exchequer, then prime minister from 1770 to 1782. A pleasant, friendly man, he preferred to seek compromise rather than conflict. This worked well in the House of Commons, but failed when North was faced with demands for independence from British colonists in America. The colonists were determined to succeed, even if it led to war. Fighting did break out in 1775, independence was proclaimed in 1776, and British troops were finally defeated in 1783. North resigned in 1782, when it became clear that the colonists were going to win the war. North's time in government was made difficult by King George III, who supported him, but interfered in unhelpful ways.

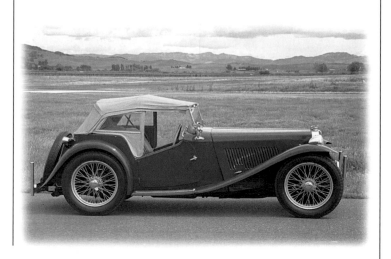

▲ MADE BY MORRIS
An early 'MG' sports car, made in Morris's factory at Oxford.

North, Marianne
(1830–1890)
Artist and scientist

From a wealthy English family, North did not go to school, but was educated by her artistic, adventurous parents. She also went with them on many journeys across Europe and the Middle East. After her father died, North began to travel alone. Her journeys had a purpose, to study wild plants and record them in detailed paintings (*right*).

North visited North and South America, East Asia, Australia, Indonesia and islands in the Pacific Ocean, recording many plants and flowers for the first time. In 1882, her paintings were housed in a specially-built gallery at the Royal Botanic Gardens in Kew, near London. There, they formed a highly important scientific resource, and were studied by experts from all over the world.

Nuffield, Viscount William Morris
(1877–1963)
Manufacturer

From poor beginnings, Morris became one of the most powerful factory-owners in Britain. He was also famous for his gifts to charity. He began his career by opening a bicycle workshop. In 1912, he built a factory to make cars; the first Morris motor was produced there the next year. His company later became famous for 'MG' (Morris Garage) sports cars, first made in 1926.

Towards the end of his life, Morris gave away much of his fortune to good causes. He founded Nuffield College in Oxford, and the Nuffield Foundation for medical and scientific research.

◀ THE CHEROKEE ROSE
Marianne North's evocative painting style.

Oates, Lawrence
(1880–1912)
Explorer

A soldier and explorer, Oates joined Captain Robert Scott's expedition (*see* page 92) to the South Pole from 1910 to 1912.

On the journey back from the pole, Oates suffered badly from frostbite, and found it difficult to keep up with the others. Rather than delay them, which would have increased the danger they were in, Oates bravely crawled out into the snow and ice to die.

In spite of Oates's brave sacrifice, the whole group died – of hunger, cold and exhaustion – just a few weeks later.

This selfless act was recorded in Scott's diary which was later found at the campsite.

Offa
(died 796)
King

Warrior and ruler of the English kingdom of Mercia, in the West Midlands, Offa took control of weaker English kingdoms, and declared himself king of the English. He ordered the building of a massive earthwork (known as 'Offa's Dyke'), to mark the boundary between his kingdom and Wales, and to display his wealth and power. Offa's Dyke was around 193 km (120 miles) long and 7.6 m (25 ft) high. Most of it still survives today. (*See* Anglo-Saxon England box.)

▲ KING OFFA
Portrayed on one of his own silver coins.

O

Olivier, Baron Laurence
(1907–1989)
Actor

Son of a clergyman, Olivier became a professional actor aged 17. With a powerful presence and a commanding voice, he achieved great success in many classic plays, and in films. He was especially famous for playing Shakespeare's heroic Henry V – the film that he starred in and directed became one of the best-known British films ever.

Oliver also directed many stage plays, and led the British National Theatre Company from 1963 to 1973. A theatre on London's Southbank is named after him.

▼ LORD OLIVIER
Photographed in 1959.

ANGLO-SAXON ENGLAND

This name is used to describe the period of history between the end of Roman rule in Britain (around AD400) and the Norman Conquest of 1066. During that time, groups of people – Angles, Saxons, Jutes and Frisians – from northwest Germany and the neighbouring lands arrived to settle in England. They lived mostly as farmers, taking over fields and farms from the existing Celtic population, and clearing new land. The country was divided into several small kingdoms, which often fought one another. They also fought against Viking invaders.

Powerful kings like Alfred the Great (*see* page 7) and Offa (*above*) tried to unite all the different kingdoms, and to encourage trade. In spite of wars and invasions, Christian missionaries, monks and nuns were very active in Anglo-Saxon England. They slowly converted the pagan German peoples to the Christian faith, and their churches and monasteries also became great centres of learning and art.

Orwell, George (Eric Blair)
(1903–1950)
Writer

The son of a senior British government official working in India, Orwell (*below*) served in the British police force in Burma, then returned to England to become a novelist and political writer. To support himself while finishing his first books, he worked at miserable, low-paid jobs, and met many unemployed people. This led him to sympathize with working-class protests, and to fight on the Republican side, against Fascists, in the Spanish Civil War. Although Orwell was a socialist, he strongly disliked communist governments, because they abused their power. His two most famous books, *Animal Farm* (1945) and *Nineteen Eighty Four* (1949) are fierce attacks on all governments that control and manipulate their citizens.

WORLD WAR I

Often described as 'the war to end all wars', World War I (1914–1918) involved most European nations, as well as Turkey and Russia. It broke out for two main reasons: first, rivalry and mistrust between Germany and other powerful European nations; secondly, political unrest in the Balkans, which threatened peaceful governments throughout Europe.

Wartime suffering was appalling. Deadly new weapons such as poison gas, tanks, aircraft and depth charges (underwater bombs) were used for the first time, and over 10 million men died. In Western Europe, enemy armies spent years fighting over land in Belgium and northern France known as the 'Front Line'. Troops sheltered from shells in muddy trenches or dug-outs (underground rooms). Many died of disease; others were killed by machine-gun bullets or trapped in razor-wire.

 ## Owen, Robert
(1771–1858)
Reformer

Remembered today as a pioneer of the co-operative movement (which encouraged workers to join together to improve their lives), Owen was the son of a Welsh draper (cloth-seller). He believed that people's character was shaped by the conditions they lived and worked in, and that ordinary people could only be 'good' if they were provided with fair wages and decent places to live.

Owen trained as a master-spinner, then took over cloth mills at New Lanark, in Scotland. He ran them as a model factory, building new houses, schools, shops and water supplies for his workers. He hoped others would follow his example. Owen also campaigned for new laws to make factories safer and healthier, and supported some of the first Trade Unions in Britain.

 ## Owen, Wilfred
(1893–1918)
Writer

One of the most important poets who took part in, and wrote about, World War I (*below*). Owen had already produced several fine poems by the time he was 21 – the year the War began. He fought as a British soldier in France, turning his horrific experiences – and those of his comrades – into bleak, bitter verses, full of anger at the tragic waste of young men's lives. Owen was killed in action one week before the end of the war. His poems still have the power to shock and move readers, and have been set to music by major composers – including Benjamin Britten, in his *War Requiem*.

Page, Sir Frederick Handley
(1885–1962)
Engineer

Page founded one of the world's first aircraft-making factories in 1909. It became famous for a number of pioneering designs, including the Halifax bomber that played an important part in World War II.

Paget, Sir James
(1814–1899)
Doctor

Paget trained as a surgeon, and invented several new techniques for operating on diseased bones. He also discovered the parasitic worm that causes trichinosis, a dangerous tropical disease. However, he is mostly remembered today as the founder of scientific pathology – the examination of dead bodies and dead tissue to discover the cause of disease, and, where possible, the cure.

Paine, Thomas
(1737–1809)
Political writer

The son of a farmer from the east of England, Paine worked as a customs officer, before being dismissed for writing a pamphlet calling for higher pay. He emigrated to America, where he edited a newspaper and wrote a book supporting the American colonists' demands for independence from British rule. After America became independent in 1776, Paine was sent to France on business, and supported anti-government protesters there.

Next, Paine travelled to London, where he published his most famous work, *The Rights of Man*, in 1791–1792. In it, he argued that kings and queens should not govern, but that all countries should be republics. He also supported the Revolution that had started in France in 1789, and had overthrown the royal government there. Paine's work outraged many people in Britain. He was accused of encouraging rebellion, and people burnt effigies (models) of him on bonfires. Paine fled to France, where he joined the revolutionary government, and helped to plan war against Britain. He returned to America in 1802.

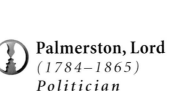

Palmerston, Lord
(1784–1865)
Politician

Palmerston began his political career as a Conservative MP, but changed his views and became a Liberal. He served as an MP for an astonishing 58 years, and was a government minister for 48 of them. His first interest was in foreign affairs, where he strengthened Britain's influence in Europe, and supported independence movements in Greece and Turkey (because he thought it would benefit Britain). He also began the Opium Wars – battles to protect English merchants (many of whom sold the deadly drug opium) – in China.

In 1852, he became home secretary. Encouraged by his progressive son-in-law, he introduced laws to improve working conditions in factories. In 1855, Palmerston became prime minister. He ended Britain's war with Russia, because it was too costly, and ordered British soldiers in India to put down a rebellion by Indian troops. His government was defeated in 1858, but Palmerston was soon back in power in 1859, with a strong team of politicians to help him introduce many new policies. These included cutting government spending, reducing taxes, and encouraging free trade (without limits or tolls) with other countries. Palmerston became unpopular when he refused to improve education for ordinary children, or to reform Parliament – at this time, few ordinary men, and no women, had the right to vote.

Palmerston remained a controversial figure throughout his life. His private life was scandalous, but, in public, he was energetic, hard-working, and never afraid to fight for what he thought was right. His unquestioning belief that Britain was superior to all other nations, however, and his unprincipled policies, won him many critics – including Queen Victoria herself.

◀ LORD PALMERSTON
Controversial PM.

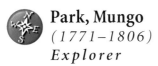

Pankhurst, Emmeline
(1858–1928)
Campaigner

Leader of the Suffragette movement, which demanded votes for women, Pankhurst – and her daughters Christabel (1880–1958) and Sylvia (1882–1960) – are remembered today for taking direct, sometimes violent, action in their campaigns. They did this because they felt that peaceful, legal demands for women's right to vote would never succeed. (*See* box)

Pankhurst was the daughter of a wealthy Manchester factory-owner, and both her parents had progressive ideas. She attended her first votes-for-women meeting aged 12, with her mother. Pankhurst married a lawyer who supported, and helped with, her campaigning. They moved to London, and made many friends among radical politicians. In 1898, Pankhurst's husband died, leaving her with three young children to support. She returned to Manchester and took a job, but continued campaigning. In 1903, with her daughter Christabel, Pankhurst founded the Women's Social and Political Union (often known as 'the Suffragettes'). From 1905, Pankhurst, her daughters, and many other women, staged dramatic protests – chaining themselves to railings, throwing bricks through windows, interrupting debates in Parliament and damaging men's sports facilities such as football grounds. They were arrested and put in prison, where they went on hunger-strike, and were brutally force-fed.

During World War I (1914–1918), Pankhurst called for the Suffragettes to stop their protest, and to work hard for their country, instead. Many Suffragettes – and other women – became volunteer nurses, drove ambulances, or worked in factories, taking over essential jobs done by men who had joined the army. They proved to be hard-working and reliable, and so, in 1918, when the war ended, the government allowed women over 30 the right to vote. The Suffragettes welcomed this, but said it was not enough. They continued to campaign, peacefully, until women were granted the right to vote on equal terms with men in 1928 – the year Pankhurst died.

VOTES FOR WOMEN

1851 Sheffield Women's Political Association founded. The first of many local political education groups

1867 Parliament rejects petition asking for votes for women. Groups demanding women's rights set up in London and other big British cities

1872 Central Committee for Women's Suffrage set up to coordinate local groups

1897 National Union of Women's Suffrage Societies formed, to plan peaceful, legal, nationwide campaign

1903 Women's Social and Political Union formed by Mrs Pankhurst and others. Aims to campaign with 'deeds not words', and will use violence if necessary. Members are nicknamed 'Suffragettes'

1908 About 250,000 women attend Suffragette rally in London's Hyde Park

1909–1913 Many Suffragettes imprisoned; they go on hunger strike and are forcibly fed. This causes public outcry

1910–1914 Suffragette protests increasingly violent – smashing windows, destroying mail, setting fire to buildings

1913 Suffragette Emily Davison dies after throwing herself in front of the king's racehorse

1914–1918 World War I. Suffragettes end protests and help war effort. Along with many other women, they prove capable and win great respect

1918 To reward them for war effort, women over 30 are allowed to vote

1928 All women allowed to vote on equal terms with men

Park, Mungo
(1771–1806)
Explorer

▶ MUNGO PARK
The explorer, being nursed by African villagers.

Born in Scotland, Park trained as a doctor, then travelled to Sumatra, in Indonesia, as assistant surgeon on a scientific survey vessel. After returning to Britain, he was recruited by a geographical society to lead an expedition to West Africa, to survey and draw maps of the river Niger. He spent two exhausting years in Africa, from 1795 to 1797. During this time, he fell seriously ill, and was captured by Arab traders. To recover his health, Park took a job as a doctor in Britain. Africa still fascinated him, however, and he returned in 1804. This time, he hoped to sail up the Niger to reach its source. Sadly, most of the men travelling with him died of fever, and Park's own boat was ambushed, then wrecked on rapids. Everyone on board died.

Parnell, Charles Stewart
(1846–1891)
Politician

A wealthy Protestant landowner, Parnell's father came from a distinguished Anglo-Irish family. However, his mother was American, and taught Parnell to hate Britain, and British policy in Ireland. Determined to help Ireland win independence, Parnell went into politics, and was elected as a British MP in 1875. In Parliament, he did all he could to obstruct government business. This was his way of drawing attention to Ireland's demands. In 1879, he became president of the Irish Land League, a body that campaigned for lower rents and better property rights for Irish people. The next year,

he was elected leader of the Irish Home Rule party. In 1885, he helped persuade Prime Minister Gladstone to support calls for Irish independence. Five years later, in 1891, Parnell's political career ended after a scandal involving a pretty Irish actress, Kitty O'Shea, and he was forced to resign.

Parsons, Sir Charles
(1854–1931)
Engineer

In 1884, Parsons designed and built the world's first industrial steam-turbine engine. It used power from coal and water to generate electricity. Soon, steam turbines were installed in many power stations. Parsons' invention transformed the way many goods were made, and also revolutionized home heating and lighting.

He also designed steam turbine engines for ships, and an experimental vessel, the *Turbinia* (1894), which used steam-power. By the early years of the 20th century, most large, fast ships were steam-turbine powered, including ocean liners and a famous series of battleships known as Dreadnoughts. Parsons also invented optical devices, such as searchlights and large telescopes.

◀ STEAM POWER
A turbine on the Aquitania

Paston, Margaret
(1423–1484)
Writer of letters

Daughter and wife of wealthy Norfolk farmers, Paston stayed at home, managing her husband's lands and their large household, while he spent months at a time in London, working as a lawyer and MP. She even defended their home against attack during the Wars of the Roses (1455–1485).

Margaret and her relatives wrote many letters to each other, describing their lives. These 'Paston Letters' are the earliest surviving collection of private family correspondence in England. As such, they are very important. They show, for the first time, what ordinary men and women thought and felt about each other and the world they lived in.

Paterson, Emma
(1848–1886)
Campaigner

A schoolteacher's daughter, Paterson trained as a bookbinder, then worked as a secretary for progressive causes, including the Women's Suffrage (right to vote) Association. She travelled to America, and studied trade union organization there. Returning to England in 1874, she set up a trade union for all women workers (the Women's Provident and Protective League), and campaigned to recruit members from many different trades. In 1875, she was the first woman to attend the Trades Union Congress (annual meeting). From 1876, she edited a women's magazine that campaigned for worker's rights, votes for women, better education, and legal reform. She also supported women's freedom to wear shorter, simpler dresses and trousers.

Paterson, William
(1658–1719)
Explorer

Born in Scotland, Paterson travelled to the Caribbean as a young man. There, he made a fortune, perhaps through piracy, perhaps by trade – no one really knows. He returned to London and, in 1691, suggested that a new national bank be set up, to be called the Bank of England. It was opened in 1694, and he became one of its first directors. However, he resigned a year later, to take part in two more exciting – but much riskier – money-making schemes. He planned a company to trade with Africa, and a new Scottish colony at Darien (in present-day Panama, Central America). Paterson sailed for Darien with his family in 1698, but his plans went horribly wrong. Many of the settlers died, including Paterson's wife and son, and the colony failed. Paterson lost his fortune, and returned to Scotland, poor, and unwell. He had a considerable share in promoting the Union of the parliaments of Scotland and England in 1707 and in 1715 was awarded £18,000 as indemnity for his Darien loss.

Patrick, St
(5th century AD)
Religious leader

Remembered today as the patron (guardian) saint of Ireland, Patrick was born in Britain, and spent his life as a Christian missionary. We know very little for certain about Patrick's work in Ireland, though many stories and legends have been told about it – for example, that he drove all poisonous snakes from the land and told them never to return. There were probably Christian communities in Ireland before Patrick arrived. He may have been sent there by the Christian church in England to help strengthen them.

Peel, Sir Robert
(1788–1850)
Politician

Son of a factory-owner, Peel became a Conservative MP, home secretary (1834–1835) and prime minister (1841-1846). He is remembered today chiefly for founding the Metropolitan Police force, to combat crime in London (*see* Law and Order box). For many years, policemen were nicknamed 'bobbies' after him.

Peel also supported free trade between Britain and other nations, and moderate reform of Parliament, although he did not agree all adult citizens should be allowed to vote. After a quarrel within the Conservative Party, Peel and his supporters formed a third party, most of whom later joined the Liberals.

Penn, William
(1644–1718)
Religious leader

A member of the Society of Friends (Quakers), Penn was imprisoned in the Tower of London in 1668 for publishing writings about Quaker beliefs. They were illegal in England at that time. Penn was put on trial, but the jury refused to convict him, and he was set free in 1670.

In 1681, the English government granted him a charter (licence) to found a settlement in North America, where he – and other Quakers – would be free to worship in the way they wanted. It was named Pennsylvania, after him, and its capital was Philadelphia (founded 1682) – 'the city of brotherly love'. In 1685, Penn returned to England, where he successfully campaigned for 1,200 Quakers to be set free from prison, but he angered the English government, and returned to Pennsylvania in 1699.

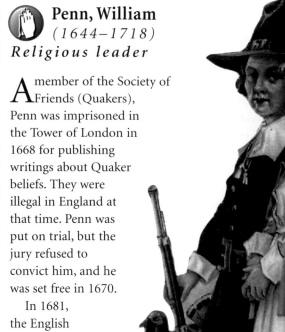

▲ **THE FOUNDING FATHERS**
Early American settlers.

▶ **SIR ROBERT PEEL**
Making a speech in Parliament.

LAW AND ORDER

From before 1066 to the 19th century, police duties were carried out by local officials. The sheriff maintained law and order in each county, and constables, helped by beadles and watchmen, were meant to 'keep the peace' in villages and towns. In many country areas, villagers had to belong to 'tithings' (groups of about 10 adult men). Each member was responsible for the good behaviour of the others and had to report all local crimes. From 1363, local judges, called justices of the peace (JPs), were appointed by the king.

By the 19th century, politicians were worried about rising crime, especially in fast-growing industrial cities. There were few local officials to control law and order in these cities, although London had a team of private policemen – known as the Bow Street Runners – appointed by local JPs. In 1829, Sir Robert Peel founded the Metropolitan Police force. It served only London, but was soon copied elsewhere. Officers known as constables took an oath that they would work for 'the prevention of crime'. Peel's force wore uniforms and patrolled the streets. The first plain-clothes detective force, based at Scotland Yard in London, was set up in 1842. Since then, police forces have been reorganized many times, but their aim remains the same.

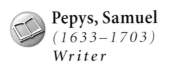

Pepys, Samuel
(1633–1703)
Writer

A senior government official, who worked for the Royal Navy, Pepys is remembered today for the wonderful diary that he kept between 1660 and 1669. In it, he recorded many dramatic national events, including the Great Plague (1665) and the Great Fire of London (1666), and descriptions of new scientific discoveries.

Even more interesting, so many readers think, is the detailed account of Pepys's private life that his diary also contains. Because he wrote in a secret code, Pepys felt safe to include in the diary his innermost thoughts about politics and the powerful people he worked for. He also revealed all kinds of information about the clothes he bought, the food he enjoyed, the music he liked to play, outings with his friends, money worries – and even quarrels with his wife, and love-affairs with his women servants.

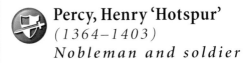

Percy, Henry 'Hotspur'
(1364–1403)
Nobleman and soldier

A famous warrior, Percy was the eldest son of the Earl of Northumberland, the most powerful nobleman in northern England. He was given the nickname 'Hotspur' for his reckless courage in battle. Together with his father, he plotted against King Richard II and helped King Henry IV to seize power in 1399. As a reward, Henry gave Hotspur and his father important army commands, patrolling England's border with Scotland. However, Henry failed to pay their wages, or let them keep the ransom money from Scottish prisoners they captured in battle. So they joined with Welsh protest leader Owen Glendower (*see* page 44) to rebel against Henry. Hotspur was killed at the Battle of Shrewsbury in 1403; his father was killed five years later, also fighting against the king.

Perkin, Sir William Henry *(1838–1907)*
Scientist

B y accident, Perkin invented a new colour – mauve – that became very popular throughout 19th-century Europe. He discovered the formula aged only 18, when he was trying to make a chemical copy of the important plant-based medicine, quinine. With his father, Perkin set up a factory to mass-produce mauve dye, and to make other synthetic dyes. They were used for clothes, furnishings and even postage stamps. Unlike earlier natural dyes, based on earth or plants, Perkin's synthetic dyes did not fade quickly when clothes were washed, or when they were exposed to bright sunlight. However, since then, artificial dyes have sometimes caused water pollution.

Philips, Katherine
(1631–1664)
Writer

B orn into a London merchant's family, Philips attended a school for girls before getting married aged 17. In her husband's home, she set up a 'salon' (meeting place) for a group of well-educated people whom she called 'The Society of Friendship'. Many writers and thinkers came to read their work and take part in discussions there. Philips wrote poems and composed literary letters; she also translated plays from French. Her work was greatly admired by members of the salon, but was not published until after her death. She became known as 'the matchless Orinda', after her pen-name.

Pitt, Lord William (known as 'Pitt the Elder')
1708–1778)
Politician

F rom a very wealthy family (his grandfather, 'Diamond' Pitt, was a merchant, trading with India) Pitt became a Whig (Liberal) MP in 1735. Although disliked by the king (and by many politicians) for his cold but powerful personality, he served as a government minister, proving to be capable and fair at a time when many other ministers were accused of self-seeking ambition and corruption.

Pitt successfully shaped government policy during the Seven Years War (1756–1763), when Britain fought against other powerful states in Europe. This earned him the nickname 'Patriot'. From 1766 until 1768, he was prime minister. However, ill health (possibly a nervous breakdown) caused him to resign.

▲ Pitt the Younger

Pitt, William
(known as 'Pitt the Younger')
(1759–1806)
Politician

Son of Pitt the Elder (*see* page 85), Pitt trained as a lawyer, then became an MP in 1781. Unlike his father, he supported the Tory (Conservative) Party. Clever and ambitious, he was soon made a government minister, then prime minister in 1783. He was only 24, and the youngest man ever to be chosen for the job. The young prime minister reformed government finances, reduced the national debt, changed the way British merchants and soldiers ran their lands in India, and increased people's respect for Parliament.

After the French Revolution of 1789, Pitt acted swiftly to stop any British people supporting the rebels in France, or discussing revolutionary ideas. Many writers and thinkers criticized him, but he was supported by the English upper classes, wealthy families and property-owners. None of them wanted revolution in their land. Pitt also worked to unite Ireland with the other countries of Britain; the law setting up this union was passed in 1800. The year after that, Pitt resigned, because the British king, George III, refused to give the Catholic people of Ireland equal religious freedom and political rights to the rest of the British people, who were mostly Protestant. Pitt returned to power in 1804, to help lead the war against Napoleon's France. He died in office, before the war ended.

Pope, Alexander
(1688–1744)
Writer

After a childhood illness, Pope was left physically disabled, and was often mentally depressed. However, he had a powerful intelligence and quick wit, which he used to criticize people whom he found foolish or pompous – especially governments and fashion-leaders. His most successful works were translations of ancient Greek epics. They were scholarly yet readable and enjoyable, and remained popular for over 100 years. They also made Pope very rich. Together with a small group of other writers interested in politics, Pope set up the Scribblers' Club. Members worked together to produce many satirical (critical but amusing) works.

Priestley, Sir Joseph
(1733–1804)
Scientist

A pioneer researcher, Priestley investigated the chemistry of gases, and discovered oxygen (the gas we need to breathe to survive) in 1774. Priestley's enquiring mind led him to question many accepted religious beliefs. He became leader of a breakaway Christian church in Birmingham in 1779, and wrote over 150 books, mostly on religion. Priestley was also a great supporter of political reform, and backed American colonists' demands for freedom from British rule. He also supported the French Revolution. Because of this, his house was attacked by mobs in 1791, and destroyed. Priestley fled to America, where he spent the rest of his life.

Purcell, Henry
(c.1659–1695)
Musician

Son of a singer in the royal chapel in London, Purcell also joined the choir, but became more famous as an organist and composer. He wrote many works specially for the royal court, such as birthday odes (songs) for the queen, and impressive pieces for choir and organ to be performed at royal coronations.

Purcell also composed many religious works, and music for the theatre. He is remembered today as the composer of the first opera in English, in 1689. Called *Dido and Aeneas*, it is a tragic love story and was written specially for young students at a girls' school.

◀ HENRY PURCELL
Composer of the first opera in English.

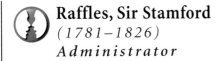

Raffles, Sir Stamford
(1781–1826)
Administrator

Raffles worked for the East India Company – an association of British merchants, trading with India and Southeast Asia, that was immensely rich and powerful. He was sent to Malaysia and Indonesia, where the company was fighting Dutch settlers. In 1811, he captured Java from the Dutch and was made lieutenant governor. After spending some time in England, Raffles returned to Asia, where he helped negotiate the British purchase of Singapore. In 1819, Singapore became a British colony, and was ruled by Raffles until 1823. He made it into the most important trading centre on the busy sea-route between Calcutta (in India) and Hong Kong.

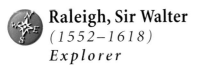

Raleigh, Sir Walter
(1552–1618)
Explorer

Born in Devon, Raleigh fought as a soldier in France, then became a courtier, serving Queen Elizabeth I. He became one of her special favourites. However, he was restless at court, planned overseas voyages, and took part in wars in Ireland. He encouraged British explorer Humphrey Gilbert to explore Newfoundland, and organized his own (unsuccessful) off the northeast coast of America (*see* The English in North America box).

After quarrelling with the queen (who was angered by his secret marriage to one of her maids), Raleigh tried to win back her favour by sailing to South America in search of treasure, and by fighting against Spanish settlers there. After Queen Elizabeth's death, Raleigh plotted against the new king, James I, and was imprisoned in the Tower of London for several years. He passed the time by writing a huge *History of the World*. He was freed in 1616, but angered the king by attacking his allies overseas. He was executed as soon as he returned to Britain.

Many romantic stories are told about Raleigh, who was a colourful, reckless and sometimes rather foolish character. He was reported to have spread his cloak over a puddle so that Queen Elizabeth would not get her feet wet, and to have introduced potatoes and tobacco to Britain. None of these stories, however, can definitely be proved.

Rambert, Dame Marie (Cyvia Rambam)
(1888–1982)
Dancer

Born in Poland, Rambert studied medicine in Warsaw and France. After seeing performances by Russian ballerina Anna Pavlova and American modern dancer Isadora Duncan, she studied dance in Switzerland and Germany. She also became a choreographer (dance designer) for leading ballet companies.

In 1917, Rambert moved to London, and became a British subject the next year. She founded a ballet school, then her own company in 1926. She attracted many exciting young dancers and designers to work for her and led her company on numerous successful international tours. In 1966, she announced that the company was to concentrate on modern, experimental dance. Famous for her high spirits and unpredictability, Rambert played an active part in the British world of dance until her late 70s. She received many honours for her inspirational work.

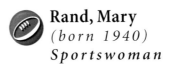

Rand, Mary
(born 1940)
Sportswoman

In the 1964 Olympics she set a world long jump record that remained unbeaten for many years. Rand also won Olympic silver and bronze medals in the pentathalon and 4 x 100 metres relay the same year.

THE ENGLISH IN NORTH AMERICA

The first attempt to establish a permanent British settlement in North America was at Roanoke Island (now in North Carolina), in 1585. It was planned by Sir Walter Raleigh. But the settlers found conditions much harder than they expected, and left after one year. A second group, of over 100 settlers, arrived in 1587. Their leader, John White, returned to England to fetch extra supplies soon afterwards. When he returned, in 1590, he found that all the Roanoke settlers had disappeared. Even today, no one is certain what happened to them.

The first successful British settlement in North America was at Jamestown, in Virginia. Pioneers arrived there in 1607. They, too, faced harsh conditions and nearly starved, but were saved by a shipload of food that arrived in 1608. From 1614, they made a living by growing tobacco and shipping it to Europe to sell.

Rathbone, Eleanor
(1872–1946)
Campaigner

The daughter of a Liverpool MP, Rathbone came from a family that was well known for its work to help poor people. She was one of the first women to study at Oxford University, then returned to Liverpool, to become a pioneer social welfare worker. She was especially eager to improve conditions for working women; she also campaigned for women to have the right to vote, and for equal pay for equal work.

Her campaigns were based on detailed scientific study of wages and conditions among poor families; she published important reports on casual labourers (women without secure jobs) and on the difficulties faced by widows. She urged governments to provide welfare benefits ('family allowances') for women with young children; these were eventually introduced in 1945. During the 1920s and '30s, she campaigned for an end to child marriages in British-ruled India. In World War II, she worked to help Jewish refugees.

Read, Mary
(1690–1720)
See Ann Bonney

 ## Reith, Lord John
(1889–1971)
Broadcaster and politician

Born in Scotland, Reith trained as an engineer. He joined the British army, and was wounded during World War I. In 1922, he was appointed general manager of the BBC (British Broadcasting Company). He was rapidly promoted, and had become director general by 1927.

A strong, stern character with a strict Christian faith, Reith took his work extremely seriously. He believed that broadcasting should be a public service, with a mission 'to inform, educate and entertain'. His ideas set a standard for radio broadcasting that was followed for many years; they also influenced the first BBC television broadcasts (*see* box). Reith remained director general until 1938. He then became an MP. During World War II, he served as a government minister, but quarrelled with Winston Churchill, and resigned. After the war, he was an adviser to several large companies, until he retired.

▲ STEEL AND GLASS
The dramatic Lloyds of London headquarters, opened in 1985.

 ## Rogers, Lord Richard
(born 1933)
Architect

Born in Florence, Italy, and then trained in Britain and the USA, Rogers won great fame with one of his earliest projects – the startlingly new Centre National d'Art et de Culture Georges Pompidou, in Paris. Rogers designed this with Renzo Piano between 1971 and 1977. Built like an industrial structure, of glass and metal, 'the Pompidou Centre' was so revolutionary at the time because it had all of its structural parts, such as stairs and drains, displayed on the outside, instead of being neatly hidden away.

Since then, Rogers has designed many more high-tech buildings. These include the new headquarters for Lloyds of London (an insurance company), the European Court of Human Rights in Strasbourg, and the controversial Millennium Dome, in London, built to mark the year 2000.

Rolls, Charles
(1877–1910)
See Royce, page 90

BROADCASTING IN BRITAIN

1922 British Broadcasting Company (BBC) founded by a group of private wireless (radio) companies
1927 BBC receives royal charter – becomes national radio station, paid for by licence fees from radio- (and later TV-) owners; aims to provide 'public service'
1932 BBC begins overseas broadcasts to British Empire
1936 BBC launches world's first regular TV broadcasts
1939–1945 BBC radio broadcasts play a very important part during World War II, providing public information and issuing morale-boosting propaganda
1946 BBC TV broadcasts start again after the war
1954 First commercial (independent) TV companies licensed; paid for by advertisements
1972 First independent radio stations licensed

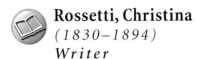

Rossetti, Christina
(1830–1894)
Writer

Daughter of an Italian political refugee and an English governess, Rossetti published her first poems aged 12. After her father became ill, she had to find work to help support her family. She taught Italian, and opened private girls' schools. Shy, nervous and deeply religious, she refused offers of marriage, preferring to live quietly at home. However, her poetry revealed a different side of her nature. It was technically very clever, rich and dramatic, and full of passionate feelings of love and loss. Rossetti also wrote many books on religion. In them, she described not only her strong faith, but also her concerns about social issues, such as poverty and unemployment. She was the sister of Dante Gabriel Rossetti (*see* below).

◀ PRE-RAPHAELITE BEAUTY
Dante Gabriel Rossetti's *La Ghirlandaia* (1873).

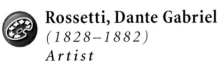

Rossetti, Dante Gabriel
(1828–1882)
Artist

Brother of Christina (*see* above), Rossetti became famous for his paintings in glowing colours and deliberately old-fashioned style. He was a founder-member of the Pre-Raphaelite Brotherhood – a group of artists and writers who admired the creative work produced in the Middle Ages in Europe (that is, from around AD1000 to 1500). They painted pictures and wrote poems on medieval topics, and copied medieval designs in their work and in their clothes, furniture and house decoration. Towards the end of his life, Rossetti concentrated on painting portraits of women in dreamy, brooding style.

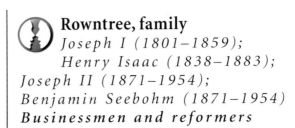

Rowntree, family
Joseph I (1801–1859);
Henry Isaac (1838–1883);
Joseph II (1871–1954);
Benjamin Seebohm (1871–1954)
Businessmen and reformers

For three generations, members of the Rowntree family were leading businessmen and social welfare pioneers. Inspired by his Quaker beliefs, Joseph I built up a grocery business, and used the profits to set up schools for poor children. His son Henry Isaac set up a very profitable chocolate-making factory. Henry's brother Joseph II used some of the money this made to found three Rowntree trusts, which paid for research into social welfare schemes. Joseph's son, Benjamin Seebohm, ran the family company, but also became famous for carrying out surveys into poverty and its causes. He hoped the results would help governments introduce policies to end poverty, or make lives better for poor people.

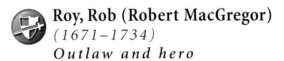

Roy, Rob (Robert MacGregor)
(1671–1734)
Outlaw and hero

'Rob Roy' (a nickname meaning 'Red Robert' in Gaelic) was born in central Scotland. He was a cattle-dealer, a skilled sword-fighter, and a supporter of the Jacobites – people who wanted the Stewart dynasty to rule Britain rather than the Hanoverians, who came from Germany (*see* George I, page 42).

In 1712, Rob Roy quarrelled with some of the men who worked for him. They ran away, taking with them money he owed to the powerful Duke of Montrose. In return, the Duke seized Rob Roy's lands, and had him made an outlaw. For several years, Rob Roy lived by stealing sheep and cattle, and by blackmailing wealthy families. He managed never to be caught. Even though he broke the law, he became a hero to many ordinary Scottish people.

In 1715, he recruited a private army to fight for the Jacobites, and because of this, the Duke of Argyll protected him for a while. Rob Roy was finally arrested in 1727, but was pardoned and set free. He spent the last years of his life peacefully at home. His story was turned into a book by famous novelist Sir Walter Scott (*see* page 92). In the 1990s, this was also made into a popular film.

Royce, Sir (Frederick) Henry
(1863–1933)
Engineer

In 1898, Royce designed and built his first automobile – one of the earliest in Britain. In 1906, he formed a business partnership with Charles Rolls (1877–1910), a fellow motoring enthusiast who had helped set up the RAC (Royal Automobile Club) in 1897. The Rolls-Royce company designed powerful, luxurious cars that became very famous. Rolls and Royce were also pioneers of flight. Rolls became the first Englishman to fly across the English Channel; Royce designed what became the Merlin engine which was used in World War II.

▲ ROLLS ROYCE CARS
From earliest days, these cars were
a symbol of power and luxury.

 ## Russell, Earl Bertrand
(1872–1970)
Writer and philosopher

Grandson of a British Whig (Liberal) prime minister, Russell won fame as a young man for his brilliant mind. He was a mathematician and philosopher, specializing in logic – the study of reason, truth and proof. However, he lost his job as a university lecturer during World War I because he believed all fighting was wrong, and because he supported other men – known as conscientious objectors – with the same views. They were all seen as traitors at that time.

From around 1920 to 1940, Russell earned his living as a writer. His massive *History of Western Philosophy*, which explained the subject to ordinary readers, was widely praised, and he won the Nobel Prize for Literature in 1950. He also supported many controversial 'progressive' causes, from votes for women to nuclear disarmament and educational reform. In 1958, he became first president of the British Campaign for Nuclear Disarmament. In 1961, he was imprisoned, aged 90, for organizing 'ban the bomb' campaigns.

 ## Russell, Dora
(1894–1986)
Campaigner

Daughter of a senior civil servant, Russell received an excellent education, and graduated from university with a first-class degree. She worked as her father's secretary when the British government sent him to New York, then returned to Britain, where she fell in love with Bertrand Russell (*see* below). They travelled to China, wrote books together (on politics and society), and married in 1921. Although many married women at that time spent their lives at home, Russell continued her feminist and socialist campaigns after she was wed. She was one of the first people to demand maternity leave and affordable birth control; she also ran a progressive school, where pupils made the rules and helped plan lessons.

Independent and free-spirited, she separated from Bertrand Russell in 1935. During World War II, Russell worked for the government Ministry of Information. In the 1950s and 1960s, she helped set up campaigning organizations, including the National Council for Civil Liberties, and the Campaign for Nuclear Disarmament. She attended her last anti-nuclear demonstration, in a wheelchair, aged 83, just a few months before her death.

◄ BERTRAND
RUSSELL
Controversial
thinker and writer.

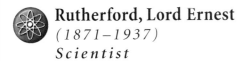

Russell, Lord John
(1792–1878)
Politician

The son of a nobleman – the Duke of Bedford, who took an active part in politics – Russell became a Whig (Liberal) MP in 1813. He was a keen supporter of Parliamentary reform. While serving as a government minister, he drew up the very important Reform Act, which was passed by Parliament in 1832. This was the first in a series of acts of Parliament that gave ordinary people the right to vote for the governments that ruled them.

Russell hoped to make further democratic reforms after he became prime minister from 1846 to 1852 and from 1865 to 1886. However, he made several important blunders in foreign affairs, and resigned

Rutherford, Lord Ernest
(1871–1937)
Scientist

Born in New Zealand, Rutherford moved to Britain to become one of the country's most famous scientists. Together with a team of experts at Cambridge's Cavendish Laboratory, he was the first to 'split the atom', in 1932. For a long time, scientists believed that atoms were the smallest particles of matter. In fact, they are made up of many smaller particles. When an atom is split up into these smaller particles, vast amounts of energy are released.

Rutherford's ground-breaking discovery led to many important inventions – including nuclear power stations and nuclear weapons.

THEORIES OF THE UNIVERSE

Between 1927 and 1930, astronomers Lemaitre (from France) and Eddington (from the UK) formulated the 'Big Bang' theory. They calculated that the universe began about 15 billion years ago with a massive explosion – the 'Big Bang'. It started to expand, and has gone on doing so ever since.

In the 1940s, some scientists challenged this theory, claiming that the universe was in a 'Steady State' instead. It had no beginning and no end, and would stay the same for ever. Today, most astronomers think that the Big Bang theory is true.

There are also different theories for how the universe might end. It might gradually stop expanding, and maybe even collapse. It might collapse, but then start again with a new Big Bang. Or it might go on expanding forever. In 2000, scientists calculated that continual expansion is most likely. However, no one can be sure.

▲ FUNDRAISING
Sue Ryder Shops are a common sight in many high streets.

Ryder, Baroness Sue
(1923–2000)
Welfare pioneer

During Word War II, Ryder worked as a volunteer nurse, and also for the army's Special Operations Executive, which trained men and women for undercover work in occupied Europe. After the War, she did welfare work in former war zones. She was so horrified by the suffering of concentration camp survivors that she set up a home in England where they could be cared for. This soon developed into a much larger organization, with homes and workers in Poland, Yugoslavia and Italy.

In 1959, Ryder married Leonard Cheshire, a disabled war hero. Together they set up 'Cheshire Homes' throughout Britain, where many people with disabilities and long-term illnesses live.

Ryle, Sir Martin
(1918–1984)
Scientist

A pioneer of radio-astronomy, Ryle studied radio waves (invisible rays of energy) given off by stars and other objects in space. In the 1950s, he produced the first-ever maps of objects sending out radio waves. He also discovered that there were many different kinds of objects producing these waves, and that they occupied different regions of space.

Ryle's discoveries were used by cosmologists (astronomers who study the age and composition of the Universe) to support the 'Big Bang' theory of how the Universe began (*see* box).

S

Saunders, Dame Cicely
(born 1918)
Doctor and welfare pioneer

A trained nurse, doctor, and social worker, Saunders is famous today as the pioneer of the hospice movement. (Hospices are places where dying people can spend their last weeks in peaceful, caring surroundings, free from pain and anxiety.) Saunders set up Britain's first hospice, in London, in 1967. Since then her ideas have been copied worldwide, and there are now thousands of hospices helping millions of dying people, and their families and friends.

Savery, Thomas
(c.1650–1715)
Engineer

A rmy engineer Savery invented the first steam-powered pumping engine, to raise water from flooded mines. His invention was taken over, and greatly improved, by his business partner Newcomen (*see* page 76).

Scott, Sir Robert Falcon
(1868–1912)
Explorer

S cott served in the Royal Navy for 20 years, then successfully commanded the British National Antarctic Expedition of 1900–1904, which explored the Antarctic territory known as King Edward VII Land. In 1911, he led a second expedition, this time to the South Pole. He arrived there in 1912, but found that the Norwegian explorer, Roald Amundsen, had reached it before him. Together with all his team, Scott died on the return journey to base camp, after struggling bravely against cold, hunger and exhaustion.

Scott, Sir Walter
(1771–1832)
Writer

S cott spent his childhood in the Scottish countryside. There, he became fascinated by traditional songs and stories, and decided that he would become a writer one day. He worked as a lawyer in Edinburgh, but also wrote in his spare time. The

▶ Ivanhoe

first collection of his poems (called *The Minstrelsy of the Scottish Border*) was published in 1802–1803; others soon followed.

After 1814, Scott began to write novels. These proved very popular; some, such as *Ivanhoe* and *Rob Roy*, are still enjoyed today. Scott became rich, and began to build a splendid stately home for his family, in romantic, mock-medieval style. He also invested money in a new publishing company. However, the company failed, leaving vast debts, and Scott was declared bankrupt. He worked frantically hard, writing more books, to pay back the money he owed but this ruined his health, and led to his death.

▼ Alexander Selkirk.

Selkirk, Alexander
(1676–1721)
Adventurer

S elkirk was born to an ordinary family – his father was a shoemaker – and ran away to sea in his teens. In 1704, he joined the crew of a pirate ship, but quarrelled with the captain. He demanded to be put ashore on an uninhabited island in the Pacific Ocean, called Juan Fernandez. Amazingly, he survived alone there for over four years, until he was rescued by a passing ship in 1709.

Selkirk returned to his home town in Fife, Scotland, in 1712, and told his story to his astonished family and friends. News of his adventures soon reached London, and inspired writer Daniel Defoe (*see* page 30) to write his famous story, *Robinson Crusoe*, which was published in 1719. Selkirk returned to the sea, and was killed in a naval battle in 1721.

Shackleton, Sir Ernest Henry
(1874–1922)
Explorer

A member of Robert Scott's 1900 expedition (*see* page 92), Shackleton led a team towards the South Pole in 1909, getting closer to it than anyone had ever been before. During Shackleton's next expedition, from 1914 to 1916, his ship *Endurance* was trapped and crushed by ice. Shackleton and his crew escaped by rowing 1,300 km (800 miles) across icy seas in an open boat. After a long, dangerous journey, they found shelter on South Georgia, an island off Antarctica.

Shaftesbury, Lord
See Anthony Ashley Cooper

▲ William Shakespeare

Shakespeare, William
(1564–1616)
Writer

The most famous English writer of all time, and, to many people, still the best. Shakespeare was born in the country town of Stratford-upon-Avon, in the English Midlands. His father was a merchant, and Shakespeare could have joined his business. Instead, he left home as a young man, to work as an actor, then a writer, in London. He also became part-owner of two of London's most popular theatres, and staged performances at the royal court.

His plays are admired as classics today, and are performed all over the world. They include love stories such as *Romeo and Juliet*, historical epics such as *Henry V*, and tragedies such as *Hamlet*. As well as plays, Shakespeare also wrote magnificent poetry, mostly about love and death. So many lines from Shakespeare's plays have been 'borrowed' for everyday speech, that he has shaped the way the English language has developed.

Shaw, George Bernard
(1856–1950)
Writer

Famous for his left-wing political views, Shaw wrote many plays about key social issues of his own time, such as women's rights, freedom, and war. He was also one of the first vegetarians to campaign for healthier food and animal welfare. Although Shaw's works had a serious purpose, they were often very witty and entertaining, and are still popular today. One of his best-known plays, *Pygmalion*, was turned into the very successful musical, *My Fair Lady*. It was also made into one of the 20th century's most famous films.

Shelley, Mary
(1797–1851)
Writer

Daughter of two radical writers, William Godwin and Mary Wollstonecraft (*see* page 108). Shelley had an unhappy childhood after her mother died. Aged only 16, she ran away to Europe with the poet Percy Bysshe Shelley (*see* page 94). One summer, they shared a house in Switzerland with other writers and thinkers, including the scandalous Lord Byron (*see* page 19). While there, Mary Shelley wrote one of the most famous horror stories of all time, about a student called Frankenstein and the terrible monster that he created.

SPEAKING SHAKESPEARE

Many words and phrases from Shakespeare's plays have entered our everyday language. Here are just a few favourites:

Hamlet
'To be, or not to be?'
'More in sorrow than in anger'
'Neither a borrower nor a lender be'
'To thine own self be true'
'To the manner born'
'Murder most foul'
'Brevity is the soul of wit'
'The lady doth protest too much'

King Lear
'More sinned against than sinning'
'The prince of darkness'
'The wheel is come full circle'

Macbeth
'Is this a dagger which I see before me?'

'Out, damned spot!'
'A charmed life'

The Merchant of Venice
'With bated breath'
'Love is blind'

The Merry Wives of Windsor
'The world's mine oyster'
'What the dickens...'
'As good luck would have it'

Midsummer Night's Dream
'The course of true love never did run smooth.'

Romeo and Juliet
'What's in a name?'
'A rose by any other name would smell as sweet.'
'Parting is such sweet sorrow'

Shelley, Percy Bysshe
(1792–1822)
Writer

The son of an MP, Shelley quarrelled with his family because of his radical views on politics and religion. He refused to believe in God, and argued that politics should be guided by people's individual feelings, rather than by strict laws or governments. He published all these ideas in his poems, which outraged many readers. Shelley's private life was also criticized. He ran away twice with very young women (his second wife was Mary Shelley; *see* page 93) and he was often in debt. He was drowned, aged only 30, in a boating accident in Italy.

Simpson, Sir James
(1811–1870)
Doctor

Simpson began to study medicine aged 14. After qualifying as a doctor, he specialized in the care of mothers and young babies. At that time, childbirth was risky and often very painful. There were no safe anaesthetics (medicines that send patients to sleep for a while, so that they do not feel pain). Simpson was determined to help women, and experimented on himself

(very dangerously!) with pain-killing chemicals.

In 1847, he pioneered the use of chloroform. Although many religious leaders objected – they believed that suffering was God's will – chloroform became widely used as an anaesthetic for operations of all kinds, as well as in childbirth. Queen Victoria herself invited Simpson to care for her while her son Leopold was born.

Slessor, Mary
(1848-1915)
Missionary

Slessor came from a poor family in northeast Scotland, and began work in a factory, aged 11. Soon afterwards, her father died and her mother became ill. Slessor had to support her three young sisters until they were old enough to find jobs.

As a young woman, Slessor decided to become a missionary. She was sent to the coast of West Africa, but she disagreed with British missionary officials there. She travelled inland, alone, and founded her own mission post in a remote area. She spent the rest of her life there, teaching her Christian faith and helping people in any way she could. She lived, dressed and ate very simply, like the local people, and studied their language and traditions. Because of this, she won their love and respect. They called her 'Ma' or 'Great Mother'.

▲ ADAM SMITH
Brilliant scholar and thinker.

Smith, Adam
(1723–1790)
Philosopher and writer

Smith is famous today for his theories on economics, which have inspired right-wing politicians in many parts of the world. A brilliant scholar, he was a professor at Glasgow University before becoming tutor to the sons of a rich and powerful Scottish nobleman.

Smith spent years travelling with his pupils in Europe, meeting many famous writers and thinkers. In 1766, he returned to Scotland, and spent the next ten years writing his most important book, *An Inquiry into the Nature and Causes of the Wealth of Nations*. In it, he discussed what made people, and countries, rich, and how wealth could be created.

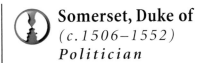

Somerset, Duke of
(c.1506–1552)
Politician

Edward Seymour, Earl of Hertford, was an ambitious, noble politician at the court of King Henry VIII. His sister, Jane Seymour, married the king (she was his third wife), and gave birth to his only son, and heir. This made Seymour the uncle of the future king, and a close friend of the royal family. He also won favour by winning battles against the Scots. In 1547, when King Henry died, Seymour plotted to get himself declared Lord Protector of England. (The new king, Edward VI, was still a very young child.) He was also made Duke of Somerset.

As Lord Protector, Somerset's policies were straightforward, brutal and self-seeking. He continued the war with Scotland, although it was expensive. Because he had Protestant beliefs, he encouraged attacks on the Catholic Church. He supported landowners who enclosed common land, even though this harmed poor people, and allowed his own brother to be executed because it was politically useful. He was forced to resign following a rebellion in the West Country, put in prison, then freed. However, he was mistrusted by other leading politicians, and executed.

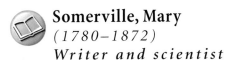

Somerville, Mary
(1780–1872)
Writer and scientist

Somerville's family believed that education was unnecessary for girls. However, she borrowed some maths books and studied secretly, on her own. When she married, her studies had to stop, because her husband also disapproved of clever women. When he died, in 1807, Somerville was free to study again. Her work was so good, that she won a national prize.

In 1812, Somerville married for a second time; her new husband supported and encouraged her. She translated and explained the discoveries of a top French astronomer, and, in 1826, gave a very important lecture to the Royal Society – a group of leading scientists and mathematicians. They were so impressed

that they made her an honorary member and arranged for the British government to pay her a pension (reward) for the rest of her life. Somerville published many books on maths and astronomy. She also supported campaigns for women's right to vote. One of the first-ever colleges for women students, at Oxford University, was named after her (*see also* box).

WOMEN'S EDUCATION

Until the 19th century, many people believed that it was wrong to provide equal educational opportunities for boys and girls. Before around 1500, only nuns and noblewomen were taught to read and write. After 1500, girls from middle-income families were often taught to read, write and keep accounts, but they were hardly ever allowed to go to day-school like their brothers, and were banned from attending boarding schools or universities where boys studied interesting, challenging subjects such as science, law, philosophy, languages and medicine.

This lack of education meant that girls could not train for well-paid, respected, professional careers. In the 18th century, a few girls-only boarding schools were opened, but they taught mostly 'feminine' subjects (such as dancing and needlework), and their standards were usually low. During the 19th century, women campaigned for the right to be educated on equal terms with men. Pioneers such as Miss Beale (*see* page 12) opened schools where girls could study the same subjects as boys, to a high level. The first university college for women was opened in London (Queen's College) around 1848.

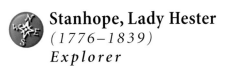

Stanhope, Lady Hester
(1776–1839)
Explorer

Born to a wealthy noble family, Stanhope was intelligent, capable and eccentric. As a young woman, she lived with her uncle, the Prime Minister, and acted as his official companion, meeting many famous people and taking an active part in politics. After he died, in 1806, she became bored with life in Britain, and decided to seek adventure abroad. She never returned home.

Dressed in Arab men's clothes, Stanhope travelled through Greece to Turkey, Syria and Egypt, and became the first European woman to visit many remote areas, and to explore many ancient monuments. She also became passionately involved in desert wars and feuds. The letters she wrote about her adventures still provide useful evidence for historians today.

Stanley, Sir Henry Morton (born John Rowlands)
(1841–1904)
Explorer and journalist

While working as a newspaper reporter, Stanley was sent to Africa in 1869 to investigate the supposed 'disappearance' of Scottish explorer David Livingstone (*see* page 64). After two years, Stanley found Livingstone, and greeted him with the now-famous question, 'Dr Livingstone, I presume?' Stanley went on, in 1874, to undertake his own expedition, to trace the course of the Congo River. He then founded the Congo Free State. Back in England, he served as an MP between 1895 and 1900.

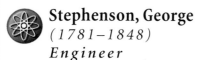

Stephenson, George
(1781–1848)
Engineer

Stephenson began his working life in coal mines. He was one of the first people to realize how steam power and railways could help the coal industry develop. He built his first steam locomotive, to haul coal trucks, in 1814. Soon afterwards, he became engineer to the pioneering Stockton and Darlington Railway Company, and drove the world's first steam-powered train along its tracks in 1825. He worked closely with his son Robert (1803–1859) to build more new steam locomotives, including the famous *Rocket* in 1829. It became the standard design, on which all later steam locomotives were based (*see* p97 box). Stephenson also designed many bridges in Britain, Canada and Egypt, including the well-known Conwy Bridge in Wales.

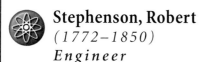

Stephenson, Robert
(1772–1850)
Engineer

Born in Glasgow, Stephenson trained as an engineer and worked for Northern Lighthouse Board – the organization responsible for building lighthouses to warn ships away from dangerous rocky coasts. He designed over 20 lighthouses, and supervized their construction in some to the wildest, loneliest, most dangerous countryside in Britain.

Stephenson invented a system of flashing lights to make it easier for sailors to identify each lighthouse and work out their position at sea, and planned many new lighting systems. Keeping lighthouse lanterns burning all night was difficult, but vitally important; at that time, there were no electricity supplies. Stephenson also used his engineering skills to design roads, canals and bridges, and took a keen interest in the newly invented railways. His sons, Alan, David and Thomas, continued his work after his death.

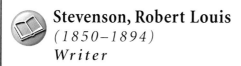

Stevenson, Robert Louis
(1850–1894)
Writer

Grandson of famous engineer Robert Stevenson (*see* above), Robert Louis studied engineering and law, but wanted to be a writer. After leaving university, he travelled in Europe, and wrote two books about his experiences. He also met an American woman traveller, whom he followed to California, where he married her.

From then on, he made his living as a writer. Some of his stories, such as *Treasure Island* and *Kidnapped*, told of exciting adventures. Others, like *The Strange Case of Dr Jekyll and Mr Hyde*, were sinister and mysterious. For most of his life, Stevenson was unwell. In 1888, with his wife, he travelled to Samoa, a tropical island in the Pacific Ocean, hoping its climate would cure him but he died there, six years later, aged only 44.

Stewart, Charles Edward ('Bonnie Prince Charlie')
(1720–1788)
'Claimant' to British crown

Charles was the eldest grandson of James VII and II of Scotland and England. In 1688, James had been forced by Parliament to give up the throne, because of his religious beliefs. (It was illegal for the king or queen of Britain to be a Roman Catholic). Charles was also a Catholic, so, in law, he had no right to rule. However, he still claimed to be the rightful king of Britain, and many people who did not like the Hanoverian dynasty (*see* George I, page 42) supported him.

In 1744, King Louis XV of France encouraged Charles to invade Britain. He hoped this would make it difficult for British troops to defend their country against French attack. Charles landed in Scotland in 1745, and led an army into England. They reached Derby, in the English Midlands, but were forced to retreat. Charles's supporters (known as 'Jacobites', from the Latin version of 'James') were massacred at the battle of Culloden, in Scotland, in 1746. Charles spent five months on the run in the Scottish highlands before Flora MacDonald (*see* page 67) helped him escape. Back in France, Charles planned another invasion, but it never happened.

▲ BONNIE PRINCE CHARLIE
Leader of the failed Jacobite invasion of England in 1745.

HISTORY OF BRITISH RAILWAYS

*c.*1700 Horse-drawn wagons on wooden rails used to carry coal in mines

1700s Development of steam engines and inventors begin to design traction (pulling) engines

*c.*1800 Iron rails replace wooden ones; are also built above ground

1825 First public railway opens (from Stockton to Darlington)

1830 Robert Stephenson's steam locomotive *Rocket* runs on newly opened Liverpool-Manchester line. Many similar locomotives built soon after

1850s Now over 11,000 km (7,000 miles) of railway in Britain

1860s–1870s 'Railway Boom'; many new lines and stations built

*c.*1870–1920 Railways most popular form of transport for people and goods

1930s–1940s Many more cars and lorries; less investment in railways; rail network becomes rundown

1947 Government nationalizes (takes over running of) railways

1963 Government enquiry (the Beeching Reports) recommends many railway closures

1996 Railways privatized (sold to business companies)

2000 Railway crisis: dangerous faults found on rails, services disrupted, accusations of bad management.

Stewart, James Edward
(1688–1766)
'Claimant' to British crown

Father of Charles Edward Stewart (*see* page 96), and eldest son of King James VII and II, James Edward was forced to flee to France when his father gave up the throne. As a Roman Catholic, he could not become king in his father's place. Instead, his Protestant sister, Princess Mary became queen, and ruled jointly with her husband, William of Orange, a Protestant prince from the Netherlands.

As a young man, James Edward fought in the French army. Then, in 1715, he led an invasion of Britain, to claim his right to rule. He hoped to join forces with a rebellion against King George I (*see* page 42), led by a Scottish nobleman, the Earl of Mar. However, he was soon defeated, and escaped, first to France and then to Spain. In 1719, he organized a second invasion, but his fleet was wrecked by storms at sea.

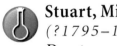

Stuart, Miranda ('James Barry')
(?1795–1865)
Doctor and soldier

Born in Edinburgh, and orphaned by the time she was 15, Stuart hoped for a career in medicine. However, women were not allowed to become doctors, by law. So Stuart disguised herself as a man, studied at medical college, and qualified in 1812. She was the first woman in Britain to do this – even though, at the time, no one knew what she had achieved.

Barry then joined the army, and served as a doctor in Canada, South Africa, southern Russia and the Caribbean. She was a good, but very strict, organizer, and was given many important and responsible posts, ending her career as inspector general of all British hospitals in Canada. She also studied traditional herbal remedies, and became an expert on South African medical plants. Stuart spent the whole of her life as a man. However, one of her army comrades suspected that she might be a woman, and, after her death, rumours started to spread. Her body was dug up and examined. When she was found to be female, the army cancelled the grand military funeral it had planned for 'James Barry'.

▲ *GULLIVER'S TRAVELS*
A book illustration showing Gulliver in the land of Lilliput.

Swift, Jonathan
(1667–1745)
Writer

Remembered today for his novel *Gulliver's Travels*, Swift was a Protestant priest who spent most of his life in Dublin, Ireland. He wrote many books and pamphlets on politics and society. Some, like *Gulliver's Travels*, comment on people's behaviour through fantasy and humour; others are more savage and critical.

Tallis, Thomas
(c.1505–1585)
Musician

Tallis devoted his entire career to composing music to be sung in churches, by choirs of young boys and men. A skilful organist, he was employed for many years at the Chapel Royal, in London, where the royal family and courtiers went to pray. His music wove several different parts (tunes) together within one piece to create a rich, mysterious and holy sound. Tallis's work influenced other British composers for hundreds of years, and is still performed today. He was so well respected, that a famous song, composed by a fellow-musician after his death, had the chorus: 'Tallis is dead, and music dies.'

Telford, Thomas
(1757–1834)
Architect

Trained as a stone-mason in Scotland, Telford also studied architecture. In 1788, he was appointed surveyor of public works in Shropshire (on the border between England and Wales). There, he supervized the construction of canals and aqueducts – including some of the most important, and difficult, building projects of his time.

In 1802, he returned to Scotland to begin a massive survey of roads and communications. He planned and designed the Caledonian Canal, which cuts right across the country, plus 1,400 km (900 miles) of road, over 1,200 bridges, large public buildings and new harbours. He also designed roads and bridges in England, Sweden and Wales. A new town in Shropshire was named after him in the late 20th century.

▼ Menai Straits Bridge

Tennyson, Lord Alfred
(1809–1892)
Writer

Appointed poet laureate in 1850, Tennyson was one of the most famous writers of the Victorian age, and a great favourite with Queen Victoria herself. After leaving university and travelling in Europe, he composed many poems in fashionable mock-medieval style. Many featured ancient legends, such as the story of British hero King Arthur. However, he also took an interest in new, scientific ideas. His best poem, called *In Memoriam*, was written after one of his friends died young. It deals with difficult subjects such as bereavement, change and memory, and links them to ideas about evolution – one of the most controversial scientific discoveries of Tennyson's day.

Terry, Dame Ellen
(1848–1928)
Actress

From a well-known theatrical family, Terry became famous for her own acting skills, and for her beautiful speaking voice. She played most of Shakespeare's great heroines, such as Juliet and Cleopatra, and also performed in many new plays; some contained roles written especially for her. In 1878, she began a stage partnership with another famous actor, Henry Irving. Together, they achieved many successes.

Thackeray, William Makepeace
(1811–1863)
Writer

Famous for witty novels that describe and criticize fashionable society, Thackeray started his career as a journalist. He began writing stories when he was faced with a financial crisis, after the savings bank where his family inheritance was kept collapsed. He also wrote satirical columns for magazines and newspapers, and gave public lectures. Thackeray's best-known novel, *Vanity Fair*, shocked many people when it first appeared, because its beautiful, fascinating heroine was also deceitful and unscrupulous. Like many of Thackeray's works, *Vanity Fair* has been made into films and TV plays.

Thatcher, Baroness Margaret
(born 1925)
Politician

The daughter of a grocer in a country town, Margaret Thatcher was intelligent and hard-working. She won a place at Oxford University, where she studied science, but decided to make a career in law. At the same time, she became passionately involved in politics. She was first elected to Parliament in 1959, as a member of the Conservative (right-wing) Party. Displaying ambition and ability, she was appointed a junior government minister within two years. She was soon given more senior posts, and became prime minister in 1979 – the first-ever British woman to lead a government.

Thatcher stayed in power until 1990. Her policies were admired by some and hated by others. She reorganized Britain's welfare system, privatized state-owned industries, and attacked trade unions. She also led Britain into a controversial war with Argentina. She was not very sympathetic to feminist ideas, preferring to use old-fashioned charm combined with iron-willed determination to get her own way.

▲ Dylan Thomas

Thomas, Dylan
(1914–1953)
Writer

Born in Wales, Thomas moved to London as a young man, to work as a broadcaster and journalist. He also wrote and recited poetry. He was an intense, dramatic performer, and was highly praised. His most famous work, *Under Milk Wood*, is a picture in words of a small Welsh town. As in all Dylan's work, the writing is simple, vivid, playful and very powerful.

MEASURING TEMPERATURE

Temperature is measured using instruments known as thermometers, and by other special devices, for example thermocouples and optical pyrometers. The first thermometers (invented by German scientist Fahrenheit; 1686–1736) were narrow glass tubes filled with mercury. As the surrounding temperature changed, the mercury rose or fell, and its level could be measured against a temperature scale.

In the 19th century, scientists discovered that an electric current will flow between a thermocouple: small pieces of different metals kept at different temperatures. When the temperature of one metal piece is known, the current flowing between them can be measured and used to work out the temperature of the other one. Optical pyrometers measure heat radiated (given off) by objects, without touching them. They change in appearance in a predictable way according to the temperature they detect.

Thomson, Sir William (Lord Kelvin)
(1824–1907)
Scientist

Born in Belfast to a famous family of scientists, Thomson began studying mathematics and physics at Glasgow University when he was only 11 years old. He became professor there aged 22. At 24, he developed one of his brightest ideas – a new scale for measuring temperature. It is still used today, and is named after him (*see also* box). The same year, with a colleague, he discovered one of the fundamental laws of physics – the second law of thermodynamics. It explains how and why heat always flows from something warm to something colder.

Thomson also made important discoveries in electricity, magnetism, refrigeration, navigation and communications. He was a keen inventor, and patented over 50 new designs. Several were useful to the new, fast-growing telegraph and telephone industries. He also supervised the first underwater electric cable to be laid across the Atlantic Ocean.

Tippet, Sir Michael
(1905–1997)
Musician

A passionate, mystical character, Tippett created unique music that blended European classics with early English songs and American jazz and blues. Tippett was also well known for his political views. A keen pacifist, he believed that all war was wrong. One of his best known works, *A Child of our Time*, was inspired by his concern for the suffering of ordinary families in war.

▲ John Tradescant the Elder and his wife Elizabeth, 1656.

 ## Tradescant, John (father and son)
(1570–1638 and 1608–1662)
Gardeners and botanists

John Tradescant was a famous gardener and plant-collector, who worked for King Charles I of England. He travelled through Russia and North Africa, looking for new flowers and ornamental plants to grow in English gardens. He also made a large collection of plants to study – at that time, little was known scientifically about the way plants grew or found food. In London, he founded a 'physic garden', where medicinal plants and herbs were grown.

His son, also called John, continued his father's work at the royal gardens. He also travelled to North America, in search of new plants and all kinds of historical and natural curiosities. He presented these to Oxford University, and they became the basis of the new Ashmolean Museum there.

STEAM POWER

All steam engines make use of a basic scientific law. When water is heated, it turns into a gas (called steam) and occupies a much larger volume than it does in liquid form. As a result, it puts pressure on anything that contains it.

The very first steam engines heated water in boilers, and used the pressure built up by the steam to push a piston, which in turn was connected to levers. This provided enough power to drive machines.

 ## Trevithick, Richard
(1771–1833)
Engineer

One of the pioneers of railway transport, Trevithick worked as a mining engineer. He invented a steam-powered engine and used it in locomotives to transport miners and coal along roads. In 1802, he built a high-pressure steam engine (*see* box). It was dangerous but powerful. In 1803, he was the first person to design an engine that could run on rails. Later, he designed steam-engines for farms.

 ## Trollope, Anthony
(1815–1882)
Writer

Remembered today for his shrewd, sly novels about middle-class life in cathedral towns, Trollope also had a successful career as a civil servant. He worked for the Post Office, and arranged for the first pillar-boxes to be built in British streets. He wrote most of his 47 novels after he had retired. The most famous include those in the 'Barsetshire chronicles' series, which were successfully dramatized for British television.

 ## Tull, Jethro
(1647–1741)
Inventor

An Oxfordshire landowner, Tull invented some of the world's first farm machines. Before his inventions, almost all work on British farms, except ploughing, was done using human muscle-power and hand-tools. Around 1701, Tull invented a seed drill (machine for planting seeds). Soon after, he travelled to Europe to study farming there. This led him to develop a horse-drawn hoe (machine for uprooting weeds), and schemes for manuring the soil to fertilize it, and to rotate (regularly change) crops, to stop the build-up of pests and plant diseases.

▼ Seed drill

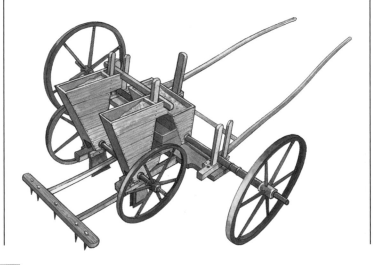

Turing, Alan
(1912–1954)
Inventor

One of the inventors of modern computers, Turing designed a pioneering computing machine in 1937. During World War II (1939–1945), he belonged to a secret British Government team of code-breakers, who worked to 'crack' (spy on and translate) messages sent by German commanders to troops attacking Europe. After the war, he worked on computers and on artificial intelligence (machines that could 'think' for themselves).

Turner, J.M.W. (Joseph Mallord William)
(1775–1851)
Artist

Turner showed artistic talent even as a young child. He began to study at art college aged 14, then spent many years travelling and sketching in Britain and Europe. His early works were pictures of landscapes, in water-colours and oil paint. Towards the end of his life, Turner lost interest in accurately recording the views he saw, and became much more concerned with portraying dramatic effects of light and shade. In many of his works, such as the famous *Rain, Steam and Speed*, sunlight and clouds make beautiful abstract patterns, and it is hard to see any precise details at all. His work was so original, and so different from anything else, that some people have called him 'the greatest British-born artist'.

▲ THE GRAND CANAL, VENICE
Turner was one of the great masters of landscape art.

THE PEASANTS' REVOLT

In 1381, large numbers of craftsmen and farm labourers from southeast England marched on London, demanding to see the king. They were protesting against new Poll Taxes, which the government had introduced in 1377. They also had other, older grievances. In particular, they were angered by a law called the Statute of Labourers, passed in 1351. It banned employers from paying high wages, even though there was a great shortage of workers following a deadly epidemic of plague – the Black Death – that had killed millions of people in Britain since it began in 1349.

The protesters in London also wanted all men and women to be free (at that time, many were still serfs, who belonged to their lords, like cattle), and for ordinary working people to be allowed to rent good farm land. The king, Richard II, rode out to meet them, and promised to grant their demands. As soon as they had gone away, however, he went back on his promise and ordered that the rebels should be punished. The rebel leader, Wat Tyler (*see* below), was killed by the lord mayor of London as he tried to talk to the king.

Tyler, Wat
(?–1381)
Rebel

Leader of the Peasants Revolt in 1381, Tyler organized farmers and craftsmen to march in protest against taxes and government corruption. At the head of an angry mob, he came face to face with King Richard II in London, and tried to force the king to give in to the rioters' demands. However, Tyler was stabbed to death by one of the king's supporters, and the protest collapsed.

Tyndale, William
(c.1494–1536)
Religious scholar

Scholar Tyndale planned the first complete translation of the Bible from Latin into English. But church leaders condemned him, and forced him to flee. He settled in Germany, close to Martin Luther, leader of the Protestant Reformation, and began printing copies of the first part of his Bible translation in 1525. After ten years, he was arrested and executed. His unfinished work was completed by other Protestant scholars, and formed the basis of many later translations of the Bible.

V

Vanbrugh, Sir John
(1664–1726)
Writer and designer

A man of many talents, Vanbrugh studied architecture, became an army officer, and then began to write for the theatre. His plays were witty satires about fashionable society, and were a great success. At the same time, Vanbrugh designed huge and very grand stately homes for important people – the most famous were Blenheim Palace (1705) and Castle Howard (1700). They are still admired by visitors today. Vanbrugh also designed (for himself) the first opera house ever built in Britain – the Queen's Theatre, which opened in 1705.

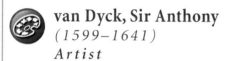

van Dyck, Sir Anthony
(1599–1641)
Artist

Born in Belgium, van Dyck moved to England to become court painter to King Charles I. There, he created magnificent portraits of the royal family and their friends. Van Dyck's paintings display the elegance and refinement of King Charles's court – and also the king's sad, rather solitary, character and his isolation from the everyday world outside the royal palace. After van Dyck died (aged only 42), his style was copied by other English painters, but their work lacked van Dyck's intelligence and psychological insight.

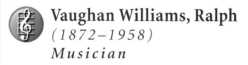

Vaughan Williams, Ralph
(1872–1958)
Musician

One of the most important British composers of the 20th century, Vaughan Williams began to write music when he was only six years old. He studied with leading European composers, but decided that his own music should be based on traditional British tunes, or inspired by British landscape, folklore and poetry. He wrote many beautiful works for singers and for orchestras, in a haunting, romantic style, and was a respected teacher and choir-master. Vaughan Williams also worked hard to preserve ancient British folk songs and instrumental works, which he feared would vanish as new 20th-century music, played on radios and gramophones, became more popular.

Victoria
(1819–1901;
reigned
1837–1901)
Queen

The longest-reigning British ruler, and one of the most successful, Victoria became queen when she was only 18 years old. Her youth and innocence won many admirers, as did her public declaration of her wish 'to do what is right'. People hoped that her reign would mark a new, and a fresh start for many British enterprises. Victoria was intelligent, practical, very determined, and had a strong sense of duty. She took an active interest in politics, although she did not support any one party.

In 1840, she married her cousin Albert, a German prince. Extremely happy together, they had nine children. Albert was also her chief adviser, as well as developing his many interests, from art to new technology. Victoria was devastated when he died, still young, in 1861, and withdrew from public life for some years. Persuaded to take up her duties again by Prime Minister Disraeli (*see* page 32), she became a popular symbol of Britain's fast-growing power and prosperity, at home and abroad (*see* box). In 1876, the British government declared her 'Empress of India' and her children married into the most important royal and noble families in Europe. The 50th and 60th anniversaries of her accession (coming to the throne) were marked by splendid celebrations, and her death was widely mourned.

THE BRITISH EMPIRE

From the 17th to the mid-20th centuries, Britain ruled other countries in many parts of the world. At its peak, around 1900, the British Empire was the largest empire ever, called 'the empire on which the sun never set.' All this began with 16th-century voyages of exploration and grew alongside British international trade. Britain first seized lands in America and the Caribbean; lands in India, Africa, Australia and the Pacific followed.

Membership of the empire had both good and bad influences on the countries involved. Many felt exploited, but also relied on Britain for help and protection at times. In the 1900s, some members, like Canada and Australia, were allowed to govern themselves; others, like India (independent in 1947), fought long campaigns for freedom. Most African colonies won independence in the 1960s. Since then, many former colonies have joined the Commonwealth of Nations – a free association of states headed by the British queen.

Wallace, Sir William
(c.1274–1305)
Soldier

A famous soldier, Wallace led the Scots to fight against King Edward I of England, who invaded their homeland. He was appointed guardian of Scotland after his troops defeated the English at the Battle of Stirling Bridge in 1297. The next year, he lost a battle against the English at Falkirk, in central Scotland, and was forced to flee. He escaped to France, where he recruited more soldiers. Wallace returned to Scotland in 1303, even though the English had declared him an outlaw, and offered a prize for his capture. He was betrayed to the English, and put in prison. Soon after, he was taken to London, tried for treason, and cruelly executed.

Wallace's life was short, and not very successful, but the Scots people remembered his brave fight for independence for many of hundreds of years, and still think of him as a national hero today. In the 1990s, a very successful film, *Braveheart,* was made about his life.

▶ WILLIAM WALLACE
Wallace fought bravely to defend Scotland from the English.

Wallis, Sir Barnes
(1887–1979)
Engineer

Pioneer engineer and inventor Wallis created over 140 new designs, mostly for aircraft and weapons. Working for the famous Vickers company (a major 20th-century aircraft-maker) Wallis designed the R100 airship (a breakthrough in the 1930s) and the Wellington bomber plane (a vital aircraft used by the British forces throughout World War II).

He also designed revolutionary 'bouncing' bombs, to smash though massive concrete dams controlling German waterways. After the war ended, Wallis helped design many new aircraft, including missiles, supersonic jets, and swing-wing planes.

▲ Sir Barnes Wallis

Walpole, Sir Robert
(1676–1745)
Politician

Walpole came from a family of country landowners. A supporter of the Whig party, he held many senior government positions, at a time when Parliament and ministers were rapidly becoming more important in deciding policy than kings or queens. He was leader of the Cabinet (group of top government ministers) for many years during the reigns of George I and George II. For this reason, he is often called 'Britain's first prime minister' ('prime' = 'first'). His policies aimed to increase British prosperity and maintain peace.

Watson Watt, Sir Robert
(1892–1973)
Scientist

Watson Watt began his career as a meteorologist (a scientist who studies the weather). After investigating radio waves given off by thunderstorms, he realized that radio signals could be used to identify the position of an aircraft in the sky, even when it could not be seen – for example, at night – and built a machine to prove this. He called his invention RADAR (RAdio Detection And Ranging) and completed the first proper RADAR machine in 1935; this could detect moving objects 160 km (100 miles away).

When World War II broke out, four years later, RADAR proved extremely useful to Britain, giving warning of approaching enemy planes. Later, RADAR was developed for use on board aircraft, and on ships at sea.

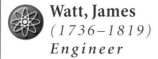

Watt, James
(1736–1819)
Engineer

Remembered today as one of the founders of the Industrial Revolution, Watt began his career as a scientific instrument-maker. In 1763, he saw a model of Newcomen's steam engine (*see* page 76), and realized that it could be improved. Around the same time, he also began experiments with steam and heat. He designed a new steam engine, but had no money to produce it, so worked for a while as an engineer, helping to design Scottish canals.

In 1774, he began a business partnership with wealthy factory-owner Matthew Boulton (*see* page 16). Together, they produced new steam-powered engines. Watt also designed new gears, new cylinders and many other devices, all of which made steam-engines more efficient and more useful. Boulton and Watt's engines were used to power machines in many factories in Britain. Watt also invented the term 'horsepower', to describe the power of a machine. Today, the Watt (another unit of power) is named after him.

▲ WATT'S ENGINE
Steam power
revolutionised industry

Webb, Beatrice and Webb, Sidney
(1858–1943 and 1859–1947)
Reformers

Husband and wife team Beatrice (*above*) and Sidney Webb were pioneer social scientists and political reformers. They devoted their lives to studying society and how it works, hoping to use this information to improve living and working conditions for ordinary people, and to encourage new, socialist ways of governing Britain. They were leading members of the Fabian Society, a socialist campaigning group; Sidney also became a Labour Party MP. Unlike many other socialist reformers, they wanted change by slow, peaceful means, not by sudden, violent revolution. Their ideas and the results of their researches helped to shape the Welfare State (*see* page 14) and the Labour Party.

Wedgwood, Josiah
(1730–1795)
Designer and manufacturer

Factory-owner Wedgwood started a new pottery-making business in Staffordshire in 1759. Working with top artists, staff in his factories produced useful and ornamental types of pottery, in striking new designs. Many were based on ancient Greek and Roman styles. Unlike many early factory-owners, Wedgwood aimed to produce very high quality goods, even though he was using mass-production techniques. Today, examples of early Wedgwood pottery – typically pale-blue, with raised white designs – are highly prized by collectors.

◄ WEDGWOOD-WARE
Pottery in blue jasper with
a raised white pattern – a
style pioneered by
Wedgwood.

THE NAPOLEONIC WARS

From 1796 until 1814, French army commander Napoleon (who declared himself emperor of France in 1804) started a series of wars against other countries in Europe. He aimed to conquer more land and establish a French Empire.

Napoleon invaded Austria, North Africa, Spain, Prussia (north Germany) and Russia. At first, he was successful, but in 1812, the bitter Russian winter forced his troops to retreat.

Britain played an important part in the Napoleonic Wars. In 1798, Admiral Nelson defeated a French fleet off the coast of Egypt in the Battle of the Nile; later, in 1805, he destroyed the French navy at the sea-battle of Trafalgar, off Spain.

On land, Britain's fight against Napoleon was led by the Duke of Wellington (*see* entry below).

From 1808, Wellington's troops fought against the French in Spain; in 1815, they won a final, famous victory against Napoleon at the battle of Waterloo, in Belgium.

 ## Wellington, Duke of
(1769–1852)
Soldier

A brilliant army commander, famous for his strict discipline (he was known as 'the Iron Duke'), his ruthless intelligence, and his dry wit. (He was reported to have said, on seeing a rough-looking bunch of British soldiers – 'I don't know whether they'll scare the enemy, but, by God! they frighten me'.)

Wellington led British troops to fight against Napoleon's France (*see* box above). His most famous victory was the Battle of Waterloo (1815), which ended French hopes to take control of Europe. After he retired from active fighting, Wellington became a Tory (Conservative) politician, serving as prime minister from 1828 to 1830, and in 1834. He did not support many of the campaigns for social and political reform at that time, but did give Roman Catholics in England full civil and political rights for the first time in hundreds of years.

 ## Wells, H. G. (Herbert George)
(1866–1946)
Writer

Trained as a scientist, Wells (*below*) became a pioneer writer of science fiction, blending his expert knowledge with exciting stories in works such as *War of the Worlds* (1898). He hoped that these would make people think – about the society they lived in, about politics, and about the benefits and dangers that science might bring. Wells was a keen member of the moderate socialist Fabian Society (*see* Webb, Beatrice, page 104), and his political hopes and fears are reflected in his work.

 ## Wesley, John
(1703–1791)
Church leader

A scholar at Oxford University, Wesley became leader of a small group with keen religious ideas. They became known as 'methodists' – a name that is still preserved today, in the church Wesley founded.

After a profound religious experience in 1738, Wesley decided to devote the rest of his life to preaching the Christian faith. However, many members of the established Church of England disliked his views, and were suspicious of his hopes of contacting people on the margins of society. So Wesley began to travel round the countryside, preaching in the open air to anyone who would listen. He was helped and supported by his brother Charles, and their friends. The Wesleys attracted many followers. He hoped they would remain within the Church of England, but this proved impossible so he founded the Society of Methodists in 1784.

Wheatstone, Sir Charles
(1802–1875)
Scientist

A professor at London University, Wheatstone is remembered today for his investigations into sound. He invented many devices that use or amplify (increase) sound-waves, including the concertina, microphone, stethoscope and electric telegraph.

Whittington, Richard (Dick)
(c.1358–1423)
Businessman

Whittington was a wealthy London businessman. He loaned money to three English kings – Richard II, Henry IV and Henry V – and was three times lord mayor of London. A traditional story tells how Whittington started life as a poor boy and travelled to London, accompanied only by his cat, hoping to make his fortune. At first, he did not succeed, and

decided to go back home. However, as he began his journey, he heard church bells ringing. They seemed to be telling him to turn back towards London. He did so, worked hard, and became rich and respected. There is no evidence to prove that this story is true, but it has been used for hundreds of years to encourage people with ambition not to give up hope, and to persevere.

Whittle, Sir Frank
(1907–1996)
Engineer

Inventor of the jet engine, Whittle revolutionized transport in the 20th century. He spent his whole career in aviation, joining the Royal Air Force as a teenage apprentice, then working as a pilot and test-pilot. His first jet-engined plane flew experimentally in 1941, and began regular flights in 1944. Almost all aircraft since then have relied on jet power.

▼ JET ENGINE
The jet engine gave birth to modern aircraft.

Wilberforce, William
(1759–1833)
Reformer

Son of a wealthy merchant, Wilberforce served as a Liberal MP. In 1785, he experienced a religious conversion to Christianity, and became deeply committed to social reform. He became convinced that slavery was wicked, and started to campaign against it.

In 1807, he persuaded Parliament to ban the slave trade in Britain. After this great success, he continued to work for slavery to be abolished throughout the world. He also supported many schemes to help poor people, and to improve religious education.

THE SLAVE TRADE

From the 16th to the 19th centuries, European traders purchased slaves in West Africa, and transported them across the Atlantic Ocean to work in new settlements in North and South America and in the Caribbean. Historians estimate that around 13 million men, women and children were traded as slaves between 1550 and 1850, although it is impossible to discover the precise figures since detailed written records were not kept.

After crossing the Atlantic, slaves were sold to farmers and landowners, and forced to work – often in terrible conditions – on sugar plantations in Brazil and the Caribbean, and on tobacco farms and cotton plantations in the southern states of North America. They were not free to leave their work, and were cruelly punished if they tried to run away. Slave-trading was banned throughout the British empire in 1807 (see Wilberforce), but was continued by other nations for many years.

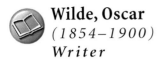

Wilde, Oscar
(1854–1900)
Writer

Born in Ireland to a cultured, well-educated family, Wilde grew up to be a flamboyant and extravagant young man, keenly interested in art and literature. Living and working in London, where he became a fashionable, although shocking, public figure, he published poems, children's stories, and a spine-chilling novel.

Wilde was most famous for his plays, especially *The Importance of Being Earnest*, and for his brilliant, witty conversation. Although married, with sons, he was also attracted to young men. In 1895, he was put on trial for homosexual behaviour. At that time, this was against the law, and he was sent to prison. On his release, many of Wilde's former friends no longer wanted to know him. Unwell, poor, and unhappy, Wilde sought refuge in France, where he died.

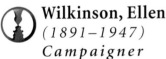

Wilkinson, Ellen
(1891–1947)
Campaigner

▲ ELLEN WILKINSON
Making a passionate speech at a protest rally.

Daughter of a cotton-factory worker, Wilkinson's family were active socialists and trade unionists. She won a scholarship to university, campaigned for votes for women, and became a public speaker for the Independent Labour Party. In 1915, during the war, she was appointed organizer for the Amalgamated Union of Co-operative Employees. She campaigned particularly hard on behalf of low-paid workers, especially women.

Wilkinson briefly joined the Communist Party, then became a socialist Member of Parliament – the first woman Labour Party MP. She was nicknamed 'Red Ellen' for the colour of her hair – and because red is the colour of revolution. All her life, she campaigned for justice, fairness and social change. She held several ministerial posts, including Pensions and Education. Along with her parliamentary duties, Wilkinson continued to support trade unions, the Co-operative Movement, and the unemployed. During the General Strike of 1926, she travelled to the USA to raise money for strikers' families. In 1935, she led the famous 'hunger march' of unemployed workers from her constituency town of Jarrow, in the northeast all the way to the capital city of London.

William I ('the Conqueror')
(1027–1087)
King

The son of Robert, Duke of Normandy, William was descended from Viking invaders who settled in northern France after *c.*AD900. After the English king, Edward the Confessor, died (*see* page 35), William claimed the right to rule England, saying that Edward had promised it to him in return for his help. However, other rivals (*see* Harold, page 48) also claimed the throne, so William invaded England in 1066. He landed on the south coast, fought a battle at Hastings, where Harold was killed, and took control of the kingdom. He put down a series of uprisings against foreign rule – the most important was led by an East Anglian outlaw named Hereward the Wake – then began to reform the English government.

William introduced French laws and methods of working, and also 'feudalism' – a way of rewarding powerful nobles with large estates, so long as they promised to help the king, and fight for him in battle, in return. Probably his most famous memorial is the *Domesday Book*, a massive survey of all England and its wealth, prepared for him in 1086, so that he could collect more taxes.

William III (of Orange)
(1650–1702; reigned 1689-1702)
King

A grandson of King Charles I, William (*below*) was a member of the Orange family, which ruled the Netherlands. He married Mary, daughter of King James II, in 1677. When James was forced to give up the throne, William and Mary ruled jointly, as king and queen. At first, they faced opposition. There were rebellions in Scotland and Ireland between 1689 and 1690. However, William and Mary won support in England, because, unlike King James, they agreed to let Parliament decide government policy. King William also successfully led Britain in a fight against France.

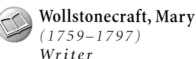 ## Wollstonecraft, Mary
(1759–1797)
Writer

An intelligent, original thinker, Wollstonecraft was unable to have an interesting career, because she was a woman. At the time she lived, women could not go to university or join any of the professions. Instead, she worked as a governess and nurse, writing in her spare time.

Wollstonecraft was sympathetic to the radical ideas of the French Revolution of 1789, and became an outspoken campaigner for equal rights for women. Her most famous book, *A Vindication of the Rights of Women* (1792) called for women's complete equality with men. It inspired many campaigners throughout the 19th century. In 1797, Wollstonecraft married a famous English revolutionary journalist, William Godwin. She died the same year, after giving birth to their daughter, Mary Shelley (*see* page 93).

 ## Wilson, Lord Harold
(1916–1995)
Politician

Determined to make a career in politics, Wilson (*right*) became a Labour Party MP in 1945. He became a government minister just two years later – one of the youngest ever. In 1963, he was elected leader of the Labour Party, and was prime minister 1964–1970 and 1974–1976.

Throughout Wilson's time in office, Britain faced serious economic problems and trade union conflicts, which he was unable to solve. He also failed to settle problems in the colony of Rhodesia (now Zimbabwe) after the white government there declared itself independent from Britain and refused to accept black majority rule. However, Wilson's governments did introduce important reforms in education, welfare, and civil rights, especially women's rights, and divorce.

 ### Wolsey, Thomas (Cardinal)
(?1472–1530)
Priest and politician

Wolsey (*right*) was a Roman Catholic priest. Like many other churchmen of his time, he received an excellent education and went to work as a government official. He held many senior positions, including lord chancellor (chief government lawyer). He helped shape England's relations with other European countries and with the leaders of the Roman Catholic Church in Rome. But after he failed to win King Henry VIII (*see* page 51) a divorce from his first wife, Catherine of Aragon, the king came to hate him, and accused him of treason. He died on his way to the trial.

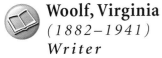 ### Woolf, Virginia
(1882–1941)
Writer

Born into a remarkable, intellectual family, Woolf became famous as a novelist and critic, and also as a member of the 'Bloomsbury Group' – a collection of writers and artists who lived in the Bloomsbury district of central London and who shared many experimental, unconventional ideas about life and creative work of all kinds.

Together with her husband, Leonard, Woolf ran a well-known company, the Hogarth Press, that published new work by unknown writers. Her own books won praise for their 'stream of consciousness' technique (written as if inside the mind of their characters) and for their feminist ideas. Throughout her life, Woolf suffered from mental illness. She committed suicide soon after completing her final novel.

 ### Wordsworth, William
(1770–1850)
Writer

One of Britain's most famous writers, Wordsworth's poems (such as 'I wandered lonely as a cloud'; 1815) are still popular today. He was born and brought up in the Lake District, in northwest England, and spent most of his life there. Its magnificent mountain scenery is described in many of his works, and strongly influenced his thoughts and feelings. He was one of the first writers to suggest that people's surroundings can affect their character and their behaviour, for good or ill.

As a young man, Wordsworth had revolutionary ideas about writing, and about politics. He deliberately used simple, natural-sounding language that did not rhyme. This marked a great change from other poetry of the time, which was full of grand, complicated words arranged in strict verse patterns. He travelled to France to show support for the French Revolution of 1789, but later changed his opinions and held conservative political views. He was made poet laureate in 1843.

▼ Dove Cottage, Grasmere, Wordsworth's home.

Wren, Sir Christopher
(1632–1732)
Architect

Trained as a scientist, Wren changed careers to become an architect. After the Great Fire of London (1666) he drew up plans to rebuild the large area of the city that had been destroyed in the blaze. These were never used, but were greatly admired. As a result, Wren was given an important position by King Charles II, and asked to build many new London churches to replace the ones damaged in the Great Fire, including St Paul's Cathedral. This was a massive project, which took many years (1675–1711) to complete.

Wren's design for St Paul's, in fashionable, 17th-century 'Baroque' style, included advanced technical features such a huge, domed roof supported on a drum-shaped stone base, wrapped in iron chains for support.

▲ Wren's 'new' St Paul's.

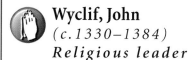

Wyclif, John
(c.1330–1384)
Religious leader

A scholar at Oxford University, who wrote many books criticizing the wealth and power of the Roman Catholic Church. Wyclif called for reforms in Church government, simpler ways of worshipping, and for the Bible to be translated from Latin into English so that ordinary people could understand it. He also said that priests and Church leaders should live purer, more holy lives.

Wyclif's ideas were spread by wandering preachers, and won many supporters, who were known by the nickname 'Lollards'. Wyclif himself, however, and the Lollards, were attacked by Church leaders and the government. Wyclif was forced to give up his job, and, after 1401, many Lollards were burned as heretics (people with dangerous beliefs).

Yeats, William Butler
(1865–1939)
Writer

Although he spent a large part of his life in London, Yeats was a keen supporter of Irish independence and very knowledgeable about Irish history, folklore and traditional culture. While working as a poet and dramatist, he helped set up societies to study Irish literature, and was co-founder of the Irish National Theatre Company.

His play, *The Countess Cathleen*, inspired many other writers to create works set in, or about, Ireland. Some of his poems – such as the well-known *The Lake Isle of Innisfree* – are on Irish topics, others are on universal themes such as love, or growing old. From 1922 to 1928, Yeats served as a senator (senior politician) in the newly formed Irish Free State. He was awarded the Nobel Prize for Literature in 1923.

Yeats had a brother Jack B (John Butler) who was a noteworthy painter and cartoonist recording Irish rural life, horses and boxing in his work.

Great Britons of the 20th Century

Adams, Gerald (Gerry)
(born 1948)
Politician
From an Irish Republican background. Leading Northern Irish political figure. Elected MP for West Belfast 1997.

Anne, H.R.H. The Princess Royal
(born 1950)
Princess
Second child of Queen Elizabeth II. Outspoken and sometimes controversial, but respected for her work with charities. Member of the British Olympic team (equestrian events) 1976.

Arup, Sir Ove
(1895–1988)
Engineer
Born in Britain of Danish parents. Designed blocks of flats, public buildings and bridges; consultant to many major projects including Sydney Opera House (1956–1973) and Eurostar Terminal, London (1990s).

Ashdown, Sir John Jeremy ('Paddy')
(born 1941)
Politician
Served in Royal Marines and as a diplomat, then became Liberal Party MP. From 1988 to 2000, leader of the Liberal Democratic Party. Keen interest in overseas policy, especially in the Balkans.

Ashton, Sir Frederick
(1904–1988)
Dancer
Trained by Dame Marie Rambert (*see* main A–Z section); danced for Britain's leading companies. Became director of Royal Ballet 1963. Created many new ballets (some of the most famous were for Margot Fonteyn, *see* main A–Z section); also choreographed for films.

Auden, W(ystan) H(ugh)
(1907–1973)
Writer
Poet and film scriptwriter. Supporter of radical causes, including anti-fascists in Britain and Germany, and Republicans in the Spanish Civil War. Later, wrote poems on religious themes.

Bacon, Francis
(1902–1992)
Artist
Flamboyant, unconventional figure; worked as an interior designer before becoming a painter. His works are dramatic, shocking, distorted and sometimes violent, but greatly admired.

Bader, Sir Douglas
(1910–1983)
Pilot
RAF pilot Bader lost his legs in an air crash in 1931. However, when war began in 1939, began to fly again, shooting down 23 enemy planes before being captured and imprisoned. Inspired many others by his courage.

Beckett, Samuel
(1896–1989)
Writer
Born in Dublin, Ireland, Beckett moved to France to live and write. His plays, in a style known as 'the Theatre of the Absurd', are strange yet compelling, forcing viewers to think and question. Won Nobel Prize for Literature 1969.

Benn, Anthony Wedgwood ('Tony')
(born 1925)
Politician
Gave up family title (viscount) to become a Labour MP. On Left wing of party; well-known for outspoken, radical, controversial views. Admired for his dedication, integrity and skill as a public speaker.

Blair, Anthony ('Tony')
(born 1953)
Politician
Trained as a barrister, became Labour MP in 1983 and prime minister in 1997. Worked hard to modernize Labour Party, and to seek 'third way' between capitalist free enterprise and socialist-style State control.

Blyton, Enid
(1897–1968)
Writer
Worked as a governess before writing over 400 stories for children, featuring popular characters such as 'Noddy' and the 'Famous Five'. Her books read and enjoyed by millions of children.

Boothroyd, Elizabeth ('Betty')
(born 1930)
Politician
Brief showbusiness career before becoming a Labour MP. The first-ever woman chosen to be Speaker of the House of Commons. Admired as warm and witty, strict but fair.

Braddock, Elizabeth 'Bessie'
(1899–1970)
Politician
Served as MP for a disadvantaged area of Liverpool for over 30 years. Famous as 'Battling Bessie Braddock' for her fiery speeches demanding better housing and education for ordinary people.

Branson, Sir Richard
(born 1950)
Businessman
Became a billionaire after setting up his own business while still a teenager. Built up enormous media and transport empire, including rail and aircraft services. Won fame for new, informal business style.

Brittain, Vera
(1893–1970)
Writer
Served as a nurse in World War I. Saw many soldiers die tragically young, and lost her only brother and her fiancé. Wrote moving autobiography, *Testament of Youth* (1933), describing wartime experiences. Spent many years campaigning for international peace.

Brook, Peter
(born 1925)
Theatre director
Won fame for his magical, experimental productions of classic plays from many civilizations. Became director of International Centre of Theatre Research.

Callaghan, James
(1912–2004)
Politician
After working for trade unions, and serving in the Navy, became a Labour Party MP 1945. A skilled negotiator and 'fixer' of deals. Prime minister (1976–1979).

Callil, Carmen
(born 1938)
Publisher
Born in Australia, moved to London to set up feminist publishing house, Virago. It found and printed many 'lost' works by women, and later encouraged new women writers.

Carey, Archbishop George
(born 1931)
Religious leader
Became archbishop of Canterbury 1991. Presided over historic decision to allow women priests in the Church of England, 1994.

Cartland, Dame Barbara
(1901–2000)
Writer
The world's most prolific novelist; published many hundreds of love stories, and created a whole new type of romantic fiction. This was often criticized but remained very popular.

Clark, Lord Kenneth
(1903–1983)
Historian
Art historian and museum director, Clark won fame as presenter of a pioneering TV series, *Civilization* (1969). It combined educational content with stunning visuals and Clark's own informative commentary.

Clarke, Kenneth
(born 1940)
Politician
Conservative MP from 1970; held government posts (including home secretary and chancellor of the exchequer) 1979–1997. Tipped as party leader, but his sympathy for closer links with Europe lost him some support in his party.

Clore, Sir Charles
(1904–1979)
Businessman
Built up huge business empire through company take-overs and property deals. Later, gave large amounts to good causes.

Cohen, Sir John (Jack) (originally Jacob Kohen)
(1898–1979)
Businessman
After serving in World War I, became a street trader, then set up successful chain of Tesco stores. Introduced self-service supermarkets to UK, from USA.

Connery, Sir Sean
(born 1930)
Actor
Became famous as star of James Bond films. Caused controversy by supporting Scottish National Party.

Conran, Shirley
(born 1932)
Writer
Designer and journalist. Famous for her book 'Superwoman' (1975), a practical guide for women, which aimed to help them lead successful careers, run a home, and care for their families, all at the same time. Later a best-selling romantic novelist.

Conran, Sir Terence
(born 1931)
Designer/ Businessman
Set up pioneering 'Habitat' shops in 1960s, to sell good modern design at affordable prices. Later, ran large retail business empire, and stylish restaurants.

Cousins, Frank
(1904–1986)
Trades Unionist
From 1956-1969, leader of the powerful Transport and General Workers' Union. Encouraged trades unions to play an active part in national politics; also supported militant action, including the 1958 national bus strike. Minister of Technology in Labour government, 1964-1966.

Coward, Nöel
(1899–1973)
Entertainer
Began his career as an actor, but soon began to write comic plays and compose witty, satirical and sometimes sentimental songs. His most famous plays include *Private Lives* (1930) and *Blithe Spirit* (1942). Also wrote successful films such as *Brief Encounter* (1945).

Cripps, Sir Stafford
(1889–1952)
Lawyer/politician
A wealthy, successful barrister, but also a radical socialist politician, with links to international communist parties. Served as government minister during World War II, introduced (and won support for) strict economic policies to help war effort.

David, Elizabeth
(1913–1992)
Writer
Pioneering cookery writer; introduced new ingredients and new styles of cooking from Europe to Britain. Revolutionized British food in the 1950s and 1960s.

Dawkins, Richard
(born 1941)
Scientist
Won fame for popular books on evolution, especially *The Selfish Gene*, 1976. From 1996, Professor of Public Understanding of Science at Oxford University.

Day, Sir Robin
(1923–2000)
Broadcaster
Chief political interviewer at the BBC in the 1970s and 1980s. Pioneered a new style of radio and TV broadcast with assertive – sometimes aggressive – questioning. Later, this was copied by many other journalists.

Diana, Princess of Wales
(1961–1997)
Princess
From an aristocratic family, married Prince Charles, heir to the Queen of England, in 1981. Marriage produced two sons; ended in divorce after she contributed to controversial books and TV programmes, describing her unhappy married life. Great outpouring of public grief after she died in a car crash.

Edwards, Robert and Steptoe, Patrick
(born 1925, and 1913–1988)
Scientists
Pioneers in field of female infertility. Produced world's first 'test-tube baby' in 1978.

Ewing, Winnie
(born 1929)
Politician
Trained as a solicitor, was elected to London Parliament as the first and only Scottish Nationalist MP in 1967. Later, a member of the European and Scottish Parliaments, campaigning for Scottish independence.

Fiennes, Sir Ranulph, OBE
(born 1944)
Explorer
After a career in the army, led series of gruelling expeditions to remote places, often experiencing extreme and dangerous conditions. Holder of ten records for exploration, has also raised millions of pounds for charity.

Fleming, Ian
(1908–1964)
Writer
Worked as a journalist, but won fame as author of popular novels featuring fictional spy, James Bond. These fitted in with the mood of US/Russian hostility (the 'Cold War' era: 1940s–1960s).

Foot, Michael
(born 1913)
Politician
A journalist and newspaper editor, became Labour MP in 1945. A left-winger, he became leader of the Labour Party in 1980, but resigned in 1983, after losing the general election to the Conservatives.

Hall, Stuart
(born 1932)
Sociologist
Born in Jamaica, moved to study in Britain. Studied links between culture and society, also politics and issues of race; professor of sociology at the Open University, 1979–1997.

Heaney, Seamus
(born 1939)
Writer
Born in Northern Ireland; moved to Irish Republic. His poems reflect the conflict in Ireland, and discuss Irish identity. Won the Nobel Prize for Literature 1995.

Hirst, Damien
(born 1965)
Artist
Creator of shocking works, including dead animals preserved in chemicals, and pictures made by throwing paint at moving canvases. Won the Turner Prize 1995.

Hoyle, Sir Fred
(1915–2001)
Astronomer
In 1948, suggested controversial new 'steady state' theory of the origins of the universe. Also wrote many popular books on science and the stars.

Huddleston, Trevor
(1913–1998)
Monk/campaigner
Anglican monk; spent years working for Church in South Africa, and campaigning against apartheid. Advised rulers of newly-independent African states.

Hume, Basil
(1923–1999)
Religious leader
A monk, was appointed Roman Catholic cardinal archbishop of Westminster in 1976. Greatly admired and respected, he worked to bring peace within the Catholic Church, and between Catholics and Protestants. Supported campaigns for justice, to help the homeless, and for overseas aid.

Hume, John
(born 1937)
Politician
Leader of the moderately nationalist Social Democratic and Labour Party; played a leading part in Northern Irish politics. From 1983, a Westminster MP. Won the Nobel Prize in 1998 for his work to end violence and also to win multi-party support for peaceful politics.

Hurst, Margery
(1914–1989)
Businesswoman
One of Britain's first successful businesswomen; set up chain of employment agencies, and became a millionaire.

Huxley, Aldous
(1894–1963)
Writer
Novelist and social critic. Best known for the alarming vision of the future portrayed in his novel, *Brave New World* (1932).

Issigonis, Sir Alexander ('Alec')
(1906–1988)
Engineer
Born in Turkey, trained as an engineer. Designed many revolutionary new automobiles, including the 'Mini' (1959) – the most successful British car ever.

Jagger, Michael ('Mick')
(born 1943)
Singer
Lead singer for rock group, The Rolling Stones, which performed with great success from the 1960s to the 1990s. Famous for his exuberant stage performances, his wild image when young, his financial shrewdness, and his controversial private life.

Jeffereys, Sir Alec
(born 1950)
Scientist
Geneticist. Invented 'DNA fingerprinting' technique, now used in medicine and to identify suspects in criminal investigations.

Jenkins, Lord Roy
(born 1920)
Politician
Became Labour MP from 1948, also served as government minister. President of the European Commission, 1976–1979. He held moderate, progressive views, and in 1981 helped set up the new Social Democratic Party. Later, chancellor of Oxford University, and adviser on electoral reform.

Jones, John ('Jack')
(born 1913)
Union leader
Trade union leader, very powerful in the 1970s. Tried to make union organization more democratic, and called for moderation in pay claims. After retirement, leader of campaign for pensioners' rights.

Kinnock, Neil
(born 1942)
Politician
Left-wing Labour MP from 1960; became leader of Labour party in 1983. Fought to remove militants from Labour Party, to modernize it, and make it more attractive to voters. After losing the 1992 general election, resigned in favour of John Smith (*see* separate entry). Became a European Commissioner in 1995.

Kitzinger, Sheila
(born 1929)
Writer/campaigner
Writer and lecturer, campaigned for better education about childbirth, to lessen women's pain and fear. Worked with the National Childbirth Trust.

Lane, Sir Allen
(1903–1970)
Publisher
In 1935, developed revolutionary new way of selling quality books cheaply, with paperback covers. His 'Penguin Press' became famous worldwide.

Lee, Laurie
(1914–1998)
Writer
Famous for his autobiographical works, especially *Cider with Rosie* (1959), which described his Cotswold childhood.

Littlewood, Joan
(1914–1999)
Theatre director
Pioneer of political theatre, she set up a 'Theatre Workshop' to stage plays with topical social themes. Her play, *Oh! What a Lovely War!*, which was fiercely critical of army leaders in World War I, was made into a successful, disturbing film.

Livingstone, Kenneth ('Ken')
(born 1945)
Politician
After serving as a Labour local councillor, became leader of the General London Council (GLC) 1981–1986. Famous for his outspoken, unconventional, radical views, he was also popular with many Londoners, and was voted the first-ever elected mayor of London in 2000.

Lloyd Webber, Lord Andrew
(born 1948)
Composer
Won fame while still a student for staging musicals, and soon became Britain's most commercially-successful composer. His best-known works include *Evita* (1978), *Cats* (1981) and *Phantom of the Opera* (1986).

McAliskey, Bernadette
(born 1947)
Politician
Active in civil rights protests and riots against the police in Northern Ireland. Was briefly MP for Mid-Ulster in the 1970s. In 1981, was shot and badly wounded by loyalist paramilitaries, but continued to remain active in Irish Republican politics.

Major, John
(born 1943)
Politician
After working as a banker, became a Conservative MP in 1979. Served in government posts, but was surprise, compromise, choice as prime minister in 1990. (After Margaret Thatcher resigned, rival groups of Conservatives could not agree on her successor.) After 1992, faced serious financial problems, also accusations of 'sleaze' (corruption) among Conservative MPs, who were also deeply divided over European policy. Lost the 1997 general election; announced in 2000 that he would resign as an MP.

Morecambe, Eric (originally Eric Bartholomew) and Wise, Ernie
(1926–1984) and (1925–1999)
Entertainers
Two of Britain's best-loved comedians, famous for their quick wit, imaginative flair and brilliant timing. During the 1960s and 1970s, their TV shows became essential viewing for many families, especially at Christmas-time.

Mountbatten, Lord Louis (Dickie)
(1900–1979)
Admiral/statesman
Descended from Queen Victoria, had an eventful, if mixed, naval career. Handsome, charming, and a skilled diplomat, he was appointed last viceroy of India, and negotiated the terms for India's independence. He later acted as adviser to the British monarchy. He was killed by an IRA bomb.

Neuberger, Julia
(born 1950)
Religious leader
The first woman in Britain to become a rabbi; also served on national committees concerned with ethics and human rights. From 1997, Chief Executive of the King's Fund, an independent organization studying health care policy.

Owen, Lord David
(born 1938)
Politician
Trained as a doctor, became a Labour MP in 1966. Achieved success as foreign secretary, but disliked many left-wing Labour policies, and left the party in 1981 to become one of the founder members of the Social Democratic Party, and later its leader. In 1987, he opposed the SDP alliance with the Liberal Party, but was out-voted. He retired from party politics, and became involved in international diplomatic missions, particularly in former Yugoslavia.

Paisley, Ian
(born 1926)
Politician
A Protestant minister, he became a Westminster MP in 1970, and founded the Democratic Unionist Party in 1971. For many years, campaigned vigorously against Irish Nationalist and Republican political parties. His party opposed the Good Friday Agreement of 1998, but took seats in the Northern Irish executive in 1999.

Pinter, Harold
(born 1930)
Writer
One of Britain's most important dramatists. Well-known for his left-wing views and for incorporating meaningful pauses and silences into his tense, sometimes menacing, plays.

Porritt, Sir Jonathan
(born 1950)
Campaigner
Trained as a teacher, became an active environmental campaigner. Director, Friends of the Earth, 1984–1990. Writer, broadcaster, and Parliamentary candidate for the Green Party and the Ecology Party.

Quant, Mary
(born 1934)
Designer
One of the leaders of the 'Swinging Sixties', opened a boutique selling fashionable, shocking, clothes in London in 1955. Her designs popularized new styles for teenagers, especially the mini-skirt.

Rattle, Sir Simon
(born 1955)
Conductor
Won first-ever John Player International Conductors' Competition, aged 19, in 1974. For many years, worked with the City of Birmingham Symphony Orchestra, transforming the musical life of the city. In 2002, became artistic director of the prestigious Berlin Philharmonic Orchestra.

Redgrave, Vanessa
(born 1937)
Actress
Famous for passionate, intelligent performances on stage and in films. For many years, involved in radical left-wing politics. Her two daughters, Joely and Natasha Richardson (born 1958 and 1963), are also successful actors.

Rotten, Johnny (originally John Lydon)
(born 1956)
Musician
Lead singer of the rock band, the Sex Pistols, popular during the 1970s. A pioneer of punk music, which was sneering, violent, and delighted to shock, Rotten used music to challenge authority figures and to publicize the negative feelings shared by many young people.

Saatchi, Charles and Saatchi, Maurice
(born 1943 and 1946)
Advertising executives
Born in Baghdad, of Jewish parents, the Saatchi brothers came to Britain as children. In 1970, they set up an advertising agency which won great success with its witty, imaginative campaigns. Charles Saatchi and his wife, Doris, also became well-known collectors of modern art.

Sen, Amartya
(born 1933)
Economist
Born in Bengal, Sen studied economics and became professor at universities in India and the UK. He specialized in investigating poverty, inequality and unemployment, particularly in developing countries, and also studied famines and how they are caused. He won the Nobel Prize for Economics in 1998.

Sieff, Lord Israel
(1889–1972)
Businessman
With his friend and brother-in-law, Simon Marks, developed the chain of Marks and Spencer stores – for many years one of the most successful retail companies in Britain. Also active in politics, as a Zionist (Jewish movement).

Sinclair, Sir Clive
(born 1940)
Inventor
Famous for selling the world's first pocket calculator, in 1972, and for other electronics inventions, including the ZX home computer and the C5 mini-car.

Smith, Delia
(born 1941)
Writer
One of Britain's most famous and best-selling cookery writers; also appeared in very popular television series. Aims to teach people how to cook, as well as introducing new recipes and unusual ingredients. A committed Christian, has also written on spiritual topics.

Smith, John
(1938–1994)
Politician
Brilliant Scottish lawyer, respected for his intelligence and integrity. Labour MP from 1973; became Labour Party leader in 1992. Determined to reform party organization and make it more democratic. His sudden death, aged 56, was widely mourned.

Steel, Sir David (Lord)
(born 1938)
Politician
A Liberal MP from 1965, supported controversial social change, including the legalization of abortion in 1967. Became leader of the Liberal party in 1976, and agreed to co-operate with the then Labour government (the Lib-Lab Pact). Also worked closely with new Social Democratic Party after 1981, agreeing a merger with them (to form Liberal Democrats) in 1988. Elected as Member of the Scottish Parliament, and its presiding officer, in 1999.

Tebbitt, Lord Norman
(born 1931)
Politician
A pilot in the RAF and for civilian airlines, became a Conservative MP in 1970. One of Margaret Thatcher's (*see* book's main A-Z section) keenest supporters, won praise and blame for his tough attitude towards trade unionists, strikers and benefit claimants, and for his typically outspoken comment that anyone unemployed should 'get on his bike' and look for work, rather than seek state aid. Displayed great personal courage when injured by IRA bomb in 1984.

Trimble, David
(born 1944)
Politician
A Northern Ireland Unionist, became Westminster MP in 1990, and leader of the Unionist party in 1995, after publicly supporting demonstrations by the Orange order. Accepted Good Friday Agreement in 1998, and was chosen as first minister of new Northern Ireland Assembly. Won Northern Ireland Peace Prize in 1998, jointly with John Hume (*see* separate entry).

Waite, Terence (Terry)
(born 1939)
Church adviser
Church worker and adviser to bishops in the UK and overseas. Acted as diplomatic representative for Robert Runcie, archbishop of Canterbury. Kidnapped in Lebanon in 1987, while on humanitarian mission to investigate the disappearance of hostages seized by Muslim militia. Survived in prison until 1991, when released.

West, Dame Rebecca (originally, Cecily Fairfield Andrews)
(1892–1983)
Writer
A feminist and socialist, West wrote articles and reviews for campaigning newspapers and magazines, also many novels and non-fiction works.

Westwood, Vivienne
(born 1941)
Designer
Became famous in the 1970s for her outrageous punk clothes designs, featuring leather, rubber and safety pins. Later, created witty, dramatic fashion garments and theatrical costumes, often drawing inspiration from the past.

Williams, Baroness Shirley
(born 1930)
Politician
Daughter of Vera Brittain (*see* separate entry), elected Labour MP in 1964. A controversial minister for education, she introduced comprehensive schools. Left Labour in 1981 to become founder member of Social Democratic Party.

Wilmut, Ian
(born 1944)
Scientist
Based at the Roslin Institute, near Edinburgh, caused a sensation by successfully producing the world's first cloned mammal, Dolly the Sheep, in 1996. Opposed to human cloning, but believes cloned animals (producing identical animals under laboratory conditions) can be useful to people.

Sports People

Abrahams, Harold
(1899–1978)
Athletics
Gold medal winner (100 metres) 1924 Paris Olympics.

Bannister, Sir Roger
(born 1929)
Athletics
First man to run a mile in under 4 minutes, 1954.

Beaumont, Bill
(born 1952)
Rugby union
Captain of England team that won the Grand Slam, in 1980.

Bennett, Phil
(born 1948)
Rugby union
Leading member of Welsh team that won three Triple Crowns, 1976–1978.

Beresford, Jack
(1899–1977)
Rowing
Won three gold and two silver Olympic medals, 1920–1936; Champion Sculler of Britain, 1920–1926.

Best, George
(born 1946)
Football
Born Northern Ireland, played for Manchester United. Most talented player of his generation. Scored 137 goals in 361 games. Member of team that won European Cup 1968.

Blanchflower, Danny
(1926–1993)
Football
Captain of Northern Ireland, played for Spurs. Made record 56 international appearances. Member of team that won the European Cup, 1963.

Boston, Billy
(born 1934)
Rugby league
First black rugby player to represent Great Britain. Scored 571 first-class tries from 565 games.

Botham, Ian
(born 1955)
Cricket
A match-winning phenomenon. Youngest player ever to reach 1,000 runs and take 100 wickets in a season. First-ever player to score a century and take 10 wickets in a test match..

Boycott, Geoffrey
(born 1940)
Cricket
A controversial character, but an unrivalled defensive batsman. Played 108 times for England between 1962 and 1984.

Braid, James
(1870–1950)
Golf
Winner of Open Championship five times between 1901 and 1910, and many other titles. Later a top golf-course designer.

Bruno, Frank
(born 1961)
Boxing
European Heavyweight Champion 1985 and WBC World Heavyweight Champion 1993. Now a popular entertainer.

Burton, Beryl
(1937–1996)
Cycling
Britain's greatest woman cyclist. Time Trials Champion for 25 years 1959–1983; also won many other medals and titles.

Busby, Sir Matt
(1909-1994)
Football
Manager, born in Scotland. From 1945, won fame as leader of young Manchester United team ('the Busby Babes'), many of whom were tragically killed in the Munich Air Disaster (1958). Busby was also badly injured, but recovered and rebuilt his team to win the FA Cup in 1963, and many other championships.

Carling, Will
(born 1965)
Rugby union
Most successful and longest-serving captain of England; leader of team that won Five Nations Championship four times 1991–1996; World Cup finalist 1991.

Carson, William ('Willie')
(born 1942)
Horse racing
Rode winners of 17 Classic races; later a sports commentator..

Chambers, Dorothea Lambert
(1878–1960)
Tennis
Won Wimbledon seven times between 1903 and 1914. Campaigner for women's right to take part in competitive sports.

Champion, Robert ('Bob')
(born 1948)
Horse racing
Rode winner of 1981 Grand National, soon after recovering from cancer. Became a national hero.

Charlton, Sir Bobby
(born 1937)
Football
Mid-fielder for Manchester United. Won 106 caps for England and scored 49 goals – a record. Member of team that won FA Cup and European Cup 1968.

Christie, Linford
(born 1960)
Athletics
Olympic gold medal-winner (100 metres) in 1992; World Champion in 1993. Later a trainer.

Clark, Jim
(1936–1968)
Motor racing
In a short career (he was killed in a race, aged 32), won 25 out of 72 Grands Prix..

Colledge, Cecilia
(born 1920)
Ice skating
Competed in Olympic Games aged only 11. World Champion 1937, European Champion 1937–1939.

Compton, Denis
(1918–1997)
Cricket
Batsman; member of England team 78 times between 1938 and 1956. Also played international football for England, and became famous for his good looks and glamorous lifestyle.

Cooper, Henry
(born 1934)
Boxing
British Heavyweight Champion 1959–1970; also won fame for courageous fights (which he lost) against world champions, including Muhammad Ali. Later a popular media personality.

Cotton, Sir Henry
(1907–1987)
Golf
Won Open Championships 1934, 1937, 1948, and many other tournaments. Writer, teacher, golf course designer.

Cousins, Robin
(born 1957)
Ice skating
British national champion 1976–1980; Olympic gold medallist and World Champion 1980.

Cowdrey, Lord Colin
(1932–2000)
Cricket
Captain of England 27 times, and president of the MCC. Popular and greatly respected.

Curry, John
(1949–1994)
Ice skating
National champion 1970–1975; Olympic gold medallist 1976, also World and European Champion.

Dalgleish, Kenny
(born 1951)
Football
Striker for Celtic and Liverpool. The only British player to have scored more than 100 league goals; awarded 102 Scottish caps – a record.

Davies, Gerald
(born 1945)
Rugby union
Welsh winger; won 44 caps and scored 20 tries – both a record.

Davies, Laura
(born 1963)
Golf
Winner British Women's Open 1986, USA Women's Open 1987 and over 50 other championships. In 1996, was first woman to win over a million pounds from golf.

Davis, Joe
(1901–1978)
Billiards and snooker
World Snooker Champion 1927–1946 – only ever beaten in a match by one person, his brother. Helped make snooker into an international sport.

Davis, Steve
(born 1957)
Snooker
World Champion 1981, 1983, 1984, and from 1987 to 1989; became one of Britain's most famous TV performers.

Dean, see Torville and Dean

Dettori, Frankie
(born 1970)
Horse-racing
Son of an Italian jockey, has ridden winners of many top races. In 1996, at Ascot, won all seven races run one afternoon – a record.

Dod, Lottie
(1871–1960)
Tennis
Won Wimbledon championship aged only 15; also a winner in many other sports – hockey, golf, tobogganing and skating. Won Olympic silver medal for archery in 1908.

Donoghue, Steve
(1884–1945)
Horse racing
Won the Derby six times; British Champion jockey 1914–1923. Only jockey ever to win Triple Crown twice.

Duke, Geoff
(born 1932)
Motorcycling
Winner of 33 Grands Prix, and 6 Isle of Man TT races. Stylish and good-looking, Duke attracted large crowds and influenced many younger riders.

Eddery, Pat
(born 1952)
Horse racing
One of the youngest British champions, Eddery was only the third jockey to ride 4,000 winners in his career.

Edwards, Gareth
(born 1947)
Rugby union
Scrum-half Edwards made a record 53 appearances for Wales, and became a national hero.

Faldo, Nick
(born 1957)
Golf
Winner of the Open Championship in 1987, 1990, 1992, and the US Masters in 1989, 1990 and 1996.

Ferguson, Sir Alex
(born 1941)
Football
After a career playing for Scottish teams, became a manager in 1974, leading his teams to victory in several championships. From 1986, manager of Manchester United, the most successful and profitable football club in Britain.

Finney, Sir Tom
(born 1922)
Football
Played for Preston North End. Scored 217 goals in 507 matches. Capped 76 times for England, was the only winger to have scored 30 goals for England.

Fox, Neil
(born 1939)
Rugby league
The highest point-scorer in the history of rugby league – he scored 358 tries and 2,575 goals. He played 29 tests for Britain.

Francome, John
(born 1952)
Horse racing
Winner of all major jump races except the Grand National; only the second jockey to ride more than 1,000 winners over hurdles. Champion Jockey 1982.

Fry, Charles Burgess
(1872–1956)
Cricket
Top run-maker for Sussex. Also holder of world long jump record for 21 years, and played football for England.

Gibson, Mike
(born 1942)
Rugby union
Born in Belfast, made a world-record 69 international appearances for Ireland, also played for British Lions.

Godfree, Kitty
(1897–1992)
Tennis
Twice Ladies Singles Champion of Wimbledon, in 1924 and 1926; also winner, with her husband, of Wimbledon Mixed Doubles, 1926, and of five Olympic medals in 1920 and 1924.

Gooch, Graham
(born 1953)
Cricket
England's leading scorer in test-matches, with 8,900 runs. Also made highest-ever score (333) by an England captain, in 1981. Played for Essex for 25 years; captained England for 34 matches.

Goodhew, Duncan
(born 1957)
Swimming
Winner of Olympic gold medal in 1980 (100 metres), also three silver medals in 1978 Commonwealth Games (100m, 200m, breaststroke).

Gower, David
(born 1957)
Cricket
Famous for his style and grace, became youngest player to achieve 100 Test caps, in 1988. Later, a TV personality.

Greaves, Jimmy
(born 1940)
Football
Scored 306 goals for Spurs, and 44 for England. Was the first division's top scorer from 1962 to 1965. Later, a TV personality.

Green, Lucinda Prior-Palmer
(born 1953)
Equestrianism
Won a record six victories at Badminton; was also a winner at Burghley Horse Trials. World Champion 1982; Olympic silver medallist 1984.

Grey, Tanni
(born 1969)
Paralympics
Winner of four gold medals at 1992 Paralympics and 1994 World Champion in wheelchair track events. Was the first athlete with disabilities to complete the London Marathon in 1994. Also campaigned to end prejudice.

Gunnell, Sally
(born 1966)
Athletics
In 1994, became only woman athlete ever to hold four championships (Olympic, World, Commonwealth and European) at the same time, for 400 metres hurdles.

Hailwood, Mike
(1940–1981)
Motorcycling
Was Britain's most successful motor cyclist, winning nine World Championships, and 76 Grands Prix races.

Hallam, Chris
(born 1962)
Paralympics
Britain's top athlete with disabilities, won Olympic medals for swimming in 1988 and 1992, and held many world records. Also successful at international level in marathon, cross-country skiing and track events. Founded charity People Versus Handicap.

Hamid, Naseem
(born 1974)
Boxing
World Featherweight Champion since 1995, has never lost a professional fight in whole career..

Hammond, Walter
(1903–1965)
Cricket
One of England's greatest batsman, he played in the national team for 20 years. Topped batting averages every year (except one) from 1923 to 1947.

Handley, Ellery
(born 1961)
Rugby league
In 1988, became first black player to captain Britain; also led his team, Wigan, to win Challenge Cup 1989–1991. Later, became British team coach..

Harris, Reg
(1920–1992)
Cycling
World Champion 1947 and Olympic silver medallist 1948, became Britain's top cyclist in 1950s. Won many titles and held world speed record for cycling 1952–1973. In 1974, won British sprint title, aged 54.

Hastings, Gavin
(born 1962)
Rugby union
Scotland's top player 1986–1995, scoring a record 667 points in 61 games. Member of victorious British Lions team, 1989. Captained Scotland to win Grand Slam, 1990.

Hemery, David
(born 1944)
Athletics
Winner of Olympic gold, 1968 (400 metres hurdles), and world record holder. Also Olympic silver medal in 4 x 400 metres relay, 1972.

Hendry, Steven
(born 1969)
Snooker
World Champion 1992–1994 and 1995–1996, and winner of many other titles.

Hill, Damon
(born 1960)
Motor racing
Winner 22 Grands Prix races, 1993–1998, World Champion 1996. Son of Graham Hill (*see* separate entry).

Hill, Graham
(1929–1975)
Motor racing
Winner of 14 Grands Prix, 1962–1969, Drivers' Champion 1962 and 1969. Father of Damon Hill (*see* separate entry).

Hobbs, Sir Jack
(1882–1963)
Cricket
Known as 'the Master', was Britain's most respected cricketer for many years. Scored 61,237 runs and 197 centuries in his career.

Hurst, Sir Geoff
(born 1941)
Football
Played for West Ham; was club's second-highest scorer of all time. Scored hat trick in 1966 World Cup Final to win the championship for England.

Hutton, Sir Len
(1916–1990)
Cricket
In 1934, scored 364 runs against Australia, setting a record that stood for over 20 years. Led England to victory in Test series against Australia, 1953.

John, Barry
(born 1945)
Rugby union
Fly-half John was generally reckoned to be the world's best rugby player in the early 1970s, and became a national hero in Wales. He scored a record-breaking 180 points on the British Lions tour of New Zealand in 1971.

Jones, Ann
(born 1938)
Tennis
Winner of ladies singles and mixed doubles at Wimbledon 1969; also many other titles, including the French Open.

Keegan, Kevin
(born 1951)
Football
Five times Footballer of the Year – a record. Played 63 times for England, often as captain. Member of Liverpool team that won European cup in 1976. Later, a manager.

Lewis, Lennox
(born 1965)
Boxing
Olympic gold medallist 1988. British, Commonwealth and European Heavyweight Champion, first became World Champion in 1993.

Liddell, Eric
(1902–1945)
Athletics
Olympic gold medallist 1924 (400 metres). Refused to compete in other events (which he was also expected to win) because they were held on a Sunday (doing this was against his religious beliefs). Remembered in famous film, *Chariots of Fire*.

Lonsbrough, Anita
(born 1941)
Swimming
Olympic gold medallist 1960 (breaststroke); also won gold, silver and bronze at Commonwealth and European Championships. Set four world records.

MacBride, Willie John
(born 1940)
Rugby union
Led British Lions on very successful tours of New Zealand and South Africa, 1971 . Won 17 test caps – a record. Also played 63 international matches for Ireland.

McGuigan, Barry
(born 1961)
Boxing
British, European and World Featherweight Champion. National hero in Ireland; also worked to improve safety for boxers.

Mansell, Nigel
(born 1953)
Motor racing
Won 31 Grands Prix in 1980s and early 1990s. World Champion driver 1992.

Matthews, Sir Stanley
(born 1915)
Football
'The wizard of the dribble'; had an extraordinarily long and successful career. Played in 701 league matches, and was member winning FA Cup team (Stoke, 1953) of two World Cup teams.

Meade, Richard
(born 1938)
Equestrianism
Winner of three Olympic gold medals, 1968 and 1972; also won Burghley Horse Trials (1968), Badminton (1970 and 1982) and many medals in European Championships.

Moore, Bobby
(1941–1993)
Football
Won 108 caps for England, and captain of the English team that won the 1966 World Cup.

Moss, Stirling
(born 1929)
Motor racing
A British hero, even though he never won the Drivers' Championship. Won 16 Grands Prix races, 1955–1962.

Offiah, Martin
(born 1966)
Rugby league
A record-breaking scorer of tries, for Widnes and Britain.

Ovett, Steve
(born 1955)
Athletics
Winner of many European and World Championships, 1973–1981, and world record-breaker for the mile (twice) and 1500 metres.

Perry, Fred
(1909–1995)
Tennis
Winner of Wimbledon men's singles 1934–1936; World Table-tennis Champion 1929. Also won US, French and Australian Championships.

Peters, Mary
(born 1939)
Athletics
Broke world record and won Olympic Gold medal for pentathlon in 1972.

Piggott, Lester
(born 1935)
Horse racing
Champion Jockey 11 times; rode 4,493 winners in his riding career.

Pirie, Gordon
(1931–1991)
Athletics
Distance runner. Set 24 British records; Cross-Country Champion 1953–1955. Olympic silver medallist 1956 (5,000 metres).

Redgrave, Sir Steve
(born 1962)
Rowing
Record-breaking winner of gold medals at five Olympics, 1984–2000, also nine times World Champion.

Richards, Sir Gordon
(1904–1986)
Horse racing
Champion Jockey 26 times between 1925 and 1953; rode 4,870 winners. Later a successful trainer.

Robson, Bryan
(born 1957)
Football
A mid-fielder, played 345 games for Manchester United, scored 74 goals. Won 90 caps for England, many as captain. Later a player-manager.

Round, Dorothy
(1909–1982)
Tennis
Twice winner of Wimbledon singles, 1934 and 1937, and Wimbledon mixed doubles 1935–1937. Top world player, 1934.

Sanderson, Tessa
(born 1956)
Athletics
First British woman and first black person to win Olympic gold in a throwing event, 1984. Three times Commonwealth Champion, eight times British Champion, set 10 British records.

Scudamore, Peter
(born 1958)
Horse racing
Most successful National Hunt jockey ever; rode 1,678 winners. Champion Jockey nine times.

Shearer, Alan
(born 1970)
Football
First Premier League player to score 100 goals, Shearer played for Southampton and Blackburn. Player of the Year 1994; PFA Player of the Year 1995 and 1997. Played for England in Euro 1996 and World Cup 1998. Has captained England. Now plays for Newcastle.

Sheene, Barry
(born 1950)
Motor cycling
World Champion twice, 1976 and 1977. Won 19 Grands Prix.

Smyth, Pat
(1928–1996)
Equestrianism
First woman rider to achieve international success; won many British and European titles, and Olympic bronze. Later a popular writer for children and adults.

Stewart, John Young ('Jackie')
(born 1939)
Motor racing
Winner of 27 Grands Prix, 1965–1973. Later a successful businessman and owner of his own race team..

Thompson, Daley
(born 1958)
Athletics
The world's greatest decathlete. Winner of two Olympic gold medals (1980, 1984), four world records, three Commonwealth Championships and many British and European titles.

Torville, Jayne
(born 1957)
and Dean, Christopher
(born 1958)
Ice skating
Olympic gold medallists 1984, and winners of British, European and World titles for ice-dancing. Achieved great fame for their grace and brilliant technique.

Truman, Fred
(born 1931)
Cricket
An aggressive fast bowler and outspoken Yorkshireman. Was the first player to take 300 Test wickets. Later a sports broadcaster.

Underwood, Rory
(born 1963)
Rugby union
England's highest-ever try-scorer, and most-capped player, 1984–1996.

Wells, Allan
(born 1952)
Athletics
Olympic gold and silver medallist 1980 (for 100 and 200 metres); also won World, Commonwealth, European and British Championships.

Whitbread, Fatima
(born 1961)
Athletics
Javelin thrower, winner of silver and bronze Olympic medals (1984, 1988), World and European Champion.

Williams, J.P.R.
(born 1949)
Rugby union
Famous as an exciting, innovative player. Fifty-five Welsh caps. Member of Welsh teams that won three Grand Slams and six Five Nations Championships.

Wright, Ian
(born 1963)
Football
Playing first for Crystal Palace, and then for Arsenal, won fame as a brilliant goal-scorer. Member of Arsenal team that won the FA and Football League Cups in 1993. Also played for England.

Nobel Prize Winners

The Nobel Prizes are named after Alfred Nobel (1833–1896), a Swedish chemical engineer who invented dynamite. His invention made him very rich, but he regretted the damage it caused when used in war. When Nobel died, he left a large amount of money to fund prizes for important scientific discoveries, for great works of literature, and for contributions to world peace. The Royal Bank of Sweden also contributes to the Nobel Prize fund. Nobel Prizes have been awarded most years since 1901. A new prize, for economic science, was awarded from 1969. Winning a Nobel Prize is a very great honour. It is a sign that the winner's work is world-class.

Chemistry

1904 Sir William Ramsay – work on gases

1908 Lord Ernest Rutherford – chemistry of radioactive elements

1921 Frederick Soddy – chemistry of radioactive isotopes

1922 Francis Aston – structure of non-radioactive elements

1929 Sir Arthur Haden – fermentation processes and enzymes (with Hans von Euler-Chelpin, of Sweden)

1937 Sir Walter Haworth – carbohydrates and Vitamin C

1947 Sir Robert Robinson – important chemicals found in plants

1952 Archer Martin and Richard Synge – invention of partition chromatography

1956 Sir Cyril Hinshelwood – understanding how chemical reactions work (with Nikolaj Semenov, USSR)

1957 Lord Todd – proteins and enzymes

1958 Frederick Sanger – proteins, especially insulin

1962 Max Perutz and Sir John Kendrew – structure of proteins

1964 Dorothy Crowfoot Hodgkin – X-ray crystallography

1967 Ronald Norrish and Sir George Porter – very fast chemical reactions (with Manfred Eigen, West Germany)

1969 Sir Derek Barton – a new chemical law, called conformation (with Odd Hassel, Norway)

1973 Sir Geoffrey Wilkinson – the structure of organo-metallic compounds (with Ernest Fischer, West Germany)

1975 Sir John Cornforth (also of Australia) – on enzyme reactions

1978 Peter D Mitchell – biological energy transformation

1980 Frederick Sanger – nucleic acids (with Paul Berg and Walter Gilbert, USA)

1982 Aaron Klug – electron microscopy

1996 Sir Harold Kroto – for discovery of fullerines (with Robert Curl Jnr and Richard Smalley, USA)

1997 John E. Walker – enzymes (with Paul D. Boyer, USA)

1998 John A. Pople (also of USA) – quantum chemistry

Physics

1904 Lord Rayleigh (John William Strutt) – density of gases; discovery of rare gas argon

1906 Sir Joseph Thomson – conduction of electricity by gases

1915 Sir William Henry Bragg and Sir William Lawrence Bragg (father and son) – analysis of crystal structure by X-Rays

1917 Charles Barkla – discovery of radiation from elements

1923 Robert Millikan – electricity and photoelectric effect

1927 Charles Wilson – electrically charged particles

1928 Sir Owen Richardson – discovery of the thermionic phenomenon

1933 Paul Dirac – discovery of new forms of atomic theory (with Erwin Schrodinger, Austria)

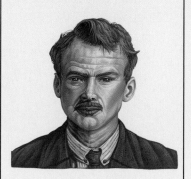

▲ PAUL DIRAC (PHYSICS, 1933)

1935 Sir James Chadwick – discovery of the neutron (sub-atomic particle)

1937 Sir George Thomson – discovery of the diffraction of electrons by crystals

1947 Sir Edward Appleton – investigating the upper atmosphere; discovering the Appleton layer

1948 Lord Blackett – discoveries in nuclear physics and cosmic radiation

1950 Cecil Powell – investigating nuclear processes and sub-atomic particles

1951 Sir John Cockcroft – investigating atomic nuclei and atomic particle (with Ernest Walton, Republic of Ireland)

1954 Max Born – quantum mechanics

1971 Denis Gabor – holograms

1973 Brian Johnson – supercurrents

1974 Sir Martin Ryle and Antony Hewish – radio astro-physics and pulsars

1977 Sir Neville Mott – theoretical physics of electricity and magnetism (with Philip W. Anderson and John H. van Vliek, of the USA)

Physiology/Medicine

1902 Sir Ronald Ross – investigating malaria

1922 Sir Archibald Hill – the production of heat in muscles

1929 Sir Frederick Hopkins – growth-stimulating vitamins

1932 Sir Charles Sherrington and Lord Adrian – how neurons (nerve-fibres) work

1936 Sir Henry Dale – chemical transmission of nerve-impulses (with Otto Loewi, Austria)

▲ ALEXANDER FLEMING, 1945

1945 Sir Alexander Fleming, Sir Ernst Chain, Lord Florey – discovery and use of penicillin

1953 Sir Hans Krebs – the citric acid cycle (Krebs cycle): how energy is used in body cells

1960 Sir Peter Medawar – immunology (how our bodies learn to fight or accept foreign substances) (with Sir Frank Burnet, Australia)

1962 Francis Crick and Maurice Wilkins – the 'double helix' structure of DNA (with James Watson, USA)

1963 Sir Alan Hodgkin and Sir Andrew Huxley – study of nerve cells (with Sir John Eccles, Australia)

1970 Sir Bernard Katz (with Ulf von Euler, Sweden and Julius Axelrod, USA)

1972 Rodney Porter – structure of antibodies (cells that fight disease) (with Gerald Edelman, USA)

1973 Nikolaas Tinbergen – social and behaviour patterns (with Karl von Frisch, West Germany, and Konrad Lorenz, Austria)

1979 Sir Godfrey Hounsfield – developing CAT scanners (with Allan Cormack, USA)

1982 Sir John Vane – investigating prostaglandins and other biologically active substances (with Sune Bergstrom and Bengt Samuelsson, Sweden)

1984 Cesar Milstein (Great Britain and Argentina) – immunology (with Georges Kohler, Germany, and Niels Jerne, Denmark)

1988 Sir James Black – pharmacology (the science of drug treatment) (with Gertrude Elion and George Hitchings, USA)

1993 Richard Roberts – genetics (with Phyllip Sharp, USA)

Literature

▲ RUDYARD KIPLING, 1907

1907 Rudyard Kipling

1932 John Galsworthy

1948 T.S. Eliot (US born, became a British subject)

1950 Bertrand Russell

1953 Sir Winston Churchill

1983 Sir William Golding

1995 Seamus Heaney

2001 V.S.Naipaul

▲ WINSTON CHURCHILL, 1953

Peace

1903 Sir William Cremer

1925 Sir Austen Chamberlain (with Charles Dawes, USA)

1933 Sir Norman Angell

1934 Arthur Henderson

1937 Lord Cecil of Chelwood

1947 Friends Service Council (Quakers) (with American Friends Service Committee)

1949 Lord John Boyd Orr

1959 Philip Noel-Baker

1976 Mairead Corrigan and Betty Williams

1995 Joseph Rotblat and the Pugwash Conference (UK/Poland)

1998 John Hume and David Trimble

Economic Science

1972 John R. Hicks (with Kenneth J. Arrow, USA)

1977 James E. Meade (with Bertil Ohlin, Sweden)

1979 Sir Arthur Lewis (with Theodore W. Schultz, USA)

1984 Richard Stone

1991 Ronald H. Coase

1996 James R. Mirrlees (with William Vickrey, Canada/USA)

1998 Amartya Sen (UK/India)

Kings and Queens

Edward the Elder 899–924

Athelstan 924–939

Edmund 939–946

Eadred 946–955

Eadwig 955–959

Edgar 959–975

Edward the Martyr 975–978

Ethelred II the Unready
978–1016

Edmund Ironside 1016

Cnut 1016–1035

Harold I Harefoot
1037–1040

Harthacnut 1040–1042

Edward the Confessor
1042–1066

Harold II 1066

William I (the Conqueror)
1066–1087 (King of
England)

William II 1087–1100

Henry I 1100–1135

Stephen 1135–1154

Henry II 1154–1189

Richard I (the Lionheart)
1189–1199

John 1199–1216

Henry III 1216-1272

Edward I 1272-1307

Edward II 1307-1327

Edward III 1327-1377

◀ EDWARD III

Richard II 1377–1399

Henry IV 1399–1413

Henry V 1413–1422

Henry VI 1422–1461;
1470–1471

Edward IV 1461–1470:
1471–1483

Edward V 1483

Richard III 1483–1485

Henry VII 1485–1509

Henry VIII 1509–1547
(England and Wales
united 1536 and 1543)

Edward VI 1547–1553

(Lady Jane Grey 1553)

Mary I 1553–1558

Elizabeth I 1558–1603

James VI and I 1603–1625
(king of England;
also king of Scotland)

Charles I 1625–1649

Civil War and Interregnum
1649–1660

Oliver Cromwell (Lord
Protector 1653–1658)

Richard Cromwell (Lord
Protector 1658–1659)

Charles II 1660–1685

▶ GEORGE 111

James II 1685–1688

William III and Mary II
1688–1694

William III 1694–1702

Anne 1702–1714 (England
and Scotland united 1707)

George I 1714-1727

George II 1727–1760

George III 1760–1820
(Britain and Ireland
united, 1800)

George IV 1820–1830

William IV 1830–1837

Victoria 1837–1901

Edward VII 1901–1910

George V 1910–1936
(Irish Free State – now Eire
– formed 1921)

Edward VIII 1936

George VI 1936–1952

Elizabeth II 1952–

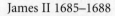

◀ JOHN

▲ CHARLES II

ELIZABETH II ▶

Prime Ministers

Robert Walpole,
1st Earl of Orford
1721–1742

Spencer Compton,
Ist Earl of Wilmington
1742–1743

Henry Pelham
1743–1754

Thomas Pelham-Holles,
4th Duke of Newcastle
1754–1756

William Cavendish,
4th Duke of Devonshire
1756–1757

William Pitt the Elder
1757–1761

Thomas Pelham-Holles,
4th Duke of Newcastle
1757–1762

John Stuart,
3rd Earl of Bute
1762–1763

George Grenville
1763–1765

Charles Wentworth,
2nd Marquess of
Rockingham
1765–1766

William Pitt the Elder
1766–1767

Augustus Fitzroy,
3rd Duke of Grafton
1767–1770

Frederick North,
2nd Earl of Guildford
1770–1782

Charles Wentworth,
2nd Marquess of Rockingham
1782

William Petty,
Earl of Shelburne
1782–1783

William Cavendish Bentinck,
3rd Duke of Portland
1783

William Pitt the Younger
1783–1801

Henry Addington
1801–1804

William Pitt the Younger
1804–1806

William Grenville,
1st Baron Grenville
1806–1807

William Cavendish Bentinck,
3rd Duke of Portland
1807–1809

Spencer Perceval
1809–1812

Robert Jenkinson,
2nd Earl of Liverpool
1812–1827

George Canning
1827

Frederick Robinson,
1st Earl of Ripon
1827–1828

Arthur Wellesley,
1st Duke of Wellington
1828–1830

Charles Grey,
2nd Earl Grey
1830–1834

William Lamb,
2nd Viscount Melbourne
1834

Robert Peel
1834–1835

William Lamb,
2nd Viscount Melbourne
1835–1841

Robert Peel
1841–1846

Lord John Russell,
1st Earl Russell
1846–1852

Edward Stanley,
23rd Earl of Derby
1852

George Gordon,
4th Earl of Aberdeen
1852–1855

John Temple,
3rd Viscount Palmerston
1855–1858

Edward Stanley,
23rd Earl of Derby
1858–1859

John Temple,
3rd Viscount Palmerston
1859–1865

Lord John Russell,
1st Earl Russell
1865–1866

Edward Stanley,
23rd Earl of Derby
1866–1868

Benjamin Disraeli,
1st Earl of Beaconsfield
1868

William Ewart Gladstone
1868–1874

Benjamin Disraeli,
1st Earl of beaconsfield
1874–1880

William Ewart Gladstone
1880–1885

Robert Cecil,
3rd Marquess of Salisbury
1885–1886

William Ewart Gladstone
1886

Robert Cecil,
3rd Marquess of Salisbury
1886–1892

William Ewart Gladstone
1892–1894

Archibald Primrose,
5th Earl of Rosebery
1894–1895

Robert Cecil,
3rd Marquess of Salisbury
1895–1902

Arthur James Balfour
1902–1905

Henry Campbell-
Bannerman
1905–1908

Herbert Henry Asquith
1908–1916

David Lloyd George
1916–1922

Andrew Bonar Law
1922–1923

Stanley Baldwin
1923–1924

Ramsay MacDonald
1924

Stanley Baldwin
1924–1929

Ramsay MacDonald
1929–1935

Stanley Baldwin
1935–1937

Neville Chamberlain
1937-1940

Winston Churchill
1940–1945

Clement Attlee
1945–1951

Winston Churchill
1951–1955

Anthony Eden
1955–1957

Harold Macmillan
1957–1963

Alec Douglas-Home
1963–1964

Harold Wilson
1964–1970

Edward Heath
1970–1974

Harold Wilson
1974–1976

James Callaghan
1976–1979

Margaret Thatcher
1979–1990

John Major
1990–1997

Tony Blair
1997–

illustrations are in italics

Abbott, Diane 6
Adam, Robert 6, *6*
Adrian IV, Pope Adrian
  (Nicholas Breakespeare) 6
Albert, Prince Consort 102
Alcock, Sir John 6, *6*
Alcuin 6
Alexander II 6
Alfred the Great 7, *7*
Anderson, Elizabeth Garrett 7
Anne of Cleves 51
Anning, Mary 7, *7*
Appleton, Sir Edward 7, *7*
Argyll, Duke of 89
Arkwright, Sir Richard 8, *8*
Ashley, Laura 8
Ashton, Sir Frederick 31
Asquith, Herbert 64
Astor, Nancy 8, *8*
Attlee, Clement 9, *9*
Austen, Jane 9

Babbage, Charles 9, *9*, 66
Bacon, Sir Francis 9, *9*
Bacon, Sir Roger 9
Baden-Powell, Robert 10, *10*
Baffin, Sir William 10
Baird, John Logie 10, *10*
Bakewell, Robert 10
Baldwin, Sir Stanley 10, *10*
Balfour, Arthur, (Earl Baldwin)
  11
Bannister, Sir Roger 11, *11*
Barnardo, Thomas 11, *11*
Barry, James (Miranda Stuart)
  11, 97
Bateman, Hester 11, *11*
Baylis, Lilian 11
Beale, Dorothea 12
Beatles, The 12, *12*
Beaufort, Lady Margaret 12, 51
Becket, St Thomas (a) 12, *12*, 50
Bede, St 13
Beeton, Isabella 13, *13*
Behn, Aphra 13, *13*
Bell Burnell, Jocelyn 13, *13*
Bell, Alexander Graham 13, *13*
Bentham, Jeremy 14, *14*
Bevan, Aneurin 9, 14
Beveridge, William 9, 14
Bishop, Isabella 14, *14*
Black, Joseph 14
Blair, Eric (see George Orwell)
  80, *80*
Blake, William 15, *15*
Boleyn, Anne 36, 51, 71
Bondfield, Margaret 15
Boniface, St 15
Bonny, Anne 15, *15*
Bonnie Prince Charlie 23
Booth, Catherine 15
Booth, William 15, *15*
Boru, Brian 16, *16*
Botham, Ian 16, *16*
Boudicca 16, *16*
Boulton, Matthew 16, *16*, 104

Boyle, Robert 53
Branson, Sir Richard 16
Breakespeare, Nicholas (Pope
  Adrian 1V) 6, *6*
Bridgid, St 17
Britten, Benjamin (Lord Britten)
  17, *17*
Brontë, Anne 17, *17*
Brontë, Charlotte 17, *17*
Brontë, Emily 17, *17*
Brown, Lancelot 'Capability' 17,
  17
Brown, Sir Arthur Whitten 6, *6*
Bruce, Robert the (Robert I) 18,
  18
Brunel, Isambard Kingdom 18,
  18
Bunyan, John 18
Burns, Robert 18, *18*
Buss, Florence Mary 12
Butler, Josephine 18, *18*
Butler, Richard 'Rab' (Lord
  Butler) 19, *19*
Butler-Sloss, Dame Elizabeth 19
Butt, Clara 19, *19*
Byron, George (Lord Byron) 19,
  19, 66, 93

Calico Jack 15
Cameron, Julia Margaret 20, *20*
Campbell, Sir Malcolm 20, *20*
Campbell, Donald 20
Campbell, Mrs. Patrick 20
Caractacus 20
Carnegie, Andrew 20
Carroll, Lewis (Charles
  Dodgson) 20
Carter, Howard 21, *21*
Cartwright, Edmund 21
Castle, Barbara (Baroness) 21, *21*
Cavell, Edith 21, *21*
Caxton, William 21, *21*
Cayley, Sir George 21
Cecil, William (Lord Burghley)
  22
Chadwick, Sir James 22
Chamberlain, Joseph 22
Chamberlain, Neville 22
Chamberlain, Sir Austen 22
Chaplin, Sir Charles 'Charlie' 22,
  22
Charles I 23, 69, 102, 108
Charles II 23, *23*, 28, 45, 110
Charles Edward Stewart 67
Charlie 'Bonnie Prince Charlie'
  23
Charlton, Sir Robert 'Bobby' 23
Chaucer, Geoffrey 23, *23*
Cheshire, Leonard 91
Chichester, Sir Francis 24
Chippendale, Thomas 24, *24*
Christie, Dame Agatha 24, *24*
Christie, Lindford 24
Churchill, John, Duke of
  Marlborough 24
Churchill, Sir Winston 9, 22, 24,
  24

Clark, James (Jim) 25, *25*
Clive ('of India'), Robert (Lord
  Clive) 25
Clive, Kitty 25
Cobbett, William 25, *25*
Cockcroft, Sir John 25
Cockerell, Sir Christopher 25,
  25
Coe, Sebastian 26, *26*
Coke, Thomas (Lord Leicester)
  26
Coleridge, Samuel 26, *26*
Collins, Michael ('The Big
  Fellow') 26
Columba, St 26
Constable, John 27, *27*
Cook, Captain James 27, *27*
Cook, Thomas 27
Cooper, Anthony Ashley (Lord
  Shaftesbury) 27, 93
Cornwallis, Charles 27
Coward, Noël 62
Cranmer, Thomas 28, *28*
Crick, Francis 28, 40
Crompton, Samuel 28
Cromwell, Oliver 28, *28*
Cromwell, Thomas 28, 51

Dalton, John 29, *29*
Dalzell, Gavin 69
Darby, Abraham 29
Darling, Grace 29
Darnley, Henry 72
Darwin, Charles Robert 29, *29*
David I 29
Davies, Emily 30, *30*
Davison, Emily Wilding 30
Davy, Sir Humphry 30, *30*
de Havilland, Sir Geoffrey 30,
  30
de Valois, Dame Ninette 31, *31*
Defoe, Daniel 30, 92
Delius, Frederick 31, *31*
Dewar, Sir James 31
Dickens, Charles 31, *31*
Dirac, Paul 31, *31*
Disraeli, Benjamin 32, *32*, 102
Dodgson, Charles (Lewis
  Carroll) 20
Dolin, Anton 70
Doll, Sir William 32
Donald II 32
Donne, John 32, *32*
Doyle, Sir Arthur Conan 32
Drake, Sir Francis 33, *33*, 36
du Pre, Jacqueline 33, *33*
Duncan I 67
Duncan, Isadora 87
Dunlop, John 33
Dunstan, St 33

Eddington, Sir Arthur 34
Edgar 34
Edward, the Black Prince 34,
  35, *35*
Edward I 18, 34, *34*, 65, 103
Edward II 18, 34
Edward III 34, 50

Edward IV 35
Edward the Confessor 35, 107
Edward V 51
Edward VI 36, 71, 95
Edward VII 35, *35*, 42
Edward VIII 37, 43
Edward VIII, King 10
Elgar, Sir Edward 36, *36*
Eliot, George (pen-name of
  Mary Ann Evans) 36
Elizabeth I 36, *36*, 61, 72, 87,
Elizabeth II 37, *37*, 43
Elizabeth, the Queen Mother
  37, *37*, 43
Engels, Friedrich 71
Epstein, Brian 12
Evans, Dame Edith 37
Evans, Mary Ann (George
  Eliot) 36
Evans, Sir Arthur 37

Faraday, Michael 38, *38*
Fawcett, Dame Millicent
  Garrett 38
Fawkes, Guy 38, *38*
Ferrier, Kathleen 38
Fielding, Henry 38, *38*
Fiennes, Celia 39
Flamsteed, John 39
Fleming, Alexander 39, *39*
Florey, Sir Howard 39
Fonteyn, Margot (Peggy
  Hookham) 39, *39*
Foster, Sir Norman 40,
Fox, Charles James 40
Fox, George 40, *40*, 65
Foxe, John 40
Francois 11 72
Franklin, Rosalind 41
Frobisher, Sir Martin 41, *41*
Fry, Elizabeth 41
Fuchs, Sir Vivian 41, *41*

Gainsborough, Thomas 42, *42*
Gaskell, Elizabeth (known as
  'Mrs Gaskell') 42
George I 42, 96, 97, 103
George II 103
George III 42, *42*, 86
George VI 37, 43, *43*
Gerard, John 43
Gibbon, Edward 43
Gielgud, Sir John 43, *43*
Gilbert, Humphrey 87
Gladstone, William Ewart 43,
  43, 83
Glendower, Owen 44, 85
Godiva, Lady 44
Godwin, William 93, 108
Goodall, Jane 44
Gordon, Charles George 44, *44*
Grace, W.G. 44, *44*
Grade, Lord (Lew) 45
Grattan, Henry 45
Greene, Graham 45
Grey, Lady Jane 45, 71
Gryffud ap Llewellyn 45, *45*
Gwynn, Nell 45, *45*

Haig, Douglas (Earl Haig) 46, 46
Halley, Edmond 46, 46
Hallowes, Odette 46
Hamilton, Lady Emma 76
Hanway, Jonas 46
Hardie, James Kier 47, 47
Hardwick, Elizabeth 47
Hardy, Thomas 47, 47
Hargreaves, James 47
Harold II 48, 48, 107
Harrison, George 12
Harrison, John 48, 48
Harvey, William 49, 49
Hastings, Selina 54, 54
Hawking, Stephen 49, 49
Hawkins, Sir John 33
Heath, Sir Edward 49, 49
Henry I 50
Henry II 50, 50
Henry IV 50, 50, 85, 106
Henry V 50, 106
Henry VII 12, 51
Henry VIII 28, 45, 51, 51, 65, 71, 74, 109
Hepworth, Dame Barbara 51, 51
Hereward the Wake 107
Herschel, Sir William 52
Hilda, St 52, 52
Hill, Octavia 52
Hill, Sir Rowland 52
Hitchcock, Alfred 52, 52
Hobbes, Thomas 53
Hockney, David 53
Hodgkin, Dorothy 53
Hooke, Robert 53, 53
Hookham, Peggy (Margot Fonteyn) 39, 39
'Hotspur' (see Henry Percy) 85
Howard, Catherine 51
Hugh of Lincoln, St 54
Hughes, Ted 54, 54
Hume, David 54, 54
Huntingdon, Countess of (Selina Hastings) 54, 54

Irving, Sir Henry 98

James I 42, 57, 87
James II 108
James IV 55, 55
James V 72
James VI 42, 55, 55
Jansky, Karl 66
Jebb, Eglantyne 55
Jekyll, Gertrude 56, 66
Jenner, Edward 56, 56
John 56, 56, 65
John of Gaunt 34, 50
John, Augustus 56, 56
John, Gwen 56
Johnson, Amy 57, 57
Johnson, Samuel 57, 57
Jones, Inigo 57, 57
Joule, James 58
Joyce, James 58, 58
Julian of Norwich 58, 58

Kay, John 59, 59
Keats, John 59, 59
Kelvin, Lord 99
Kempe, Margery 59
Kenneth I (Kenneth MacAlpine) 59, 59
Kent, William 59, 59
Kidd, William 60, 60
Kingsley, Mary 60
Kipling, J. Rudyard 60, 60
Kitchener, H. Herbert (Lord Kitchener) 60, 60
Knox, John 61, 61
Krebs, Sir Hans Adolf 61

Lanchester, Frederick 61, 61
Langland, William 61
Larkin, Philip 61
Lawrence, D.H. 62
Lawrence, T.E. ('Lawrence of Arabia') 62, 62
Leakey, Louis 44, 62, 62
Leakey, Mary 62
Leakey, Richard 62
Lean, David 62
Lee, Baroness Jennie 63
Lennon, John 12
Lessing, Doris 63, 63
Leverhulme, Lord William 63
Linacre, Thomas 63, 63
Lind, James 63
Lister, Lord Joseph 64, 64
Livingstone, David 64, 64, 95
Lloyd George, Lord David 64, 64
Lloyd, Marie (Matilda Alice Victoria Wood) 64, 64
Llywelyn the Great (Llywelyn ap Iorwerth) 65, 34
Locke, John 65
Lockyer, Sir J. Norman 65
Lonsdale, Dame Kathleen 65
Louis XV 96
Lovelace, Countess Ada 66
Lovell, Sir (A.C.) Bernard 66, 66
Lowry, L.S. 66
Lutyens, Sir Edwin 56, 66
Lynn, Dame Vera (born Vera Margaret Lewis) 66

MacAdam, John 67
MacAlpine, Kenneth (see Kenneth 1) 67
Macbeth 67, 67
MacDonald, Flora 67, 96
MacDonald, J. Ramsay 67
MacGregor, Robert ('Rob Roy') 89
MacKenzie, Sir Alexander 68
Mackintosh, Charles 68
Mackintosh, Charles Rennie 68, 68
Mackintosh, Margaret 68, 69
Macmillan, Harold 68
Macmillan, Kirkpatrick 69, 69
Macmillan, Margaret 69, 69

Macmillan, Rachel 69
Makin, Bathshua 69
Malcolm III 'Canmore' 67, 69, 70
Malthus, Thomas Robert 69, 69
Mar, Earl of 97
Marconi, Guglielmo 10
Margaret, Princess 43
Margaret, St 70, 70
Markova, Dame Alicia (Lilian Marks) 70, 70
Marlborough, Duke of (see Churchill. John) 70
Marlowe, Christopher (Kit) 70, 70
Martineau, Harriet 71
Marx, Karl Heinrich 71
Mary 97, 108
Mary 1, (Bloody Mary) 36, 40, 71, 71
Mary of Guise 72
Mary, Queen of Scots 36, 55, 61, 72, 72
Matthews, Sir Stanley 72, 72
Maudslay, Henry 72
Maxwell, James Clerk 72
McCartney, Sir Paul 12
Mill, J.S. 73
Milton, John 73, 73
Montfort, Simon de 73, 73
Montgomery, Lord Bernard 74, 74
Montrose, Duke of 89
Moore, Henry 74, 74
More, Sir (or St) Thomas 74, 74
Morris, William 74, 74

Nelson, Lord Horatio 76, 76
Newcomen, Thomas 76, 76, 104
Newman, J.H. 76
Newton, Sir Isaac 46, 77, 77
Nightingale, Florence 77, 77
Normandy, Robert, Duke of 107
North, Lord Frederick 78
North, Marianne 78, 78
Nuffield, Viscount William Morris 78, 78
Nureyev, Rudolph 39

Oates, Lawrence 79
Offa, 79, 79
Olivier, Baron Laurence 79, 79
Orwell, George (Eric Blair) 80, 80
O'Shea, Kitty 83
Owen, Robert 80, 80
Owen, Wilfred 80, 80

Page, Sir Frederick Handley 81
Paget, Sir James 81
Paine, Thomas 81
Palmerston, Lord 81, 81
Pankhurst, Christabel 82
Pankhurst, Emmeline 82
Pankhurst, Sylvia 82

Park, Mungo 82, 82
Parnell, Charles Stewart 83, 83
Parr, Catherine 51
Parsons, Sir Charles 83, 83
Paston, Margaret 83
Paterson, Emma 83
Paterson, William 83
Patrick, St 84
Pavlova, Anna 87
Peel, Sir Robert 84, 84
Penn, William 84, 84
Pepys, Samuel 85, 85
Percy, Henry 'Hotspur' 85
Perkin, Sir William Henry 85
Philip II of Spain 71
Philip, Prince 37
Philips, Katherine 85
Pitt, Lord William (known as 'Pitt the Elder') 85, 85
Pitt, Wiliam (known as 'Pitt the Younger') 86, 86
Pope, Alexander 86
Priestley, Sir Joseph 86
Purcell, Henry 86, 86

Raffles, Sir Stamford 87
Raleigh, Sir Walter 36, 87, 87
Rambert, Dame Marie (Cyvia Rambam) 87
Rand, Mary 87
Rathbone, Eleanor 88
Read, Mary 15, 15, 88
Reber, Grote 66
Reith, Lord John 88
Richard II 85, 106
Richard III 12, 51, 51
Rizzio, David 72
Robert, James 6, 6
Rogers, Lord Richard 88, 88
Rolls, Charles 88, 90
Rontgen, Wilhelm 53
Rossetti, Christina 89, 89
Rossetti, Dante Gabriel 89
Rowntree Benjamin Seebohm 89
Rowntree, Henry Isaac 89
Rowntree, Joseph 11 89
Rowntree, Joseph 1 89
Roy, Rob (Robert MacGregor) 89
Royce, Sir (Frederick) Henry 90, 90
Russell, Dora 90, 90
Russell, Earl Bertrand 90, 90
Russell, Lord John 91
Rutherford, Lord Ernest 91
Ryder, Baroness Sue 91, 91
Ryle, Sir Martin 91, 91

Saunders , Dame Cicely 92
Savery, Thomas 92
Scott, Robert 79
Scott, Sir Robert Falcon 79, 92, 92, 93
Scott, Sir Walter 89, 92, 92
Selkirk, Alexander 92, 92
Seymour, Edward (Duke of Somerset) 95
Seymour, Jane 51, 95

Shackleton, Sir Ernest Henry 93
Shaftesbury, Lord (see Anthony Ashley Cooper) 93
Shakespeare, William 70, 93, *93*
Shelley, Mary 93, 94, 108
Shelley, Percy 93, 94, *94*
Simpson, Sir James 94
Slessor, Mary 94
Smith, Adam 94, *94*
Somerset, Duke of (Edward Seymour) 95
Somerville, Mary 95, *95*
Stanhope, Lady Hester 95
Stanley, Sir Henry Morton (born John Rowlands) 95
Starr, Ringo (Richard Starkey) 12
Stephenson, George 96
Stephenson, Robert 96
Stevenson, Robert Louis 96
Stewart, Charles Edward ('Bonnie Prince Charlie') 23, 96
Stewart, James Edward 97
Stuart, Miranda ('James Barry') 97
Swift, Jonathan 97, *97*

Tallis, Thomas 98
Telford, Thomas 98, *98*
Tennyson, Lord Alfred 98
Terry, Dame Ellen 98, *98*
Thackeray, William Makepeace 98
Thatcher, Baroness Margaret 99
Thomas, Dylan 99, *99*
Thomson, Sir William (Lord Kelvin) 99
Thomson, William 58
Tippet, Sir Michael 99
Tradescant, John (father & son) 100, *100*
Trevithick, Richard 100
Trollope, Anthony 100, *100*
Tull, Jethro 100, *100*
Turing, Alan 101
Turner, J.M.W. (Joseph Mallord William) 101, *101*
Tyler, Wat 101
Tyndale, William 101

van Dyck, Sir Anthony 102
Vanbrugh, Sir John 102
Vaughan Williams, Ralph 102
Victoria 32, 35, 81, 94, 98, 102, *102*
von Richtoven, Frieda 62

Wallace, Sir William 34, 103, *103*
Wallis, Sir Barnes 103, *103*
Walton, James 25
Watson Watt, Sir Robert 103
Watson, James 28, 41
Watt, James 16, 76, 104, *104*

Webb, Beatrice and Sidney 104, *104*
Wedgwood, Josiah 104, *104*
Wellington, Duke of 105
Wells, H.G. ((Herbert George) 105, *105*
Wesley, John 105
Wheatstone, Sir Charles 106
Whittington, Richard (Dick) 106, *106*
Whittle, Sir Frank 106, *106*
Wilberforce, William 106, *106*
Wilde, Oscar 107, *107*
Wilkinson, Ellen 107, *107*
William I ('the Conqueror') 48, 107, *107*
William III (of Orange) 97, 108, *108*
Wilson, Lord Harold 108, *108*
Wollstonecraft, Mary 93, 108, *108*
Wolsey, Thomas (Cardinal) 29, 51, 109, *109*
Woolf, Leonard 109
Woolf, Virginia 109, *109*
Wordsworth, William 26, 109, *109*
Wren, Sir Christopher 110, *110*
Wyclif, John 110

Yeats, William Butler 110, *110*
Yeats, Jack 110

The publishers would like to thank the following artists whose work appears in this book:

Nicholas Forder
Terry Gabbey/AFA
Sally Holmes
The Maltings Partnership
Janos Marffy
Martin Sanders
Peter Sarson
Guy Smith
Rudi Vizi
Mike White/Temple Rogers

The publishers would like to thank the following sources for the use of their photographs:

Page 6 (T/C) Courtesy Castrol; 7 (B/R) Hulton Deutsch Collection/Corbis; 8 (C) Hulton Deutsch Collection/Corbis; 10 (B/L) Hulton Deutsch/Corbis; 11 (B/L) Bettmann/Corbis, (T/R) Courtesy Barnardo's Photographic Archive; 13 (B/L) Hulton Deutsch Collection/Corbis; 14 (T/L) Courtesy University College, London, (T/R) The Royal Geographical Society, 15 (T/R) Courtesy The Salvation Army; 16 (B/L) Patrick Eager; 17 (B/R) London Aerial Photo Library/Corbis; 19 (B/L) Hulton Deutsch Collection/Corbis, (C) Hulton Deutsch Collection/Corbis; 20 (T/C) Historical Picture Archive/Corbis, (C/R) Corbis, (B/L) Courtesy Castrol; 25 (T/C) Courtesy Team Lotus Ltd. 1968, (B/L) Bettmann/Corbis, (C/R) Corbis; 26 (T/L) Neal Preston/Corbis; 27 (B/L) Corbis; 28 (T/L) Bettmann/Corbis; 30 (T/L) The Mistress and Fellows, Girton College, Cambridge; 31 (T/L) Robbie Jack/Corbis; 32 (T/R) Mary Evans Picture Library; 33 (B/L) Hulton Deutsch Collection/Corbis; 35 (B/L) Pictorial Press Ltd; 37 (T/L) Hulton Deutsch Collection/Corbis, (B/R) Hulton Deutsch Collection/Corbis; 39 (T/R) Hulton Deutsch Collection/Corbis; 40 (T) IN-press Photography; 41 (B/R) Bettmann/Corbis; 49 (B/L) Michael S. Yamashita/Corbis, (C/R) Bettmann/Corbis; 51 (B/R) Cordaiy Photo Library/Corbis; 52 (T/L) Patrick Ward/Corbis, (B/R) Hulton Deutsch Collection/Corbis; 53 (T/R) Hulton Deutsch Collection/Corbis; 54 (C/L) Caroline Forbes; (T/R) Bettmann/Corbis; 56 (B/R) Hulton Deutsch Collection/Corbis; 63 (C/L) Bettmann/Corbis, (T/R) Archivo Iconografico/Corbis; 64 (T/R) Hulton Deutsch Collection/Corbis; 65 (B/R) Hulton-Deutsch Collection/Corbis; 66 (B/L) The University of Manchester; 69 (C/L) Bettmann/Corbis, (B/R) Bettmann/Corbis; 70 (B/R) Hulton Deutsch Collection/Corbis; 72 (T/R) Hulton Deutsch Collection/Corbis; 74 (B/R) Massimo Listri/Corbis; 78 (B/C) Reproduced with permission of the Trustees of the Royal Botanic Gardens, Kew; 82 (B/R) Macduff Everton/Corbis, (C/L) Corbis; 83 (B/L) Hulton Deutsch Collection/Corbis; 85 (B/R) Mary Evans Picture Library, (B/R) Corbis; 86 (T/L) Michael Nicholson/Corbis, (B/C) Bettmann/Corbis; 90 (T/R) Hulton Deutsch Collection/Corbis; 91 (T/R) Topham Picturepoint, (B/R) Hulton Deutsch Collection/Corbis; 94 (B/L) Hulton Deutsch Collection/Corbis, (C/R) Bettmann/Corbis; 95 (B/L) Bettmann/Corbis; 97 (C/R) Corbis; 98 (C/R) Hulton Deutsch Collection/Corbis; 99 (C/L) Hulton Deutsch Collection/Corbis, (B/R) Hulton Deutsch Collection/Corbis; 100 (T/L) Ashmoleon Museum, Oxford/Bridgeman Art Library, (T/R) Hulton Deutsch Collection/Corbis; 103 (T/C) Hulton Deutsch Collection/Corbis; 104 (C/L) Hulton Deutsch Collection/Corbis; 106 (C/L) Bettmann/Corbis, (B/L) Mary Evans Picture Library; 107 (C/L) Underwood & Underwood/Corbis; 108 (T/R) Bettmann/Corbis; 109 (C/L) Hulton Deutsch Collection/Corbis, (B/L) Patrick Ward/Corbis; 110 (B/R) Underwood & Underwood/Corbis.

All other images from MKP Archives